their shadow over the promise of the future. [Commager and Morris, 1959: ix]

The United States nearing the turn of the twentieth century was a country in the process of rapid and profound change. Expansion of the population had reached geographical limits in the last decade of the old century, but had only begun to approach its human ones by that date. The federal government had quietly announced – after the 1890 Census – the exhaustion of free public land in the West, and thus had declared the "closing of the frontier" (Turner, 1921).

Yet, immigrants continued to appear at ports of entry, seeking a share of the still considerable burden of nation building, and a share, too, of its rewards. An historic influx from southern and eastern Europe was, over the next three decades, to increase vastly the number of foreign-born urban residents. Native inhabitants of rural areas and small towns likewise converged on the cities, and with the newest immigrants swelled the populations of America's industrial centers. Industry quickly exploited this newly available pool of labor to propel the United States materially into the twentieth century. Public education and social services were altered accordingly, as age-old systems of schooling and welfare were gradually adapted to render literate the peasantry of old Europe and the Old South alike, to prepare workers for the unaccustomed rigors of industrial employment, and to accommodate the national culture to a widely lamented condition of persistent diversity.

The appearance of a decidedly new form of social life accompanied the rise of the city. Concentration of the labor force under manufacturing, and improved systems of transportation and communication diffused cultural innovations within and well beyond the spreading boundaries of cities. Demanded in return of urbanites, current and prospective, was a flexibility in adaptation to rapid social change, a malleability in accordance with the new structural conditions of urban living (Turner, 1940: 238–239). For "urbanization no longer denotes merely the process by which persons are attracted to a place called the city and incorporated into its system of life," wrote Louis Wirth (1938: 5), one of the foremost American urban sociologists. "It refers also to that cumulative accentuation of the characteristics distinctive of the mode of life which is associated with the growth of cities." The mode of life to which Wirth alluded contains many traits representative of cultural modernity: a prevalence of impersonal social relations, the application of rationality to increasingly numerous phases of everyday existence, cognizance of widespread diversity (and recognition of an obligation to tolerate it), and a thoroughgoing secularization of tradition (cf. Simmel, 1950).

The experience of sweeping social change at the turn of the century

# "As Slavery Never Did"

## American Religion and the Rise of the City

After the conclusion of the nineteenth century's most important social crusade, the one which sought to liberate thousands of Americans from legal though involuntary servitude, Wendell Phillips,[1] a prominent abolitionist and a farsighted reformer, predicted that "the time will come when our cities will strain our institutions as slavery never did" (quoted in Strong, 1898: 101–102). Indeed, the pace of change implied by urban growth in the late nineteenth century was to try severely the social institutions transplanted from the countryside and established in a more settled time. One of those institutions, organized religion, is the subject of this study. A social historian notes of this period that "the growth of the metropolis, with all that it implied in secularism and anti-traditionalism, gave the churches the greatest challenge in their history" (Wish, 1952: 148). In fact, the development of the city, as another historian (Abell, 1943: 3) has observed, tested the structure of American religion "to the breaking-point."

"The decade of the [eighteen-] nineties," Henry Steele Commager and Richard B. Morris have written, "was the watershed of American history."

On the one side stretches the older America – the America that was overwhelmingly rural and agricultural, that devoted its energies to the conquest of the continent, that enjoyed relative isolation from the Old World, that was orthodox in religion, optimistic in philosophy, and romantic in temperament. Over the horizon, on the other side, came the new America – an America predominantly urban and overwhelmingly industrial, inextricably involved in world politics and world wars, experiencing convulsive changes in population, economy, technology, and social relations, and deeply troubled by the crowding problems that threw

1

dens of harboring an academic like me. They endure them, and me, rather well.

An article of mine, drawn in part from Chapters 2 and 3, examines the historical origins of the data used in this book, inspects the data for accuracy, and suggests how the information on denominations that they contain may allow a reconsideration of the historical role of organized religion in American society. That article was published in *Social Science History* 8 (Fall, 1984): 341–370. I am grateful to James Q. Graham, Jr. and Robert P. Swierenga, managing editors of this journal, for granting permission to reprint here most of my earlier essay.

KEVIN J. CHRISTIANO

how he analyzed diversity in his own dissertation, a study of Protestantism in Los Angeles between 1850 and 1930.

Besides the persons noted above, James R. Beniger, Kathleen Biddick, Jay P. Dolan, Maureen T. Hallinan, Martin E. Marty, John R. Sutton, Andrew J. Weigert, and Michael J. White discussed my research with me at various moments and freely gave of their time to help me to improve it. Each was able to see some things in this work worth talking about, and these exchanges, in turn, kept me talking – and thinking in between.

All the while that I talked and thought, Robert S. Cox, John F. Kuzloski, and Wesley M. Shrum neither ignored the obligation they bore as my colleagues to criticize my work nor dismissed the inclination they shared as my friends to respect what it meant to me. They were perhaps less delicate than I in handling matters to which rules were attached, but in no important sense were they ever really cavalier.

This project commenced in the last of three years of financial support that I received from the National Science Foundation (NSF) under its predoctoral fellowship program in sociology. For one year thereafter, I was designated a Charlotte Elizabeth Procter Honorific Fellow by the Fellowship Subcommittee of the Faculty Committee on the Graduate School of Princeton University. Much later, preparation of the manuscript for the publisher was completed at Princeton – where it all began – during the first weeks of a year I enjoyed on leave from my teaching responsibilities at the University of Notre Dame. My return to Princeton as a Visiting Fellow was occasioned by a kind invitation from the Department of Sociology and its chairman, Marvin Bressler. I wish to thank the NSF, Princeton, and Notre Dame for the assistance that each institution has extended to me over the course of this research.

Back at Princeton, Clifford I. Nass furnished expert advice about dealing with the mainframe computer, aid that was above and beyond even his own elevated standard of duty to users of that machine. Cynthia Gibson typed many of the more complicated tables in the manuscript with diligence and dispatch.

A host of other friends served this work and its author importantly by resonating, in their conversation and their laughter, a sound that Hawthorne identified as "the echo of God's own voice, pronouncing 'It is well done.'" Ann and Rick Blanc, Joe and Moy Burns, Calum Carmichael, Michelle Alberti Gambone, Sarah Hewins, Bill Lehrman, and Mark Stanton all fell (or were pushed) into this role, and they never (or seldom) complained.

Finally, I must thank my siblings (this time by name, they demanded): Steve, Patty, Maureen, and Donna. Along with our parents, to whom this book is dedicated, they have assumed with unflagging patience the bur-

appeared in the imagination, long before it became a book; thus I know as well that much of the credit for any merit to be found in this finished study is not mine. The people I list below, thankfully, intervened.

Foremost among those who deserve mention is Robert Wuthnow. To him I owe intellectual and personal obligations which (like the federal deficit) seem to grow daily, and at a compound rate. Fortunately (and also as with the national debt), payment in full is not expected in the near term. On this project, Wuthnow was the one who first directed me to the Censuses of Religious Bodies and persuaded me not to flinch at the historical study and statistical analyses that would be required to digest the data and to tell their story adequately. More generally, he has been, across the ten years of our association, always careful of thought, calm in judgment, and generous with praise.

Robert C. Liebman was instrumental in demonstrating to me how I could better integrate this study's historical contents and sociological themes. He provided attentive and detailed comments on drafts of all the chapters, even when a transatlantic research trip of his own loomed. Not incidentally, these comments were accompanied at all times by ample doses of good humor.

Throughout the writing of this work, John F. Wilson proved to be a temperate and judicious critic. His careful attention to this project often led him to suggest further authorities for me to consult, or alternative arguments with which I ought to contend. Above all, he maintained a sense of charity while he managed this sociologist's instruction in the subtlety of the historian's craft.

I was fortunate, as this work took shape, to have taken part in an informal discussion group in which sociologists shared some results of their research and addressed common problems. Among the participants in this group were Karen A. Cerulo, Muge Gocek, Beth Kaplowitz, William G. Lehrman (who drew my attention to the data available in the Censuses of Manufactures), Ann Shola Orloff, Laura Shill Schrager, Catherine Leeco Stern, Steven Wemer (who offered several helpful references on statistical procedures), and David E. Woolwine. I thank them all.

At least four segments of this work were delivered, in preliminary form, as papers at meetings of the Society for the Scientific Study of Religion, the Association for the Sociology of Religion, or the Social Science History Association. Albion M. Urdank, Richard Perkins, and Marsha Rosenblit acted as discussants at these sessions, where they contributed much constructive criticism, not all of which I could incorporate in the book. In addition, a number of scholars read an early report of the findings and graciously commented on it. Stanley Lieberson described how I could adapt for use with church membership data the linguistic diversity measures he has refined, and Gregory Holmes Singleton explained to me

turing, and falling levels of illiteracy diversified the religious environments of urban communities. The analyses in addition depict how a form
of religious diversity prevalent at the beginning of the twentieth century
established the bases for competition by and commitment to churches in
modern America. Importantly, the religious patterns that resulted can
today still be recognized in the denominational system of the United
States.

In summary, this study finds that such generic types of social change as
population growth and industrialization in themselves had little discernible and consistent influence on the religious profiles of American cities
around the turn of the century. Rather, diversity appears more to have
been a product of a city having sheltered certain racial or ethnic
subcommunities and having supported a culture with widespread literacy. Religious diversity, for its own part, was a condition which inclined
cities toward secularization, as well as a catalyst for the consolidation of
the parties to nineteenth-century sectarian conflict.

This book was conceived several years ago as a doctoral dissertation in
the sociology of religion at Princeton University, though the manuscript
has been revised repeatedly since its submission for the degree. Revisions
were carried out to promote clarity in expression, to correct minor
errors, and to cite research which has only recently come to light. Of
these purposes, the first was also the most serious. The text deals in
places with matters that are highly technical, even for professionals in
sociological research. Yet, because it also combines religious history with
social science theory, the manuscript was rewritten for this book with a
broader audience in mind. Portions have been revised more than once to
improve readability, and the inevitably dense descriptions of method and
justifications for technique have been placed almost entirely in notes and
appendixes. Trying to make one's work acceptable to one's peers in the
discipline is difficult; trying to make it intelligible to others is doubly so.
All the same, if more than one kind of reader can actually read this book,
the effort will have been worth it.

As scholarly books go, this one is not very long. Nevertheless, it took a
long time to produce it, and many people helped along the way. I recognize that to acknowledge the contributions of others to this research by
naming them at the start is neither to implicate them necessarily in its
results nor to compensate them fully for their trouble.

In candor, I suspect that those who helped, recognize this (especially
the part about inadequate rewards) as well as I do. Their cooperation in
spite of this foreknowledge is all the more reason why I as the author am
bound to repeat that much of the blame for what may be wrong with this
study is not theirs. As the author, I alone know how raw this project

# Preface

In the years immediately preceding the turn of the twentieth century, the United States stood not merely on the threshold of a new chronological period. The nation was poised, more crucially, at the beginning of a radically different era for its social institutions, because trends initiated in this era would ultimately modify many of the structures of American life, shaping contours which persist to this day.

Social change in the latter part of the nineteenth century was as rapid as it was profound. During that time, America had moved increasingly from a native to an immigrant population, from rural to urban residence, and from agricultural to industrial production. As one consequence of this movement, American institutions, whose essential features were determined under more settled circumstances, faced for the first time the task of accommodating the most prominent product of change: greater cultural diversity. Organized religion in particular was severely tested by the urbanization, industrialization, and diversity of American society in this period.

This book provides an account of religion's response, on the structural level, to the new social conditions that arrived with the twentieth century. While not strictly an historical study, it utilizes sophisticated methods of analysis to test propositions which are central to historical writing on religion in the turn-of-the-century period. Because much of what has been published in the past on the history of religion in America is really a brand of intellectual history, this book augments and complements other religious histories with a quantitative assessment of changes taking place in urban populations and their institutions around 1900.

One goal of this study is to explain the effects of the rise of American cities on the religious organizations within them. Statistical models analyze government census data on cities and their churches, probing ways in which the nature and growth of populations, the expansion of manufac-

and, more pointedly, an encounter with the diversity it produced, must have been bewildering. The new urban dweller was impressed in numerous ways and repeatedly that

America was strange. Democracy: since he had never experienced such a novel idea in Europe, the immigrant could hardly conceive of political responsibility. Religion: one encountered here an almost unbelievable variety of faiths, each equally acceptable, and none officially supported; such practices seemed odd especially to Catholics and Lutherans accustomed to a state church. Language: in America one met innumerable strange tongues and people who couldn't understand one's own language. Customs: in the new country one found little respect for the established, time-honored practices, handed down with reverence and awe from ancestors who lived in the same place, even in the same dwellings, centuries ago. Instead, in America everything was in flux, nothing seemed permanent, and traditions became lost in the midst of rapid change. Certainly the new land was a peculiar place. [Hays, 1957: 96]

Cultural diversity was especially salient with respect to religion. Not only did the foreign-born bring with them to this country Old World religious practices, but rural migrants as well adapted to the city forms of worship heretofore alien to urban life (Singleton, 1975). The unique culture of the expanding city, moreover, was itself the catalyst for the founding of a number of religious groups, like Christian Science (Pfautz, 1964), whose appeals were specialized to the spiritual needs of the urban populace. Together, these developments represented a strong challenge to the prevailing Protestant establishment in nineteenth-century cities. French Canadians in New England, for instance, "added to the already large Irish Catholic contingent," and in the view of one historian (Schlesinger, 1933: 75), "seemed to threaten the traditional Puritan and Protestant character of the section." In more general terms, urbanization, industrialization, and cultural modernity all seemed to contribute to the creation of a new environment for American religion as it moved toward the next century (Hammond, 1983: 282–283).

This study relates these large-scale changes in American society to the creation of religious diversity, and in so doing, traces the sociological and social-historical roots of the current system of denominationalism in the United States. The study's particular focus is urban America in the period between 1890 and 1906, and its specific intent is to explain the effects of the composition and development of American cities on the fortunes of religious organizations within them. A series of statistical analyses using Census data on cities and their churches probes the ways in which population growth, industrialization, and increasing rates of literacy changed

the religious environments of urban communities. The analyses in addition suggest how these changes fixed the organizational bases of religious competition and commitment in America at the beginning of the twentieth century.

The central variables in this study are a pair of measures of religious diversity in 122 American cities for both 1890 and 1906. Examined first are how the size and composition of city populations, the scale and scope of their manufacturing activity, and the dimensions of urban cultural development (as reflected in rates of literacy) furthered the construction of social structural arrangements more or less supportive of a diversity of affiliations within a city's population of church members. The effects of this diversity across two decades on levels of urban religious allegiance (or secularization) and on relations between religious groups are then assessed. Discussion places the findings in historical context and explains how the events of this period established institutional patterns which are today characteristic of American religion.

Two purposes of this opening chapter are to introduce the turn of the century as a turbulent historical period, and to describe the urban settings to which the analyses of religion appearing later in this study pertain. To begin, the magnitude of demographic and cultural change coinciding with the turn of the century is conveyed in figures, and the response of religious institutions and actors to urban expansion is depicted. Then, a brief description of the cities chosen for analysis in this study is provided. Finally, growth in organized religion in this period is summarized quantitatively, in anticipation of the more thorough discussion of the uses and pitfalls of church statistics which is presented in the second chapter.

## A Statistical View of Turn-of-the-Century Urbanization

The process of urbanization was not new to America at the turn of the century. "The modern city had been taking shape for some time," historian Harold U. Faulkner (1959: 278) notes, "but it was not until the nineties that people began to see that the United States was no longer a land of farms and villages; that the future belonged to the city." What produced this change in public opinion was in part a massive change in urban populations and their composition.[2] This section traces that change and its implications using historical data from the United States Census.

The Census data relevant to urbanization around the turn of the century exhibit two seemingly contradictory trends: a considerable growth in the number of small towns being established at that time, but also a consistent move toward concentration of the population in cities of

Table 1.1. *Numbers of places in the United States, by size of place, in 1890, 1900, and 1910*

| Size of place | Number of places in | | |
|---|---|---|---|
| | 1890 | 1900 | 1910 |
| 1,000,000 or more | 3 | 3 | 3 |
| 500,000–999,999 | 1 | 3 | 5 |
| 250,000–499,999 | 7 | 9 | 11 |
| 100,000–249,999 | 17 | 23 | 31 |
| 50,000–99,999 | 30 | 40 | 59 |
| 25,000–49,999 | 66 | 82 | 119 |
| 10,000–24,999 | 230 | 280 | 369 |
| 5,000–9,999 | 340 | 465 | 605 |
| 2,500–4,999 | 654 | 832 | 1,060 |
| 1,000–2,499 | 1,603 | 2,128 | 2,717 |
| Less than 1,000 | 4,887 | 6,803 | 9.113 |
| Total number of places | 7,838 | 10,668 | 14,092 |

*Source:* Bureau of the Census (1975: 11).

larger size. Between 1890 and 1910, Table 1.1 reveals, the number of cities in the United States with 25,000 or more inhabitants nearly doubled, increasing from 124 in 1890 to 228 in 1910. Roughly the same observation could be made about smaller places, however. Was America becoming more urban, then, or really maintaining its previous rural character? Table 1.2 helps to clarify the picture. From this table, one may see that the aggregate population of several of the larger classes of cities actually doubled over the twenty-year period, a phenomenon caused both by the expansion of populations of existing urban places, and by the promotion of cities to higher population categories as a result of growth. In particular, the population of cities of over 25,000 persons increased from slightly below 14 million in 1890 to over 28½ million two decades later.

A clearer record of the progress of turn-of-the-century urbanization is provided in Table 1.3, which expresses the data from the table that precedes it in terms of percentages. From these calculations, a movement toward consolidation of the national population in larger cities between 1890 and 1910 is apparent. Twenty-two percent of the American people in 1890 resided in places with 25,000 or more people; by 1910, that proportion had increased to 31 percent. An inverse effect was felt by smaller towns. In 1890, places with fewer than 1,000 inhabitants embraced 61 percent of the population of the United States, whereas such places could claim only half of all Americans as residents in 1910.

Table 1.2. *Population of the United States, by size of place, in 1890, 1900, and 1910*

| Size of place | Population (in thousands) in | | |
|---|---|---|---|
| | 1890 | 1900 | 1910 |
| 1,000,000 or more | 3,662 | 6,429 | 8,501 |
| 500,000–999,999 | 806 | 1,645 | 3,011 |
| 250,000–499,999 | 2,448 | 2,861 | 3,950 |
| 100,000–249,999 | 2,782 | 3,272 | 4,840 |
| 50,000–99,999 | 2,028 | 2,709 | 4,179 |
| 25,000–49,999 | 2,269 | 2,801 | 4,023 |
| 10,000–24,999 | 3,451 | 4,338 | 5,549 |
| 5,000–9,999 | 2,384 | 3,204 | 4,217 |
| 2,500–4,999 | 2,277 | 2,899 | 3,728 |
| 1,000–2,499 | 2,509 | 3,298 | 4,234 |
| Less than 1,000 | 2,249 | 3,003 | 3,930 |
| Other rural areas | 36,083 | 39,533 | 41,809 |
| Total population | 62,948 | 75,992 | 91,971 |

*Source:* Bureau of the Census (1975: 11–12).

Table 1.3 *Proportions of the population of the United States in places of varying sizes, in 1890, 1900, and 1910*

| Size of place | Percentage of total population in | | |
|---|---|---|---|
| | 1890 | 1900 | 1910 |
| 25,000 or more | 22 | 26 | 31 |
| 1,000–24,999 | 17 | 18 | 19 |
| Less than 1,000 | 61 | 56 | 50 |
| Totals | 100 | 100 | 100 |

*Source:* Calculated from Table 1.2.

What caused this change? At least three factors can be isolated: "natural" increase in the population (i.e., fertility), rural-to-urban migration, and immigration from abroad to the United States. Of particular interest are the latter two forces. Initially, analysts of the rise of the city in this period attributed fully 65 to 70 percent of new urban population to immigration, and 10 to 15 percent to migration to the city from rural areas (Gillette, 1911: 649, 651). As demographic research methods were refined and applied to this problem, such high estimates were revised to place more emphasis on rural-to-urban migration and to rely less on the

role of the immigrant in explanations of urbanization (Clark, 1915; Gillette and Davies, 1915; cf. Thernstrom, 1968). However, studies confined to larger cities and to the more heavily industrialized states (e.g., Chapin, 1914; Gillette and Davies, 1915: 650–653) established that in those ecological contexts, immigration was the predominant cause of urban expansion. This factor therefore deserves closer examination.

Between 1891 and 1900, the United States accepted more than 3½ million immigrants from beyond North America, making the decade of the 1890s the period of the second heaviest immigration to the United States recorded by that date. Only in the preceding decade had America yet seen more immigrants approach its shores (Faulkner, 1959: 4). Table 1.4 provides raw counts of total immigration and of immigration from Europe by region of origin for the years 1880 through 1906. The sheer volume of humanity involved in this migration is staggering. In no year reported in Table 1.4 did the United States process fewer than 200,000 arrivals. In the peak year of the time series – 1906 – more than 1.1 million were admitted.[3] In every year, Europe accounted for the vast majority of immigrants to the United States.

The most striking aspect of these statistics is obscured by their detail, however, and requires for its comprehension reference to Table 1.5. This table reports the proportions of total immigration to the United States in each year attributable to several regions of Europe. A substantial shift over time in the composition of the immigrant stream is clearly in evidence. In 1880, a scant 4 percent or so of immigrants to America came from eastern or southern Europe; almost half hailed from the northwestern corner of that continent. By 1906, a reversal had taken place: about one new arrival in six was born in northwestern Europe, while almost 49 percent were derived from eastern or southern Europe.

Figures 1.1 and 1.2 depict graphically this change in the makeup of the turn-of-the-century's tide of immigration. Each chart presents a superimposition of four trend lines, corresponding to the four categories of origin used to divide the totals in Table 1.4.[4] The meaning of Figure 1.1, which graphs the raw data from Table 1.4, is relatively clear. In 1880, newcomers to America who had migrated from homes in northwestern Europe were slightly less than an absolute majority of all immigrants. By 1890, however, a change had begun to take place: the line representing northwestern European immigration dips precipitously. It falls throughout most of the decade, recovering a positive slope just prior to the turn of the century, and then only in response to an increased volume of immigration from all sources. Conversely, immigration from southern and eastern Europe was maintained at comparatively low levels through the 1880s and into the 1890s. Late in the 1890s, though immigration in total had

Table 1.4. *Total immigration to the United States, and immigration from Europe by region of origin, 1880–1906*

| Year | Total immigration | Region of origin | | | |
|---|---|---|---|---|---|
| | | Northwestern[a] Europe | Central[b] Europe | Eastern[c] Europe | Southern[d] Europe |
| 1880 | 457,257 | 225,575 | 104,082 | 5,049 | 13,985 |
| 1881 | 669,431 | 262,183 | 244,034 | 5,143 | 17,185 |
| 1882 | 788,992 | 312,545 | 284,452 | 17,052 | 34,137 |
| 1883 | 603,322 | 254,357 | 224,422 | 10,072 | 33,736 |
| 1884 | 518,592 | 200,790 | 220,783 | 13,077 | 19,036 |
| 1885 | 395,346 | 163,944 | 154,837 | 18,099 | 16,203 |
| 1886 | 334,203 | 171,020 | 117,022 | 18,470 | 23,017 |
| 1887 | 490,109 | 246,684 | 153,258 | 33,017 | 49,870 |
| 1888 | 546,889 | 287,380 | 161,354 | 34,880 | 54,517 |
| 1889 | 444,427 | 233,063 | 138,634 | 35,061 | 28,032 |
| 1890 | 455,302 | 193,697 | 159,699 | 36,321 | 55,963 |
| 1891 | 560,319 | 204,242 | 212,093 | 48,648 | 81,102 |
| 1892 | 579,663 | 181,624 | 236,641 | 82,842 | 69,769 |
| 1893 | 439,730 | 155,600 | 152,550 | 42,935 | 78,239 |
| 1894 | 285,631 | 94,665 | 94,568 | 40,305 | 47,514 |
| 1895 | 258,536 | 109,302 | 66,364 | 36,675 | 38,001 |
| 1896 | 343,267 | 105,637 | 97,679 | 52,399 | 73,352 |
| 1897 | 230,832 | 67,585 | 59,729 | 26,759 | 62,324 |
| 1898 | 229,299 | 62,002 | 61,634 | 30,904 | 63,246 |
| 1899 | 311,715 | 72,471 | 79,967 | 62,720 | 82,191 |
| 1900 | 448,572 | 85,212 | 133,354 | 97,639 | 108,495 |
| 1901 | 487,918 | 94,059 | 135,041 | 93,456 | 146,681 |
| 1902 | 648,743 | 110,396 | 200,293 | 115,581 | 192,798 |
| 1903 | 857,046 | 163,603 | 246,097 | 148,693 | 256,114 |
| 1904 | 812,870 | 171,007 | 223,536 | 157,897 | 215,493 |
| 1905 | 1,026,499 | 222,452 | 316,267 | 195,919 | 239,635 |
| 1906 | 1,100,735 | 178,251 | 302,702 | 234,317 | 303,095 |

[a]Belgium, Denmark, France, Great Britain, Iceland, Ireland, Luxembourg, Netherlands, Norway, Sweden, and Switzerland.
[b]Austria, Germany, Hungary, and Poland.
[c]The Baltic States, Bulgaria, Romania, Russia, and Turkey (Europe).
[d]Greece, Italy, Portugal, and Spain.
*Source:* Bureau of the Census (1975: 105–106).

slowed, numbers of southern and eastern European immigrants increased dramatically. The trend lines for these two groups sweep upward after 1898, and continue to climb into the first decade of the new century.

The relative proportions of immigrants embraced by each of the four origin groups are followed over time in Figure 1.2, which is a graph of the data in Table 1.5. Here, the influence of general changes in absolute

Table 1.5. *Immigration from Europe to the United States, 1880–1906, by region of origin, expressed as a percentage of total immigration*

| | Percentage of total immigration from | | | |
|---|---|---|---|---|
| Year | Northwestern Europe | Central Europe | Eastern Europe | Southern Europe |
| 1880 | 49.3 | 22.8 | 1.1 | 3.1 |
| 1881 | 39.2 | 36.5 | 0.8 | 2.6 |
| 1882 | 39.6 | 36.1 | 2.2 | 4.3 |
| 1883 | 42.2 | 37.2 | 1.7 | 5.6 |
| 1884 | 38.7 | 42.6 | 2.5 | 3.7 |
| 1885 | 41.5 | 39.2 | 4.6 | 4.1 |
| 1886 | 51.2 | 35.0 | 5.5 | 6.9 |
| 1887 | 50.3 | 31.3 | 6.7 | 10.2 |
| 1888 | 52.5 | 29.5 | 6.4 | 10.0 |
| 1889 | 52.4 | 31.2 | 7.9 | 6.3 |
| 1890 | 42.5 | 35.1 | 8.0 | 12.3 |
| 1891 | 36.5 | 37.9 | 8.7 | 14.5 |
| 1892 | 31.3 | 40.8 | 14.3 | 12.0 |
| 1893 | 35.4 | 34.7 | 9.8 | 17.8 |
| 1894 | 33.1 | 33.1 | 14.1 | 16.6 |
| 1895 | 42.3 | 25.7 | 14.2 | 14.7 |
| 1896 | 30.8 | 28.5 | 15.3 | 21.4 |
| 1897 | 29.3 | 25.9 | 11.6 | 27.0 |
| 1898 | 27.0 | 26.9 | 13.5 | 27.6 |
| 1899 | 23.2 | 25.7 | 20.1 | 26.4 |
| 1900 | 19.0 | 29.7 | 21.8 | 24.2 |
| 1901 | 19.3 | 27.7 | 19.2 | 30.1 |
| 1902 | 17.0 | 30.9 | 17.8 | 29.7 |
| 1903 | 19.1 | 28.7 | 17.3 | 29.9 |
| 1904 | 21.0 | 27.5 | 19.4 | 26.5 |
| 1905 | 21.7 | 30.8 | 19.1 | 23.3 |
| 1906 | 16.2 | 27.5 | 21.3 | 27.5 |

*Source:* Calculated from Table 1.4.

numbers is removed; the course of each group over a quarter century may be compared directly with those of the others. The dual impressions imparted by this second figure are, again, a markedly decreasing numerical contribution by northwestern Europe to the pool of immigrants to the United States between 1880 and 1906, and an increase of similar importance in the immigrant flow from southern Europe, a flow whose fraction of the total surpasses that of the historically dominant group not long before the turn of the century.

These statistics reflect the change in kind which historians have characterized as the "new immigration" – that is, the appearance for the first

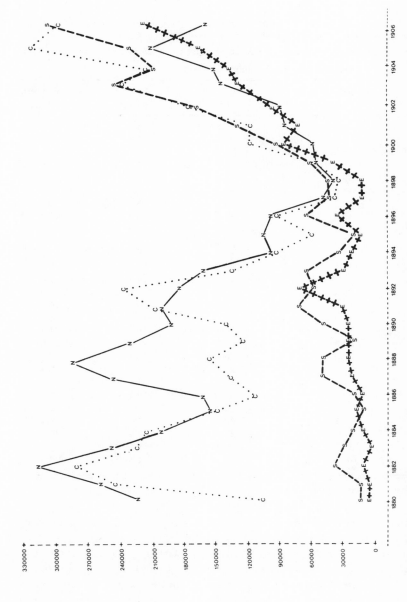

Figure 1.1. European immigration to the United States, 1880–1906, by region of origin: N, northwestern Europe; C, central Europe; E, eastern Europe; S, southern Europe (*Source*: Derived from Table 1.4)

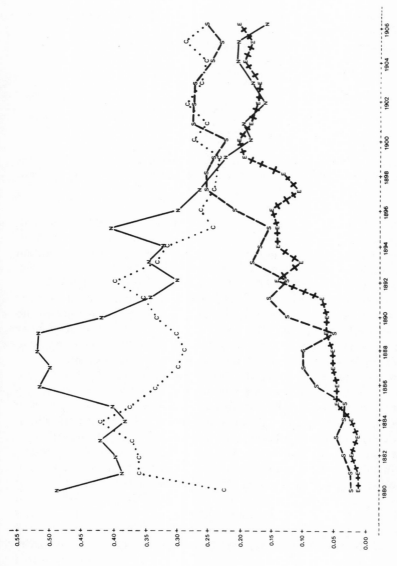

Figure 1.2. European immigration to the United States, 1880–1906, by region of origin, expressed as a percentage of total immigration: N, northwestern Europe; C, central Europe; E, eastern Europe; S, southern Europe (*Source*: Derived from Table 1.5)

Table 1.6. *Percent illiterate*[a] *among persons at least ten years of age, by race and nativity, 1890, 1900, and 1910*

| | | White | | | |
| | | | Native | Foreign | Non- |
| Year | Total | Total | born | born | white |
| --- | --- | --- | --- | --- | --- |
| 1890 | 13.3 | 7.7 | 6.2 | 13.1 | 56.8 |
| 1900 | 10.7 | 6.2 | 4.6 | 12.9 | 44.5 |
| 1910 | 7.7 | 5.0 | 3.0 | 12.7 | 30.5 |

[a]Illiteracy was defined by the Census Bureau as the inability to write in any language.
*Source:* Bureau of the Census (1975: 382).

time in America of enormous numbers of persons descended from cultures radically distinct from its dominant Anglo-Saxon Protestant ethos. The American population, and even more relevantly, the American urban population, was not simply growing in the 1890s: it was growing at a fast rate, growing increasingly by the admission of foreigners, and growing by adding foreigners, further, with backgrounds unlike native predecessors. The result was a high degree of cultural diversity. "It was only in the nineties," Faulkner (1959: 278) points out, "that men began to ponder the changes wrought in American life by the introduction of vast numbers of people new to all that was familiar to American experience."

Table 1.6 suggests one implication of this trend. Tabulated there are Census statistics on illiteracy among persons at least ten years of age, by race and nativity, across the two decades positioned astride the turn of the twentieth century. Illiteracy declined between 1890 and 1910 within all categories of the population, and it declined especially substantially among nonwhite residents. However, since the Census defined illiteracy as the inability to write in *any* language (and not specifically as an inability to write English), the number of foreign-born persons who could not communicate effectively in the wider world, and thereby participate in the national culture, was certainly underestimated. Yet, even with this qualification, foreign-born whites were two to four times more likely than native-born white Americans to be found to be illiterate, a disparity that widened over time. On the national level, this situation meant that the American people and their institutions were forced to accommodate a greater degree of diversity than they had historically known, without the assurance for nativists of overwhelming numerical superiority or the possibility for reformers of immediate recourse to means whereby diverse elements in the population could be readily assimilated.

The growth of American cities in the late nineteenth century was "a

concomitant of radical institutional and technological changes that altered the social and physical environment and the way people were conditioned by the environment" (Glaab and Brown, 1967: 133–134). The import of these changes was not missed by leaders of organized religion. The section which follows describes their reactions to urbanization and its assumed consequences for religion in this period, and details how they guided the church through – or became victims of – "significant modification in the new environment" (Glaab and Brown, 1967: 134).

## Religion Reacts to the City

"We must face the inevitable," insisted Josiah Strong, a Congregational minister and one of the earliest spokesmen for what was to be known as the Social Gospel in America (see Ahlstrom, 1975b: 265–266; Handy, 1966a: 9; Marty, 1970: 155–165; Muller, 1959). "The new civilization is certain to be urban," he said, "and the problem of the twentieth century will be the city... Something must be done. Something *will* be done. What is done depends on who does it – the Christian Church or the frenzied mob" (Strong, 1898: 53; cf. Strong, 1907: 241). Charles Stelzle, Superintendent of the Northern Presbyterians' Bureau of Social Service, agreed, if in less dramatic terms: "If the city is to dominate the nation – and it will – and if the Church continues to lose in the city, it does not require a prophet to foretell the inevitable result" (Stelzle, 1912: 24). The Northern Methodist bishops, in a statement drafted in 1900, likewise concluded that "how to reach the heart of the city and to change its life is, indeed, the question of questions" (quoted in Handy, 1971: 144).

Thus did much of organized religion in America conceive the challenge posed to it by the prospect of twentieth-century urbanization. Masses of new urban dwellers appeared mostly to be insensitive to traditional religious obligations, and in the generic small-town culture which a then dominant Protestantism embodied, where orthodox religious belief and regular religious practice were thought not just to foster respectability but to undergird public order and morality itself, this neglect alone was ample reason for alarm (Frank, 1986: 32–54). "The cities are exceptionally exposed to perils," Strong advised. "In them the great conservative influences are exceptionally weak" (Strong, 1887: 11).

But the religious reaction to American urbanism was animated, at least in part, by a consideration more momentous than a simple defense of tradition: namely, a sense of the city as a God-given opportunity as much as a diabolical threat. This view, which was formulated admittedly out of immediate worries, and which offered no less urgent a reading of current events, nevertheless bore an emphasis more millennial than apocalyptic.

Religion, many churchmen feared, was giving way to secularization at precisely that point in history at which God had ordained and had orchestrated the advent of a new Kingdom on earth (Strong, 1913). They optimistically regarded the rapid urbanization leading up to the turn of the century as purposive, even if the theological purpose of the city was not entirely clear, and even, further, if the full revelation of its end demanded their obedient labor toward an unspecified goal. A century shy of the second millennium, a kind of social millennialism took hold in American religion, and the Social Gospel movement sank its first roots through the pavement of the nation's cities (Ahlstrom, 1975b: 250–273).

The Social Gospel creatively drew upon the Protestant tradition in America—and particularly its evangelical and prophetic dimensions—to place the church in a position to construct actively the anticipated new age (see, e.g., Strong, 1893; cf. Handy, 1966a; White and Hopkins, 1976: xiii-xv). To be sure, Social Gospel advocates were concerned about the same range of urban problems as were more conservative churchmen, primarily because of what those problems implied for Protestant church membership, and—relatedly, it was felt—for the survival in America of democratic institutions.

But additionally, theorists of the movement saw contemporary social trends as signifying collective sin, as evidence of evils for which society even then was being held under divine judgment. For example, *If Christ Came to Chicago!*, a popular book of the 1890s by muckraking English journalist William T. Stead (1894), contemplated what the Redeemer's opinion of American society would be if He were to visit, unannounced, one of the more irredeemably urban locations in the United States. Although Christ was not universally expected soon to descend from above to commence the millennium, the Social Gospel taught that it was the religious duty of Americans to act together as if He might and to build an urban society that by its obvious goodness would welcome the event. In this way, the Social Gospel fused traditional religious values with a Progressive politics of reform (Muller, 1959). American Protestantism in turn seized the Social Gospel as one means by which rural virtue could ride atop a wave of industrial modernity into the twentieth century.

As a sign of the onset of a new era, America's growth promised not simply social institutions of a larger scale, but begged ones of a new kind altogether. Religion would not be immune to the influence of such change; rather, religious leaders assumed that they had been called out to direct its course (Hopkins, 1940: 102–105). Strong for one took notice of the portents of a spreading urbanism, immersed himself in Census statistics on the religious and social conditions of the American people, and in 1891 published the second edition of a tract entitled *Our Country: Its Possible Future and Its Present Crisis* (Strong, 1891).[5]

A vigorous polemic against the perils of immigration, "Romanism," socialism, and intemperance—all of which, Strong (1891: 172) observed, festered most intensely in the cities—*Our Country* became one of the best-selling books of its day. It was, moreover, a book addressed *to* its day. "The closing years of the nineteenth century" Strong ranked as one of the "great focal points of history . . . second in importance," he insisted, only to the time of the birth of Christ (Strong, 1891: 13). Austin Phelps, the aging seminary professor who wrote the introduction to *Our Country,* was equally convinced of the gravity of the immediate future. His warning was direct: "Five hundred years of time in the process of the world's salvation may depend on the next twenty years of United States history" (quoted in Strong, 1891: 13).

Later, more dispassionate scholars would stress the significance, in organizational terms, of these times. In dubbing the years between 1875 and 1900 "A Critical Period in American Religion," the distinguished historian Arthur M. Schlesinger, Sr. framed concisely the problem facing religious organizations in the last decades of the nineteenth century. "In an age of rapid, not to say fearful, urban and industrial development," Schlesinger (1932: 524) wrote, "the church was fast losing its appeal." A fateful question followed: "Was Protestantism to be sequestered in the small towns and rural districts or could it adjust itself to the requirements of megalopolis?" As "the product of a rural, middle-class society . . . American Protestantism faced a range of problems for which it had neither experience nor aptitude" (Schlesinger, 1932: 531).

Winthrop S. Hudson, in his study of the voluntary principle in American churches, concurred in Schlesinger's analysis, labeling the 1890s "decisive as a time [of] transition between the old and the new" (Hudson, 1953: 158).

While it is true that the period from 1890 through World War I represents the peak of Protestant influence and activity in America, these years also constituted the great testing period which was to determine whether the vigorous advance of the past century was to continue into the new century. [Hudson, 1953: 198–199; cf. Hammond, 1983]

Similarly, Timothy L. Smith has suggested that the years 1895 and 1905 bound one of the four "most significant" decades in American religious history,[6] crucial periods during which "Christianity made major adjustments of thought and practice to cope with new social conditions" (Smith, 1960: 9).[7]

Not long before the turn of the century, then, American clergymen and social activists were troubled by "the menace to our civilization" (Strong, 1891: 172) which came to be called *The Challenge of the City* (Strong,

1907). Most detected the old order receding; a few were soon occupied with the task of fashioning new and different answers to the threat an expanding, apparently unchurched, and seemingly irreligious urban population represented. Some, like the evangelists Dwight L. Moody and William A. "Billy" Sunday, preached a withdrawal from urban secularism and a return to "Bible religion" (McLoughlin, 1959). Some, like the innovators of the "institutional church," made the transformation from religion to community work. These activists threw open the church doors to aid the poor, to educate the immigrant, to agitate for the worker, and to promote personal piety and thereby shape the characters of the rising generation of city dwellers (Abell, 1943; Cross, 1967: xxxv-xxxix; Faulkner, 1931: 204–228; Hopkins, 1940; May, 1949; Reimers, 1968; Schlesinger, 1932, 1933: 320–348; Wish, 1952: 148–173). Others, however, simply grew more alarmed, and lapsed into suspicion, political reaction, and nativism (Davis, 1973; Higham, 1955; Kinzer, 1964).

At the very least, as accounts of national life and culture circa 1890 make clear, religious ideas were coming under closer scrutiny (courtesy of German Biblical criticism and the Darwinian theory of evolution); at the same time the groups which championed them were facing broad challenges on the social front in emerging cities. Of these two modes of attack on organized religion, the latter was the more significant and has had the more enduring effects. As Commager (1950: 170) has argued, "the challenge which the new urban, industrial, and corporate order presented to the church was less dramatic, but more immediate and complex, than that with which either Darwinism or the Higher Criticism confronted it." Church leaders in varying ways took up the defense of religion, and participated—wittingly or not—in the transformation of both its ideology and its organization.

This study provides several measurements of religion's response, on the social structural level, to the new urban environment. It is designed to augment and to complement the social and intellectual histories of this period with a quantitative assessment of changes taking place in urban populations and institutions at the turn of the century. The two sections that follow specify more precisely the populations and institutions, respectively, which are of interest in this effort.

Following in the next chapter is a complete evaluation of the strengths and weaknesses of the type of data analyzed here, including an extensive discussion of their previous uses in studies of American religion. Chapter 3 advances to the subject of American religion itself, and undertakes in a brief history to describe what is undeniably one of its principal attributes—its diversity. A pair of measures for quantifying the historical evidence on religious diversity is proposed near the end of the third chapter.

Data analyses in Chapters 4 through 8 put these statistical methods to

work, explaining the relationships between religious diversity and social change across the turn-of-the-century period. Chapters 4 through 6 trace the structural causes of religious diversity in American cities by reference to the diverse components of urban populations, to their different economic enterprises, and to their varying levels of literacy.

Chapters 7 and 8 look in turn at diversity's consequences. How did the obvious example of religious plurality in turn-of-the-century cities affect the maintenance of church memberships in these settings? And how did diversity in church memberships lay the foundations for conflict and cooperation between American churches and their members at the onset of a new historical era? As the conclusion to the study, Chapter 9 summarizes the statistical results and draws together themes and theories about the course of diversity and its role in the development of American religious life.

## Cities as Units of Analysis

The units of analysis in this study are 122 American cities with 25,000 or more inhabitants in 1890.[8] This set of cities is not truly representative of the United States as a whole in 1890, nor are its members typical of the many hundreds of urban places in America in the decade before the turn of the century. Rather, these cities together represent the highest stage of nineteenth-century urbanization.

A lack of available religious data in the Census required that, for selection, cities' populations meet a minimum size of 25,000. The 122 cities that qualified for inclusion in the group are therefore mostly places that had amassed large populations and considerable urban experience by 1890. Hence, older and more populous urban places predominate as units of analysis. Among these cities, the median date of municipal incorporation is 1847, the median 1890 population being just under 46,000.[9] Together, these cities encompass more than 22 percent of the United States' population in 1890 (see Table 1.3). The oldest and largest city, New York, was formed by Dutch merchants in 1653, fully 237 years before the 1890 Census; it is also one of three cities in the United States to enter the twentieth century with a population exceeding one million.[10] On the other hand, some newly settled and rapidly urbanizing areas were overlooked by the Census in its tabulations of data on religious bodies because they had not by 1890 reached or passed the lower population limit.

These 122 cities were also far more heavily industrialized than were the remainder of American towns in 1890. Indeed, some of the cities, such as Fall River, Lawrence, and Lynn, Massachusetts, and Paterson, New Jersey, were the more important factory towns of their day (Cumbler,

1979). Today, however, they are noteworthy primarily for their role in the history of manufacturing in America; they no longer are urban centers of national significance. Conversely, many cities which since the turn of the century have grown in importance to the national economy (e.g., Miami) are not included in this group.

The cities selected for analysis are further unrepresentative of the nation in that they are not geographically dispersed. Approximately three-quarters of them are located in New England, the Middle Atlantic states, or the Midwest. (The South and the West supply the other quarter.) Just one in five of the cities lies west of the Mississippi River. In all, thirty-six states are represented in the group, but only five[11] contribute five or more of their cities to the analysis.

In addition, the inhabitants ten years of age and over of these cities, when race and nativity are controlled, were marked by lower rates of illiteracy than were suffered in 1890 by the United States as a whole. Slightly more than 1 percent of native whites in the 122 cities in 1890 could not write, compared with over 6 percent nationally (cf. Table 1.6). Approximately 11 percent of foreign-born whites residing in one of the cities were illiterate, while the national proportion for such persons was marginally greater, at 13 percent. Urban nonwhites were also more literate than national statistics for their race suggested. Thirty-five percent in these cities were classified as illiterate, while nearly 57 percent of nonwhites at large met that determination. In this respect, the cities selected for analysis in this study were several decades ahead of the country in a national trend toward a better educated citizenry.

This is in spite of the fact that these cities in 1890 were also much more densely populated with foreign-born individuals than was the nation. For example, about 15 percent of the American population ten years before the turn of the century had been born abroad, but in San Francisco, with sizable Asian and European immigrant communities, the ratio of foreign-born to the total population was .42. In Chicago, the percentage of foreign-born persons in 1890 was nearly 41; in Boston, it was over 35, and in Philadelphia, persons of foreign nativity accounted for 26 percent of the city's population (Clubb, Austin, and Traugott, 1981: 126–128; Weber, 1967: 306).

Given the empirical peculiarities already acknowledged, it is not surprising that the distribution of church affiliations among persons living in these cities was unrepresentative of the national pattern before the turn of the century. Primarily because of their large foreign-born populations, the cities selected for analysis were host to greater-than-average proportions of Jews, Roman Catholics, and German Evangelical Protestants. They contained lesser than likely proportions of Lutherans, Congregationalists, and Baptists (Weber, 1967: 400–401).

Nevertheless, such divergences do not really reduce the appropriateness of these cities as cases illustrating turn-of-the-century social change and its religious consequences. On the contrary, they enhance it. This study seeks to explain social processes, and not necessarily to describe a static historical situation which these units of analysis are thought to exemplify. Therefore, to ascertain the effects of factors like urbanization and industrialization on religious diversity, it is reasonable to seek as examples of these dynamics cities where the social processes were underway on the largest scale and where their religious effects presumably were most acute. "Urbanism will assume its most characteristic and extreme form," Wirth (1938: 9) postulated nearly fifty years ago, "in the measure in which the conditions with which it is congruent are present. Thus the larger, the more densely populated, and the more heterogeneous a community, the more accentuated the characteristics associated with urbanism will be." How large the scale of urban religious change was at the turn of the century is a question pursued in the next section.

## Urban and Religious Growth, 1890–1906

Data on population and total church membership published by the Census for 1890 and 1906 are summarized in Tables 1.7 and 1.8.[12] These and similar data are used throughout this study to measure changes within organized religion and in the wider society as well. The Census religious data are described in more detail in Chapter 2; this section is intended simply to convey the magnitude of the changes in American religion that occurred over the short time examined in this study. Inspection of the two tables reveals that church growth in the period spanning the turn of the century was substantial. This impression is sustained even after consideration of the large increase in the national and urban populations realized in this period, less than one generation in length.

As Table 1.7 reports, the population of the United States between 1890 and 1906 climbed from almost 63 million to over 84 million, an increment of more than one-third. Table 1.8 indicates that the aggregate population of those of the cities selected for analysis for which full data are available grew at an even faster rate, moving from a total figure of about 13½ million in 1890 to almost 21 million in 1906. Taken together, these cities, according to Census statistics, were half again as big in 1906 as they were in 1890. Of 117 cities, just two lost total population in the sixteen years between 1890 and 1906;[13] nine cities in the group more than doubled in size.[14]

At the same time, church membership in America burgeoned. Tables 1.7 and 1.8 show that church growth around the turn of the century outstripped population growth, and that urban church growth was espe-

Table 1.7. *Population growth and religious statistics for the continental United States, 1890–1906*

| Variable | 1890 | 1906 | Percent increase |
|---|---|---|---|
| *Total population* | 62,947,714[a] | 84,246,252[b] | 33.8 |
| *Total church membership* | 20,597,954 | 32,936,445 | 59.9 |
| Protestant | 14,007,187 | 20,287,742 | 44.8 |
| Roman Catholic | 6,241,708 | 12,079,142 | 93.5 |
| Jewish | 130,496 | —[c] | — |
| *Church membership as a percentage of population* | 32.7 | 39.1 | 19.6 |
| *Church organizations* | 165,151 | 212,230 | 28.5 |
| Protestant | 153,054 | 195,618 | 27.8 |
| Roman Catholic | 10,239 | 12,482 | 21.9 |
| Jewish | 533 | 1,769 | 231.9 |
| *Members per church* | 125 | 155 | 24.0 |
| Protestant | 92 | 104 | 13.0 |
| Roman Catholic | 610 | 968 | 58.7 |
| Jewish | 245 | — | — |

[a]"Includes the population of Indian Territory and Indian reservations."
[b]Estimated by the Bureau of the Census.
[c]Jewish membership figures for 1890 and 1906 are not strictly comparable; the latter year's counts, which are not shown here, include only heads of families (cf. Engelman, 1947: 147).
*Sources:* Bureau of the Census (1909, 1910); Carroll (1894).

cially great. Total church membership grew 60 percent nationally between 1890 and 1906, and increased more than 87 percent in the cities. Roman Catholic membership, in particular, roughly doubled over this period, in the beginning of a trend later described as "the most spectacular development in American religious history after the decade of the eighties" (Commager, 1950: 189; see also Canevin, 1917; O'Hara, 1922; Shaughnessy, 1925).[15] Church membership expressed as a percentage of population registered a healthy increase as well. By 1906, 39 percent of Americans belonged to some church, while over 46 percent of city residents were affiliated with a local congregation. The number of church congregations nationwide rose, and rose especially in urban areas, where the rate of growth was nearly double the national pace.

Indeed, about the only statistic for which the urban performance in this time interval was inferior to the national record is that for the

Table 1.8. *Population growth and religious statistics for 117 principal cities in the United States, 1890–1906*[a]

| Variable | 1890 | 1906 | Percent increase |
|---|---|---|---|
| *Total population* | 13,449,529 | 20,749,227 | 54.3 |
| *Total church* | | | |
| *membership* | 5,108,325 | 9,564,897 | 87.2 |
| Protestant | 2,031,238 | 3,487,516 | 71.7 |
| Roman Catholic | 2,886,912 | 5,824,663 | 101.8 |
| Jewish | 108,651 | —[b] | — |
| *Church membership as* | | | |
| *a percentage of* | | | |
| *population* | 38.0 | 46.1 | 21.3 |
| *Church organizations* | 9,867 | 15,033 | 52.4 |
| Protestant | 7,291 | 10,990 | 50.7 |
| Roman Catholic | 1,451 | 1,909 | 31.6 |
| Jewish | 386 | 773 | 100.3 |
| *Members per church* | 518 | 636 | 22.8 |
| Protestant | 279 | 317 | 13.6 |
| Roman Catholic | 1,990 | 3,051 | 53.3 |
| Jewish | 281 | — | — |

[a]Population in 1890 > 25,000 ($N = 122$). Census 1906 population estimates for Los Angeles and San Francisco are unavailable; Roman Catholic Church data for Auburn, Elmira, and Rochester, New York are not reported separately for 1906.
[b]Jewish membership figures for 1890 and 1906 are not strictly comparable.
*Sources:* Bureau of the Census (1910); Carroll (1894).

increase in members per church. However, this comparison largely reflects two coincident trends: the consolidation of rural churches with dwindling memberships, and the more frenzied activity of denominations in establishing new churches for growing city populations. The Census religious data thereby highlight the entrepreneurial nature of urban religious expansion against a background of cooperation in country church contraction.

But Census religious data are themselves problematic, and any attempt to draw inferences from them should first address their obvious inadequacies as well as their special usefulness. It is to this preliminary task that this study turns in Chapter 2.

# "Numbering Israel"

## United States Census Data on Religion

The first recorded descriptions of attempts to determine the size of a religiously distinct population appear, appropriately, in the Bible. The planning, execution, and results of these attempts, furthermore, typify how sets of religious statistics have been assembled and have come to be regarded to this day. For the Bible is pocketed with descriptions of human pride and human fallibility, and of catastrophic mixtures of the two; it is heavy with stories of grand schemes gone awry and of conflict following on confusion. So is the history of statistics on religion.[1] In the Biblical accounts of how the "numbering of Israel" was several times undertaken and accomplished lies evidence of recurring problems in the collection of data on religious membership (cf. Price, 1967; Wolfe, 1932: 358).

The Old Testament's Book of Numbers (chapters 1 and 2) recounts how the God of the Israelites, fresh from leading His people out of Egypt and into the Sinai wilderness, commanded His prophet Moses to recruit a specific assistant from each tribe and, along with His priest Aaron, to register all men in their midst over the age of twenty, "all in Israel who are able to go forth to war, you and Aaron shall number them, company by company" (Numbers 1: 3). Together, the account claims, the fourteen original census takers counted more than 600,000 warriors for the nation of Israel. Only the Levites, whom the Lord had specially designated as guardians of the tabernacle, escaped this initial enumeration.[2]

The efforts of the Israelites at data gathering, whether for purposes of military planning or for the management of ministerial personnel, did not, however, serve them well. The congregation only strayed, and its members, in their disarray, balked at entering Canaan, "a land which flows with milk and honey" (Numbers 14: 8). For although God had chosen this land for the Israelites, it was inhabited already by fearsome peoples. Those who in their cowardice and wickedness opposed the Lord were

22

then barred by Him from ever reaching their new home; instead, the Lord declared, "your dead bodies shall fall in this wilderness" (Numbers 14: 32). A delayed move by the Israelites to approach Canaan from the south was repelled in a crushing military defeat at Hormah.

This development, while disastrous, was not as directly attributable to census-taking activities as were the grave consequences of King David's census of Israel and Judah about 500 years later (2 Samuel 24: 1–25, 1 Chronicles 21: 1–27). Exactly who was responsible for initiating this project is unclear: second Samuel (24: 1) says the Lord "incited David against" Israel; first Chronicles (21: 1) blames Satan, who "stood up against Israel and incited David to number Israel." In any event, it was a task David assumed with obvious relish, though he delegated the actual work of the census to the commanders of his army. His personal enthusiasm is not explained, however, nor was it universally shared. "Why does my lord the king delight in this thing?" asked David's general (and nephew), Jo'ab (2 Samuel 24: 3). "Why," he objected, "should he bring guilt upon Israel?" (1 Chronicles 21: 3). David nevertheless persisted, and Jo'ab withheld full cooperation, eventually returning incomplete figures "because the king's command was abhorrent" to him (1 Chronicles 21: 6).

Almost ten months of canvassing revealed, according to second Samuel, that "in Israel there were eight hundred thousand valiant men who drew the sword, and the men of Judah were five hundred thousand" (2 Samuel 24: 9). The findings of the same census, reported elsewhere (1 Chronicles 21: 5), are read differently: "In all Israel there were one million one hundred thousand men who drew the sword, and in Judah four hundred and seventy thousand who drew the sword." It is not known if David himself encountered these conflicting figures—if he detected, for example, a discrepancy nearing 40 percent in the total for Israel. But he regretted on other grounds having ordered the census. The Bible (2 Samuel 24: 10) records that "David's heart smote him after he had numbered the people," the King confessing that "I have done very foolishly."

In order to compensate, David was given by God a choice of one of three plagues to invite upon his nation: three years of famine, or three months of defeat at the hands of Israel's enemies, or three days of pestilence and mass destruction. David deferred to the Lord, who, in adopting the third option, killed tens of thousands before the King could successfully intercede with Him to halt the slaughter.

As is often the case with the use of narratives from the Bible, these accounts are repeated here not to assess their value as history, but to identify a broader theme. Elements of these particular stories, taken as a composite, unfortunately describe as well patterns in the subsequent

history of efforts to compile religious statistics. First, these researches all are launched at the command of a distant authority. The idea is received with some hesitation, if not met with open resistance. The work is quickly delegated, and in the process some compromise is made between familiarity with the group to be enumerated, on the one hand, and on the other, technical capacity to execute the count efficiently and accurately. Much time and money are expended, and finally the sought-after totals are calculated and released. But the summaries are inconsistent on their face, and are therefore suspect; few who awaited the statistics are pleased.

Like problems have so regularly hampered the collection of religious statistics that contemporary historians normally hold them in disrepute (Landis, 1957). "Nothing is more elusive in church history," Franklin Hamlin Littell (1971: 36) has written, "than honest statistics." Henry Steele Commager (1950: 166) goes farther: "church statistics," he charges, "attain an unreliability that would be a penal offense in a corporation." For this reason, "the world of church statistics" is, according to a prominent inhabitant (Landis, 1959: 348), "one that most social scientists would generally label 'crude.' " Counts of church membership, it is true, have often proven to be inaccurate. Their lack of precision derives from no single source, but is due rather to a multitude of conflicting factors.

This chapter identifies a number of these factors, and examines when and why they are present. At the same time, this chapter introduces the historical religious data available in the United States Census, "the most complete body of statistics of American religion" (Burr, Smith, and Jamison, 1961: 34). The origins and history of Census statistics on religion are explained, the validity of the data is evaluated, and illustrations of how such information has been employed in previous social research are provided.

## Data on Religion in Nineteenth-Century United States Censuses

The United States Census has maintained a long and conflict-ridden relationship with religious matters. Religion, in fact, presented trouble to the Census from the start. Popular piety in part impeded the first decennial Census of the United States, conducted in 1790. The experience of David in numbering Israel was not lost on a proportion of the new Americans: many devoutly religious former colonists resisted Census enumerators, citing Biblical precedent in their defense against the government's intention to number the people of God (Bureau of the Census, 1915: 9; Merriam, 1905: 11).[3] To seek to know the size of God's dominion, many felt, was, in effect, to try to measure His glory by earthly standards and thus, in the end, to claim to have comprehended its limits. The Census, they

reasoned, was little more than a bold temptation to man's pride. Indeed, viewed in this light, any census was an affront to divine authority in a nation whose special mission it was to do God's will in the world.

Scriptural injunctions notwithstanding, between 1850 and 1936, or for more than half of the initial century and one-half of census activity in the United States, religion was an official subject of interest to government statisticians. Inquiries about churches were added to census schedules by the mid-nineteenth century, and were continued as the federal government's involvement in collecting "social" statistics of all types was encouraged by changing national priorities, improving statistical technology, and increasing professionalism among statistical scientists.

The United States Census had grown from a simple enumeration of the young nation's inhabitants in 1790 to include, by 1840, tables on agriculture, manufacturing, education, and welfare. So extensive had the data gathering become that, emboldened by the lifting of cash fines for nonresponse to certain categories of questions, and fearful of the power imparted to the federal government by personal information (particularly information which could constitute the basis for direct taxation), some citizens had eventually refused to cooperate (Lunt, 1888–1889: 82). In other respects, too, the censuses of the early nineteenth century were judged to be unsatisfactory. The amount of error in the results of the 1840 Census alone was a major point of complaint by committees of both the House of Representatives and the Senate (Cassedy, 1984: 172–177; Cohen, 1982: 175–204; Deutsch, 1944; Eckler, 1972: 8; Grob, 1971: 44–48; W. S. Holt, 1929: 14). Two remedies were available: to narrow the boundaries of any future census inquiry, or to impose greater rigor on its conduct (or both).

As plans for the Seventh Census (1850) were being drawn in 1848, therefore, a proposal was made to abbreviate the schedule of questions, which had expanded incrementally from decade to decade, and whose very breadth was seen then to threaten popular support for the census enterprise (Lunt, 1888–1889: 80–83). Prominent statisticians protested, however, and concurrent legislative activity set the Census permanently on a different course, a course emphasizing a systematic census over an unnecessarily streamlined one. Congress in 1849 established the Department of the Interior, and a year later shifted responsibility for the Census to a new office in that department. Also in 1849, an independent board, consisting of the Secretary of State, the Postmaster General, and the Attorney General, was created to oversee preparations for the approaching census. The Senate followed this flurry of reorganization and impaneled a technical committee to help plan the 1850 Census, with assistance from a group of statistical consultants brought to Washington especially for this purpose (W. S. Holt, 1929: 14–15; Lunt, 1888–1889: 83–84).

The value of these precautions and of the deliberate approach to adminis-tration they signified was demonstrated several years later in the produc-tion of what was "commonly known as the first reasonably modern cen-sus" (Rossiter, 1919: 289).

The innovations of the 1850 Census "constituted an epoch in the history of census taking in this country" (Wright, with Hunt, 1900: 47). One of the innovations was the first attempt to compile government data on religion nationwide. Six separate census schedules were designed for 1850. In the last schedule, entitled "Social Statistics," religion was intro-duced in the form of directions to federal marshals and assistant marshals (who acted then as census takers) to return information from local offi-cials on the number of churches in their localities, the denominations they represented, their seating capacities, and the value of church-held property (Wright, with Hunt, 1900: 46, 121, 647, 649–650).[4] Supplemen-tary investigations in 1850 counted religious periodicals, Sunday schools, and church libraries (Good, 1959: 4).

Questions on religious organizations became a fixture in succeeding censuses, although those subsequent efforts did not easily match the scope and ambition of the 1850 undertaking. Hence, the quality of gov-ernment data on churches is not uniform throughout the nineteenth century. The bulk of the work of the 1860 Census was completed before the outbreak of war between North and South, but the conflict prevented full publication of the results (Good, 1959: 4). The 1870 canvass suffered in the Civil War's aftermath, as the chore of collecting data amid the disruption of social life the hostilities had caused fell to political patron-age appointees and, in the South, to untrustworthy agents of Reconstruc-tion governments (W. S. Holt, 1929: 20; Rossiter, 1919: 290). As a result, the Census of 1870, despite its accomplishments in presenting printed social data in charts and on maps, was, in the words of one critic, "per-haps the poorest of the modern group" (Rossiter, 1919: 290). In particu-lar, its religious statistics were judged to be "more or less imperfect" (Carroll, 1912: xxxvi).[5]

New regulations insulated the Census of 1880, in contrast, from such overt political influence. Census-taking duties were at last transferred from United States marshals to enumerators who were local residents appointed "without reference to their political or party affiliations" (quoted in W. S. Holt, 1929: 22, and Lunt, 1888–1889: 92). Professional-ism advanced further when, in the planning of the counts and in the tabulation of the results, Census personnel were allowed assistance from "special agents," temporary consultants hired for their specific knowl-edge or expertise (W. S. Holt, 1929: 24). Equally as important were changes instituted in the content of the census inquiry. By the addition of numerous questions, "the scope of the census was extended to encyclo-

paedic proportions" (W. S. Holt, 1929: 21), making the Census of 1880 "the most ambitious effort ever made up to that date, expensive and elaborate" (Rossiter, 1919: 290).

This ambition was clearly reflected in the attention accorded religion in the 1880 Census. Gone was the brief series of blanks in which the enumerator was to enter the details of local church organizations and the buildings in which their membership met. It was replaced by a lengthy schedule, calling for 372 items of information (Wright, with Hunt, 1900: 122),[6] the outline of a project which remains, a century later, one of the most comprehensive national studies of local religious organizations ever performed. The schedule solicited an array of information about church facilities and other property, but supplemented these inquiries with questions which more adequately convey the modern image of the individual church as a functioning organization, with problems of leadership, management, membership, and programing. These more practical matters about which the Census asked included the numbers and statuses of clergy and other church staff, the number of church members,[7] the criteria for membership in the congregation, the average attendance at various services, and the church's income, expenditures, and debt. Two questionnaires appended to the main schedule dealt, respectively, with educational programs conducted by religious bodies (Sabbath and "industrial" schools and their enrollments, libraries, and teachers) and church-affiliated men's and women's associations.

The growing diversity of American religion in the late nineteenth century is openly acknowledged by still two more special inquiries on churches in the 1880 Census. The first was directed to pacifist sects, and so the respondents were assured that their answers merely "may be of interest to the general public" and bore "no relation whatever to taxation or to military enrollment" ("Special Schedule: Inquiries Relating to Peace Denominations," reprinted in Wright, with Hunt, 1900: 793). The second sought to gain an understanding of the organization and activities of spiritualist societies.

But what most strongly establishes the sophisticated and unconventional approach of the 1880 Census's special schedule on churches are its initiatives in gathering evidence on religious life over time and in ecological context. Interest in religious change is indicated by requests for the date of the church's founding and the number of charter members, as well as for membership totals of a decade ago. A concern for the measurement of the immediate religious environment is apparent in questions about the proportion of the population of the town where the church is located which attends *any* church, and the number of other churches within a three-mile radius.

What was otherwise "one of the most successful efforts made by any

country in the way of statistical and social science" (Lunt, 1888–1889: 92), however, limped to a strangely inconclusive finish. The loss thereby to students of historical church statistics is incalculable. In 1879, the Superintendent of the Census, Francis A. Walker, motivated by what he later termed "an overweening desire to make the then approaching enumeration at once both the best and the cheapest" submitted to the Congress, he himself confessed, an "absurdly low estimate of the cost" (Walker, 1888: 140).

By the middle of the 1881 fiscal year, the original appropriation for the tabulation and publication of the results of the 1880 Census was depleted. Some 700 Census clerks moved to "voluntary" duty and accepted government certificates in lieu of paychecks until additional funds could be approved by Congress (W. S. Holt, 1929: 25; Wright, with Hunt, 1900: 68). The impact of Walker's (1888: 141) "ambitious folly" was softened by these extraordinary appropriations, but never was enough money put forward to complete the Census as it was conceived. The extensive statistics on churches the Census Office had compiled languished in an unpublished state.

In the meantime, Walker's successor as Superintendent of the Census (and the man under whose scrutiny the 1880 data were being arranged for publication), Colonel Charles W. Seaton, died. It was said of Seaton that he "spoke contemptuously" of the job of organizing the church statistics from the 1880 Census, and "scoffed at" the requirement that he fill pages of census volumes with such "stuff" (Hull, 1889: 414, 419). While the "hostility and prejudice of Col. Seaton," it was charged, slowed the preparation of the Census's religious statistics, his death could not but have aggravated the "indisposition" he demonstrated toward the assignment (Hull, 1889: 414, 413).[8]

Dwindling resources, and leadership which was lethargic and uncooperative when it was not absent, drove the Census into trouble. Many publications were delayed, and some were, in time, canceled altogether. Among the latter were the reports on churches (W. S. Holt, 1929: 26; Wright, with Hunt, 1900: 68). Interim officers of the Census, however, denied any negligence in the matter of church statistics. H. L. Muldrow, Acting Secretary of the Interior, excused himself with the claim that the 1880 religious data were "not . . . regarded by the Department as either reliable or complete" (quoted in Hull, 1889: 415). "These statistics were found to be in such unsatisfactory condition," he told an inquiring Congressional committee chairman, "that it was some time since determined that the Department would not be justified in directing their publication" (quoted in Hull, 1889: 417).

Official statements like Muldrow's were met with skepticism – especially among some veterans of the Census Office. They viewed the quick

dismissal of the 1880 Census's vast collection of religious statistics as a serious lapse in duty. Indeed, this ultimate omission qualified as one of two "outright failures of the census of 1880," in the blunt admission of Superintendent Walker (1888: 143n).[9] Religious professionals as well were distressed. "It is an agnostic Census," complained one clergyman (Hull, 1889: 419), "and the omitted part referred to is placed just where Robert C. Ingersoll[10] would have it."

All that survives in published form of the statistics on religious organizations of the 1880 Census is some information in the volumes on *Social Statistics of Cities* (e.g., Waring, 1887) describing the churches of selected major cities by denomination (Schmeckebier, 1925: 140).

The Census of 1890, relative to the one which preceded it, is both a relief and a disappointment to the historian. Its statistics *were* eventually and completely published, but they were, in their very conception, comparatively fewer and more limited.

In 1889, Henry K. Carroll, an experienced church statistician, was engaged by the Census Office as a special agent to direct the collection and compilation of religious data for the Census of 1890.[11] Carroll was strongly intent on not replicating the overly ambitious Census of 1880. Rather, he declared himself "determined to make the scope of the inquiry broad enough to embrace the necessary items of information, and narrow enough to insure success in collecting, tabulating, and publishing them" (Carroll, 1912: xi).

Consequently, the extent of the 1890 investigation was modest. In all, the Census of that year carried only thirteen items pertaining to churches (Wright, with Hunt, 1900: 122, 794–795). More important than what the Census overlooked in 1890, however, is what it provided and how it did so. For the first time, a census successfully published, in an impressive oversized volume (Carroll, 1894), information on the membership (defined as numbers of "communicants") of American religious bodies.

Another innovation was the manner in which these data were gathered. Carroll's background in organized religion led him to bypass the system of federal marshals and local officials relied upon in previous censuses for information on churches. The Census Office, at their Special Agent's direction, instead recruited clerks and secretaries of regional administrative districts of church groups (such as dioceses, synods, conferences, and presbyteries) to survey all the individual congregations they served. The local churches, in turn, handed up figures on their membership and property, figures which were then transmitted to Washington. Unaffiliated churches (such as those composed by independent Lutherans) were located by requests to ministers of like tradition, but of churches affiliated with a higher denominational body, to report other congregations they knew of in their vicinity. "This method proved to be

quite practicable, and very satisfactory," Carroll (1912: xii-xiii) concluded. "Several thousand agents thus gave information which they were best qualified to secure, and the results were found, when tests were applied, to be full and accurate."

## Censuses of Religious Bodies, 1906–1936

Until the twentieth century, the Census Office was a temporary – though regularly recurring – organization, constituted by an ad hoc order before the turn of each decade and withering into a kind of bureaucratic receivership at the conclusion of its work. Each census was commenced from scratch, and its apparatus was some years later dismantled without great ceremony, often only shortly before the whole process was to be repeated. Soon thereafter, another superintendent had to be engaged, and the entire central staff rehired or assembled anew. The discontinuity caused by the Census Office's temporary mandate was severe: as Robert P. Porter, Superintendent of the Census of 1890, recalled, "When I was appointed, I had nothing but one clerk and a messenger, and a desk with some white paper on it" (quoted in W. S. Holt, 1929: 27).

Reservations about the efficiency of this practice, coupled with a desire for an ongoing agency to coordinate federal statistical activity, prompted Congress, in 1902, to pass "An Act to Provide for a Permanent Census Office."[12] The Act both reorganized the structure and respecified the duties of the Census Office. In the course of these changes, efforts at gathering certain types of statistics were removed from the decennial census and relocated in the intercensal period, to distribute more evenly the workload of the redefined agency. By this shift were inaugurated, in 1905, the Census of Manufactures, and in 1906, the first of four Censuses of Religious Bodies (Eckler, 1972: 55; W. S. Holt, 1929: 118).

The Censuses of Religious Bodies represented both a quantitative and a qualitative break from the government's pattern of religious data gathering in the nineteenth century. These counts, conducted in the first four decades of this century (in years ending in the numeral "6"), sought the collection of more information from more officials than was achieved in the 1890 Census. Planners of the Censuses of Religious Bodies had devised a continuing project which, though quite direct in its methods, is mind-boggling in its proportions, even today.

Essentially the same procedure was followed in all four Censuses of Religious Bodies. In brief, the process entailed first securing from official representatives of American religious bodies, large and small, orthodox and not, and from their directories and yearbooks, exhaustive lists of their churches and pastors, including their addresses. This information was then manually transferred to, and stored on, a set of nearly a quarter

of a million individual file cards—one for each reported congregation (W. S. Holt, 1929: 118). Next, a short schedule was designed by the Census Bureau, in consultation with leaders of various religious organizations, and, with the aid of the file cards, a massive correspondence was undertaken. Its purpose was simple: to solicit statistics on membership, property, and activities, directly, via a mailed questionnaire, from *every known local church organization in the nation.*

If no response was returned by the congregation's pastor or clerk, a reminder was sent. In some cases, second and third reminders were dispatched, along with a duplicate copy of the schedule. If still no information was forthcoming, the Census called upon denominational officers to intervene to encourage cooperation. Telegrams bearing pleas to churches to participate were issued by the hundreds. And when these means failed, the full resources of the government were mobilized. Local postmasters were enlisted to help locate and to prod nonresponding pastors in their jurisdictions, and some "recalcitrant" churches were paid personal visits by field agents of the Census (Bureau of the Census, 1930: 5–6; Fry, 1930b: vi). Additional data on groups that were difficult to enumerate, such as Jews (Engelman, 1935, 1947; Linfield, 1938), were obtained through the appointment of special agents, persons trusted in and knowledgeable about these religious communities.

These efforts combined to induce very high rates of response for the first three Censuses of Religious Bodies—in 1906, 1916, and 1926. "Census information about the number of churches," boasted C. Luther Fry (1930b: vi), the most experienced student of Census church statistics, "is virtually 100 per cent. complete." "There were ... relatively few criticisms of the compilations for the years 1906 and 1916," and the 1926 data, by virtue of their completeness and accuracy, are generally considered to exemplify statistical work on churches in its highest stage of methodological refinement (*Information Service,* 1945: 4; Landis, 1957: 3; cf. Stark, Bainbridge, and Kent, 1981). The counts from each administration of this census were aggregated by cities, counties, and states, and were published with authoritative and detailed historical sketches of the denominations encompassed in the totals.

The sole flawed edition in this series occurred in 1936, in connection with what turned out to be the final Census of Religious Bodies to be published. The Census in that year came close to being canceled before it started. Committee action in the House of Representatives removed the appropriation for the Census from a longer bill, but President Roosevelt stepped in and endowed a more modest budget for the project from the WPA "work relief funds" at his discretion. Underfunded and late, the Census of Religious Bodies returned for the fourth time in 1938 (*Information Service,* 1945: 4; Landis, 1940: 1–2; Weber, 1939: 1).

The enumeration which was eventually accomplished was conceded to be "seriously incomplete" (Murphy, 1941: 48), perhaps because of social dislocations associated with the Depression (Bainbridge and Stark, 1981: 40; Singleton, 1975: 210n).[13] A more likely cause of the lower totals, however, is organized resistance to reporting. Extremist churchmen were said to fear "that the New Deal would soon do to the churches what Hitler had just done to them in Germany" (*Information Service,* 1956: 1).[14] More concretely, they viewed as a provocation by the state a routine addendum to the Census schedule in 1936 which reminded pastors that they were compelled by federal law to respond fully and truthfully to all questions; the penalties for noncompliance were spelled out in detail (Landis, 1940: 2; Sperry, 1946: 66–67). Whether in spite of the warning or because of it, many clergy did not cooperate.

A wave of civil disobedience, supported by religious libertarians and joined by conservative and fundamentalist clergy, ultimately crippled the inquiry. Some estimates hold that as many as 20 percent of American churches may have gone uncounted in the 1936 Census (Bureau of the Census, 1975: 389–390; *Information Service,* 1961: 5; Landis, 1957: 3, 1959: 340, 1960: 3). Later analyses showed nonresponding churches to be concentrated in rural areas, in the South and West, and within the Methodist and Southern Baptist denominations (*Information Service,* 1956: 2; Reuss, 1943).

Whereas the 1936 Census of Religious Bodies yielded undercounts, the 1946 Census fared worse yet: it brought forth nothing. An initial appropriation for the canvass was secured from Congress, and schedules were prepared for mailing to local churches in early 1947. The Census had to be aborted when it was more than 60 percent completed, however, because money to support the latter phases of the project was denied by Congress.[15] No statistics from the 1946 Census were ever published (Eckler, 1972: 55; *Information Service,* 1956: 2, 1961: 6, 1963: 5; Landis, 1957: 3, 1959: 340, 1960: 3; United States Department of Commerce, 1954: 55; Whitman and Trimble, 1956). Indeed, involvement of the Census Bureau in collecting and distributing church membership statistics ended abruptly with the 1946 failure. Efforts have since been mounted by church groups to revive the Census of Religious Bodies (see, e.g., *Information Service,* 1963), but to no avail.[16] "It seems safe to predict," a former director of the Census Bureau (Eckler, 1972: 55) has ventured, "that the 1936 report will remain the final one in this series."[17]

## Validity and Value of Census Church Membership Data

"There simply are no reliable historical statistics on church membership," writes Charles Y. Glock (1959: 39), "and it is extremely doubtful

that accurate statistics can be produced through manipulating the unreliable ones." Census statistics on church membership may not deserve inclusion in Glock's generalization, but as the products of a legacy riddled with conflict and confusion, data on religion from the United States Census merit regard with a special skepticism. The statistics qualify, further, for careful evaluation to check their validity. Accordingly, this section assesses the data's integrity. Below are identified a number of sources of possible error (cf. Dollar and Jensen, 1971: 30–31; Jacob, 1984). Estimates of the extent to which these factors may have biased the data are furnished. In addition, past criticisms of Census data on religion are collated and addressed.

## Varying Definitions of Membership

The element of church membership statistics that is most troublesome to quantitative research is the definition of membership itself: what do the numbers signify? The definition varies markedly both across religious bodies and within them over time. Unless close attention is paid to these differences, any analysis of church statistics is prone to erroneous conclusions (Brown, 1922: 67; Currie, Gilbert, and Horsley, 1977: 18–19; Demerath, 1968: 354; Fry, 1930a: 1044; Hall, 1930: 267–268; Hudson, 1955b: 1495; *Information Service*, 1961: 4–5; Landis, 1957: 3, 1959: 337, 1960: 4; Lipset, 1959: 18, 1967: 165; Moberg, 1962: 29, 36; Petersen, 1962: 168, 170; Silcox and Fisher, 1934: 27–28).

Religious groups recognize different classes of their adherents as members, and which persons a group will designate as qualified normally depends on its history and polity, or system of church government (see VanderMeer, 1981). Roman Catholicism and "liturgical" Protestantism (i.e., Episcopalianism and Lutheranism) are the descendants in America of old European universalist or established church systems, wherein church membership was the formal companion to, and virtual equivalent of, national citizenship (Kieffer, 1928). These traditions practice infant baptism, and have counted as full members all persons so admitted to their ranks.

In contrast, most American Protestant churches are more restrictive in their conception of membership. They consider affiliation with a congregation to be the personal and voluntary decision of a mature individual, and they often require that it be accompanied by a public profession of faith or by some discernible evidence of religious conviction. This commitment, expected though it might be, seldom takes place before early adolescence. Thus, "pietistic" Protestant bodies rarely regard as regular members churchgoers below the age of 13.

The statistical picture is clouded further when Jews and Eastern Ortho-

dox church members are examined. Because these traditions are organized around common ethnic group membership, it is presumed to be
evident to persons within them who belongs as a coreligionist and who
does not. Hence, formal definitions of voluntary membership, after the
Protestant fashion, have never had to be constructed. The definitions that
exist are premised on hereditary qualifications.

Indeed, the idea that membership for Jews and Orthodox Christians is
adopted rather than acquired was, until recently, an alien notion. The
same thing may be said of Catholicism as well. The bases of membership
in these groups reverse the sequence of affiliation used as a model by
Protestants. As Oscar Handlin (1951: 119) explains it, "The Church gave
no reasons for being; it was. Its communicants were within it not because
they had rationally accepted its doctrines; they had faith because they
were in it." In these traditions, membership is ascribed, and it is disaffilia-
tion which is voluntary (though sometimes difficult).

The record of the Census in controlling for differences in conceptions
of membership is mixed. In 1890, churches were asked to report the
numbers of "communicants" on their rolls—that is, the sum of persons
whose membership was sufficiently advanced as to permit them to participate in the most common ritual in the Christian tradition. A similar effort
was made in 1906 to restrict reporting to full members. In what has been
termed "a noble but necessarily crude standardization" (Demerath, 1968:
354), 15 percent of total Catholic membership in both years was sub-
tracted to remove noncommunicating Catholic children (Bureau of the
Census, 1909: 13; Carroll, 1912: 71).[18] Latter-day Saints (Mormons) correspondingly restricted their membership counts to persons over eight
years of age. The instruction to return communicants thus reduced the
inequities generated by the habit in some denominations of counting
small children, but it afforded little guidance to Jews and other non-
Christian bodies, or to Protestant groups that shun ceremony, such as
Quakers.

Nevertheless, statistical definitions of Jewish membership were con-
trived for census purposes. In 1890, pewholders in Jewish synagogues
were counted as analogous to Christian communicants. By 1906, Jewish
membership figures were limited to heads of Jewish families.[19] In 1926,
the biggest change of all was effected: the Census Bureau expanded its
conception of Jewish membership to embrace an estimate of all persons
of Jewish background residing in communities served by a synagogue
(Engelman, 1947: 134–135, 159–162; cf. Engelman, 1935; Linfield,
1938; Robison, 1949: 186n). Over time, membership totals for Eastern
Orthodox churches have come to be based on just such a "cultural
population" count (Bureau of the Census, 1975: 389; *Information Service,* 1961; Landis, 1957: 3, 1959: 337; Moberg, 1962: 36), although these

estimates have been termed "too general to be regarded as even an 'educated' guess" (Hudson, 1955b: 1494).

In 1916 and after, the Census simply left it to the churches (with the exception of Jews) to decide themselves whom to count. The subsequent tables reflect the statistical opportunity the government's subjectivism had created. Following the 1906 Census of Religious Bodies, several Protestant denominations altered their membership criteria, both lowering the minimum age at which full membership could be achieved and relaxing the rules governing the processes of adult affiliation (Fry, 1930a: 1047–1048). That American Protestants were gravitating toward a European standard of church membership at the same time that they faced numerical competition from European-origin groups, such as Catholics, with inclusive definitions of membership, was not accidental. "While the reasons advanced for the changes made by the various denominations in their membership standards did not allude to such competitive considerations," Seymour Martin Lipset (1967: 167n–168n) argues, "there can be little doubt that these played a role." Statistical solipsism prevailed in Census religious counts after 1906, and the fact that some churches exploited it renders the later statistics more difficult to interpret.

Even conceding the historical importance of artifactual changes in reported church membership, calculations using 1926 Census of Religious Bodies data for seventy-eight large cities (Bainbridge and Stark, 1981: 41) have shown that neither variations among denominations in age restrictions on membership nor a broadly inclusive definition of Jewish membership affects overall church membership rates greatly. The crude membership rate and the same rate adjusted for these two irregularities are very highly correlated.

Falsification of Membership Statistics

Although the various censuses differed in the level of the official to whom they appealed for religious statistics, the ultimate sources of those statistics were the same: local church membership rosters. The integrity of these records is subject to ambivalent pressures. That pastors pad their membership statistics so as to create for their superiors the illusion of a thriving congregation is, to many critics, beyond any doubt. "Ecclesiastical statistics are exceedingly untrustworthy," historian Thomas Cuming Hall (1930: 212) has warned. His recommendation is to deduct 15 to 20 percent from all church membership totals, because "the temptation for the individual church to exaggerate its numbers for the higher courts and assemblies is overwhelming and seldom resisted" (Hall, 1930: 213n).

On the other hand, in many denominations, the costs of the central administrative body's activities are distributed among the constituent

churches in proportion to the size of the congregation. A fraudulently large congregation's phantom members not only do not contribute to the church, they may under such a plan harm its financial well-being. This practice, then, is a disincentive to deliberate inflation of membership totals (Fry, 1930a: 1046, 1930b: 9; Fry and Jessup, 1933: 1020; Silcox and Fisher, 1934: 28; Weber, 1939: 5). In Roman Catholic churches, a further disincentive to reporting large numbers is present: the fear that a growing parish might be subdivided and that resources would thereby be spread too thinly over an increasing number of territorially based administrative units (Shaughnessy, 1925: 200). Thus, the urge to falsify church statistics does not uniformly push the totals in one direction. Whatever bias that is introduced into church membership data in this way is not clearly systematic (cf. Currie et al., 1977: 16–17).

The Census's religious data anyway are probably freer than most from fraud, for two reasons. First, that the enumerations were carried out by an authority of the federal government apparently encouraged honesty and diligence on the part of those queried, at least early in the series (Fry, 1930b: v-vi). Second, beginning with the first Census of Religious Bodies in 1906, statistics were transmitted from the local churches directly to the Census Bureau; they did not pass up through the denominational hierarchy and were not open to its inspection. Much less therefore depended on the numerical growth or decline of any one congregation, and so inducements to tamper with the figures were not as pronounced.

## Bad Record-Keeping by Churches

Probably more common than deliberate falsification of membership figures, however, is error which enters the data simply as a result of poor accounting. Churches, even highly rationalized ones, are not businesses, and they do not exist primarily to keep records and amass archival material. Few resources are available in local churches to set up an elaborate system of information on church members or to train personnel to maintain one in place. In some churches, the clergy are doubly clerical, in that they assume the additional role of clerk. And, as church statistician Benson Y. Landis (1957: 3; cf. *Information Service,* 1961: 4) has charitably observed, "it has often been said that pastors, priests, and rabbis are not distinguished for their work with figures."

Individual churches are thought to experience particular difficulty in keeping membership records current. As *The Nation* (1883: 443) editorialized in 1883:

It is notorious that nearly every individual church, as well as every considerable denomination, has upon its records the names of many persons whom it reports as communicants, yet who have no right to be numbered

among our distinctively Christian population. Some of them have lapsed from the faith and never show their faces inside a church, out of sheer indifference and unbelief. Others are non-resident, who may be dead, or agnostics, or members of other churches, for all that anyone knows, and yet their names stand in the books year after year.

No matter how serious this problem was one hundred years ago, it probably has not improved with time ( cf. *Information Service*, 1936). Modern patterns of residential mobility, sociologists (e.g., Welch, 1985: 9–33; Welch and Baltzell, 1984; Wuthnow and Christiano, 1979) have noted, have damaged the interests of settled social institutions like the church. Church records reflect this injury: as more people move, a greater proportion of any church's currently registered membership will be unaccounted for, or will be duplicated on the rolls of another church, and a greater proportion of its future constituency will escape detection (Demerath, 1968: 356; Glock, 1959: 36; Hudson, 1955b: 1495; Landis, 1957: 3, 1959: 348, 1960: 4; Lipset, 1967: 165n; Moberg, 1962: 35). Census church statistics, then, compare favorably with religious statistics of any era, although there is still no solution to the problem of tracking accurately a highly mobile population of American church members.

Inadequate Coverage by the Censuses

The statistics of local churches may be intact and accurate, but this is of little import if the church is overlooked in the census. Any project which attempts to communicate with a population of organizations on the same massive scale as the Censuses of Religious Bodies did will doubtless miss some number of them. More crucially, these neglected organizations will share certain traits, features which predisposed them to exclusion from notice by other religious bodies and by the government. Uncounted churches will probably be relatively new, rather small, and unaffiliated with any larger body. They will more often than not be located in sparsely settled areas, and will draw their membership from the lower social strata and from among persons marginal to the community.

It is difficult to estimate the extent of any possible Census undercount of religious organizations. The Census planners worked from information supplied by denominations, and if the completeness of the censuses is judged with respect to these statistics, the government counts were remarkably successful. Fry ( 1930b: vi), to illustrate, revealed in his book summarizing the results of the 1926 Census of Religious Bodies that

in no case did the Government figures for membership differ from the denominational returns by as much as 10 per cent., while the average

difference was only 2 per cent. So far as church expenditures are concerned, the average difference was only 1.5 per cent.

The single effort in the sociological literature to validate independently Census data on religious organizations (Reuss, 1943) corroborates Fry's conclusion. The analysis is concerned solely with the state of Washington as reported in the 1936 Census of Religious Bodies, which, as has been noted, was marred by widespread nonresponse. Still, the discrepancies between the total numbers of churches counted by the Census and the normally larger numbers claimed in denominational directories averaged only about ten percent, "a favorable showing in view of the methodological obstacles" (Reuss, 1943: 345). This positive evaluation assumes, further, that the denominational statistics are not themselves inflated. Urban areas, it was found, were more thoroughly enumerated than regions outside of cities. Since cities are the units of analysis in this study, the Census religious data for them seem acceptably comprehensive.

Yet, there were religious groups operating in cities that were not on any of the original lists of the censuses. For example, Rodney Stark et al. (1981: 139) have found that the 1926 Census of Religious Bodies provided no data on scores of cult movements whose existence they have verified from historical sources. The groups that were omitted from the census tabulations are likely, however, to have been so tiny as not to influence the church membership profiles even of small geographical units like cities. Indeed, although a staggering heterogeneity of faiths is depicted by the groups the censuses did enumerate, the majority of church members in America have historically belonged to one of a few very large denominations. In the five religious censuses between 1890 and 1936, the proportion of national church membership accounted for by the five largest religious divisions hovered each time at around three-fifths; the fraction included in the ten largest groups likewise remained stable across the decades, at slightly more than three-quarters.[20] Therefore, it seems likely that the Census statistics adequately represent the main historical contours of organized religion in the United States.

Errors in Tabulation

Census religious statistics, like all quantitative data, are susceptible to errors in tabulation. How many such errors exist in the printed tables is difficult to determine. One gauge is available through checks on internal consistency: do the figures for all subgroups and all cases on all variables sum to the totals reported in the printed tables? Tests conducted on data from 1890 and 1906 as a prelude to the empirical analyses in this study uncovered only one obvious tabulation error: the transposition of 1890

membership totals for Quakers in Portland, Maine and Portland, Oregon. Of course, there may be still more errors embedded in the tables and not reflected in inconsistent marginals and subtotals. However, their number is likely to be small, because the facilities of the Census Office were the most sophisticated of their time in America. For example, the Hollerith punched-card system of data tabulation, the forerunner of the modern IBM card reader, was developed in collaboration with the Census. It was first used to collate data from the Census of 1890 (Truesdell, 1965).

Other Criticisms of Census Data

Possibly the most enduring of the several criticisms of Census data on religion emanates from two textbooks by T. Lynn Smith (1947, 1948), a rural sociologist and demographer. The books contain segments that describe the religious composition of, respectively, rural American society and the American population as a whole. In each case, Smith prefaces his clear exposition with a history and critique of Census religious statistics. The history is not extensive, but the critique of Census methods and their products is vigorous:

Not only is the procedure followed clumsy, incomplete in results, much more expensive than need be, and unable to secure comparability from denomination to denomination, but it fails to give a complete inventory of the religious affiliations or preferences of the population which can be studied in relation to the other characteristics of the people. The entire population is not included, and the results are divorced from the data on the other fundamental population characteristics. [Smith, 1947: 90]

If by this, Smith means to accuse the Censuses of Religious Bodies of being counts of church membership and not surveys of religious identification, he is accurate, but the blame is misplaced. The law which authorized the censuses stipulated that religious organizations, and not individuals more or less religious, be the subjects of the canvasses. A second object of Smith's complaint could be the placement of the Censuses of Religious Bodies in mid-decade, between the more inclusive Censuses of Population. There, he suggests, the censuses are statistically adrift, excluded from the relevant time referents of most other federal population statistics, and comprising data on organizations—not individuals—at that. The consequence, he insists in the second book (Smith, 1948: 176), is that the data which the Censuses of Religious Bodies yielded "are almost impossible to correlate with other census data."

Actual analysis of the data indicates otherwise. Research experience with the data, as the section which follows makes clear, has demon-

strated that the charge that Census data on religion cannot usefully be analyzed in conjunction with other Census data is largely incorrect. These other data must of necessity be presented at the aggregate level, but this quality does not impair their value. In instances in which the charge might be sustained, it is still exaggerated. While population estimates for intercensal years either do not exist or are difficult to secure, the Census's religious information is as temporally proximate to successive editions of important social structural data (such as those on manufacturing activity, which alternately are the products of a mid-decade census) as is the decennial census. What is more, church membership rates for geographical units have exhibited stability over time (Bainbridge and Hatch, 1982: 244), thereby weakening Smith's objection that religious data cannot be related to other Census statistics of a few years prior or a few years later.

Smith's critique, which is nearly forty years old, is unfortunate not so much because it is wrong, but because it did not, from all appearances, result from attempts at statistical manipulation of these data, because it has been repeated uncritically by authors equally disinclined to test it, and because this echo has reverberated long enough to discourage the initiation of much potentially fruitful research. "Shifts in definition are so numerous as largely to invalidate comparison," Dorothy Good (1959: 8) complains, thus ratifying Smith's dissatisfaction with the Censuses of Religious Bodies. "Correlations with data on other characteristics," she adds, "are generally lacking." David O. Moberg, writing in one of the first textbooks on the sociology of American religion, points out that "the data are incomplete and lack internal consistency and comparability. It is almost impossible to correlate them with other census data" (Moberg, 1962: 28).[21]


## Summary

This section has reviewed the "relatively meager documentation on the limitations or defects" of historical statistics of religious affiliation (Landis, 1959: 336), and, proceeding from it, has tried to ascertain the validity of United States Census data on church membership. General criticisms of church membership statistics, it was found, are not especially applicable to Census data on religion. These censuses were the grandest research projects ever undertaken in the quantitative study of American religion, and they possess a level of rigor more than appropriate to their scale. The extensive follow-up procedures employed by the Censuses of Religious Bodies testify to the care with which these data were gathered. Attention was devoted, particularly early in the series, to ensuring that

the counts from the censuses would be comparable across religious groups and over time. Church record-keeping was no less reliable then than it is now, and natural incentives to falsify the data were absent. Furthermore, criticisms specific to these data appear, upon examination, to be weak or even mistaken.

Census statistics on church membership are, then, "by far the most complete and dependable source of information in this field" (Fry, 1930b: vii). In contrast, many individual denominations did not generate and distribute their own statistics, and none that did could match the scope and scale of the government's efforts. The denominations either did not canvass on the level of local congregations, or did so irregularly, or in regularly doing so did not use consistent methods, or did not disaggregate their totals by small geographical units and publish them widely (*Information Service,* 1956: 2; Landis, 1957: 3, 1959: 339–340, 1960: 3).

Data Selected for Analysis

For the purposes of this study, data from the 1890 decennial Census (Carroll, 1894) and the 1906 Census of Religious Bodies (Bureau of the Census, 1910) were chosen for statistical analysis. These two data sets qualified for further examination on grounds of quality, utility, comparability, and historical importance. As the brief history of Census religious statistics in this chapter suggests, "the data prior to 1890 are especially suspect" (Demerath, 1968: 354). Even if they were of greater validity, data from earlier nineteenth-century censuses would not be helpful to this project, because tabulation of religious statistics for principal cities did not commence until the publication of the returns of the 1890 Census. In fact, church membership totals, as distinguished from estimates of church seating accommodations, were not released in any form until the 1890s (Finke and Stark, 1986). Data after 1906, in turn, are rendered inappropriate for longitudinal study by changes in the bases by which critical concepts such as membership were defined; these changes are described as well in this chapter.

Luckily, the data which are most suitable for this analysis, from a methodological standpoint, are also those which are historically the most relevant. The 1890 and 1906 data straddle the turn of the century, and overlap what has been thought, in a classic interpretation, to be a "critical period" in the development of American religion (Schlesinger, 1932). In this regard, the data contain evidence of the effects on the structure of organized religion of its initial responses to surging urbanization and of its first contacts, on a large scale, with an alien immigrant population.

## Previous Uses of United States Census Data on Religious Bodies

Some recent social scientific studies analyzing data on religion from United States Censuses bemoan the fact that these data have been "almost wholly neglected" (Stark and Bainbridge, 1981a: 131n). The authors lament that Census data "have languished relatively unused for many decades in university libraries" (Stark et al., 1981: 138), "sadly neglected and forgotten" (Stark and Bainbridge, 1981b: 360). "If sociologists noticed these data when they appeared," a team of investigators (Stark, Bainbridge, Crutchfield, Doyle, and Finke, 1983: 10) declares, "they were not prompted to use them in research." "And," they add, "there is no evidence that sociologists in recent decades have even known the data existed" (Stark et al., 1983: 10). Social scientists even now, it is claimed, "have only begun to exploit" these data (Bainbridge and Stark, 1981: 39).

It is evident that the newest uses of Census religious statistics are among the most inventive and informative, and it is the consensus of opinion among analysts that the data permit much promising sociological research on American religion to be undertaken in the future. In heralding the rediscovery of these data by social scientists, however, researchers have been hasty to imply that little had been accomplished with them in the past. In fact, data on religion from United States Censuses have for about a century functioned in a variety of applications, depending on the purposes of the user.

This section identifies a succession of census users and describes what they sought to demonstrate with these data. Applications range from immediate and literal quantitative description to more advanced social scientific analyses. While most of these applications do not realize fully the data's newly recognized potential for informing the history of American religious groups, it is not accurate to suggest, either, that Census religious statistics have until now been totally ignored.

The earliest and in some respects most impassioned uses of Census religious data were on the surface descriptive, but beneath had a hortatory motivation. They appeared not long after each edition of the data was released, because those who so quickly seized them had urgent arguments to make. The users were church leaders, religious commentators, social critics, and reformers (or all of these), and they saw in the census a factual basis for the rhetoric they had pronounced in support of an increasingly beleaguered evangelical Protestantism and the various versions of "applied" or "social" Christianity it offered in defense of its capacity to address contemporary crises. Among those who sounded the alarm against the perils of modern urbanism using Census data were Samuel Lane Loomis (1887), Charles Stelzle (1912), and Josiah Strong (1891). Indeed, Strong's most famous work, *Our Country,* was originally

published in 1885, but was specially revised by the author after the 1890 Census and reprinted in a new edition, with more up-to-date statistics, in 1891. Strong in particular was praised as an author who "invested church statistics with human interest, and the figures of the census, the departments of government, the board of trade, and of organized labor with religious significance" (Graham Taylor, quoted in Muller, 1959: 190).

But as the social issues which the Census was thought to illuminate receded in religious significance, when the Social Gospel and related movements were gradually assimilated by the progressive wing in American domestic politics, interest in these data was still sustained. Their utility, if not always their validity, was so widely accepted that they came to constitute a national and interdenominational baseline of religious measurement (see Bass, 1929: 329–343; Brown, 1922: 65–72; Fry, 1930a, 1930b; Fry and Jessup, 1933; Hart, 1942; A. E. Holt, 1929; Landis, 1935; Pearl, 1931; Swift, 1938).[22] The Census was, after all, the sole source for comprehensive information on church membership, Christian and non-Christian, nationwide—no single denomination could hope to duplicate it. So important, in fact, were the Census data to ongoing research in church planning and administration that religious bodies and cooperative agencies became chief advocates for their continued and improved collection (see, e.g., *Information Service,* 1945, 1946, 1963; cf. Good, 1959: 4; Moberg, 1962: 28–29).

Among scholars, by far the most frequent users of Census data on religion have been historians. Yet historians, by and large, have failed to employ these data in any but the most limited way. Though historians are normally more analytical than are social reformers, they likewise confined the data to the work of simple description. Seldom, for instance, have the data been examined by historians for systematic trends or related in their works to emerging conditions or coincident events. More common is an almost casual resort to the Census tables for a number or several to insert into an otherwise impressionistic narrative on a certain religious group or a general social history of a particular region or period. Martin E. Marty's historical survey of American Protestantism, *Righteous Empire* (1970), for example, does feature a discussion of nineteenth-century church statistics, but does not mention by name the Census's efforts at the collection of such data (Marty, 1970: e.g., 168–171, 211–212; cf. Hudson, 1965: 354–355). And Sydney E. Ahlstrom's mammoth *A Religious History of the American People* (1975a, 1975b) contains just a single reference to them, in a footnote near the end of the book's thousand-plus pages (Ahlstrom, 1975b: 595n). Census data on religion are used extensively, however, as the basis for numerous maps and graphical displays in Edwin Scott Gaustad's *Historical Atlas of Religion in America* (1976).

A more sophisticated appreciation of the descriptive possibilities of Census data on religion is embodied in their use as what would today be called a social indicator. A fifty-year-old example is the inclusion of selected data on religious affiliation from the 1926 Census of Religious Bodies in a series of articles by Charles Angoff and H. L. Mencken in a popular magazine, *The American Mercury*. Angoff and Mencken's irreverent aim was to determine, by quantitative means, which of the United States suffered the worst quality of life. The pair noted that homicide and, specifically, lynchings were correlated strongly with the percentage of Baptists in a state's population; they concluded more broadly that "the density of Baptists runs in inverse ratio to the general wealth and culture," while the negative relationship "between the density of Methodists and the cultural rank of the States is but less striking" (Angoff and Mencken, 1931: 360). That these correlations were almost certainly spurious was not stated as directly.

Later uses of Census religious statistics in the construction of social indicators were both more rigorous in interpretation and less mocking in tone. The results were also more confusing. E. L. Thorndike, the pioneer psychometrician, calculated four different indexes of church membership for 1926 in his analysis of "What Makes a City Good" (Thorndike, 1939: 55–118). He then reported (Thorndike, 1939: 96–98), for a sample of approximately 300 American cities, correlations he was sure would "astound many": membership in religious bodies as a proportion of a city's population was negatively related to his measures of quality of life, and individual proportions of Catholics and Jews bore little relation to the "goodness" of a city as a place in which to live. "Few even of those who thought that they were fully aware of the great decline in influence of the churches compared with other human organizations," Thorndike (1939: 97) conceded, "would have believed this possible."[23]

The ratio of church membership to the population was associated negatively with school enrollment among persons aged 16 to 20, as well as with the circulation of books from public libraries and sales of "reputable" magazines per capita. Organized religion did seem, nevertheless, to reinforce "typical features of traditional morality, if not . . . the broader aspects of welfare": high levels of church membership were accompanied in Thorndike's sample of cities by lower rates of illegitimate births, deaths from venereal diseases, and homicide (Thorndike, 1939: 99).

Thorndike's (1939: 99) reluctant speculation that "churches are clubs of estimable people and maintainers of traditional rites and ceremonies rather than powerful forces for human betterment" was supported a dozen years later by Robert Cooley Angell (1951). Angell's meticulous research attempted to gauge, by aggregating a lengthy list of social indicators, the "moral integration" of American communities—that is, the ex-

tent to which communities exemplified solidarity in promoting general welfare, and how much they collectively discouraged deviant behavior.

Using data from the 1936 Census of Religious Bodies, Angell measured religion's influence in two ways: first, as the percentage of a city's population belonging to any church, and second (proceeding from Durkheim's belief that Catholics are less individualistic and more group-oriented than Protestants), as the size of the Catholic fraction among all church members. However, in neither form did religion contribute statistically to moral integration, and Angell (1951: 18–19) eventually discarded the measures.

Another manner in which religious data from the Census have been employed is in social scientific research to explain, at an ecological-level of analysis, varying rates of incidence of phenomena which presumably are generated by some aspect of the social environment. Here, that the religious counts are aggregated into totals for places is important not merely for descriptive purposes, but additionally as a suggestion that traits of whole social collectivities can be related to them. Just as suicide rates, to choose an example, are "social facts," characteristic of a level of reality above that of individual behaviors, so, too, may the religious climate in which are committed the individual acts that make up the rates equally be a macro-level fact.

Census religious data have been used in the past to describe the religious climate of an area and to discover its secular causes and consequences. With data by state from the 1936 Census of Religious Bodies, Austin L. Porterfield (1952) found that total church membership and numbers of churches correlated negatively with numbers of suicides,[24] and with homicides and other serious crimes. A general secularization index Porterfield constructed for each state using the 1936 data included a component for the size of its unchurched population, a factor he took to be "indicative of a type of institutional dislocation closely related to the breakdown in the mores" (Porterfield, 1952: 333). This index strongly predicted the incidence of suicide, but was inversely related to homicide and the commission of serious crimes.[25]

Data from the Census of Religious Bodies have been further used to explain patterns in aggregate voting statistics, particularly in elections where religious issues were prominent (e.g., Gray, 1970; Lichtman, 1979; Ogburn and Talbot, 1929; Silva, 1962; Stange, 1970). Other ecological level analyses with Census church data as indicators of the independent variable have detected religious contributions to the political cultures of cities (Bernard and Rice, 1975) and states (Johnson, 1976), but no religious influence on the structural probability for women in the United States of advancement into higher professional occupations like banking, law, and medicine (Bainbridge and Hatch, 1982). John W. Meyer and his

colleagues (Meyer, Tyack, Nagel, and Gordon, 1979) employ historical Census data on church affiliations to test for the effects of religiously formed orientations toward the polity on the expansion of public schooling in America during the late nineteenth and early twentieth centuries.

George M. Thomas (1978, 1979) takes the religious climate instead as his dependent variable. He believes that the evidence of episodes of revivalism reflected in nineteenth-century Census religious statistics indicates the success of religious individualism; he explains the spread of this ideology by reference to a trend toward increasing economic individuation, culminating in a triumph for principles of rational exchange in the marketplace. A recent analysis by Linda K. Pritchard (1984: 253–261; cf. Pritchard, 1980: esp. 178–213) also examines the effect of regional economic development on religious revivalism, but for an earlier period in American history. Also James M. Inverarity (1976) has investigated the effects of Populism and the threat it posed to stable community life on outbreaks of lynching in late nineteenth-century Louisiana parishes (counties). Community solidarity is not measured directly in Inverarity's study, but its magnitude is implied in part by a measure of religious homogeneity derived from Census data.

Finally, there exist a number of studies that use Census data on religion to describe the organization and functions of American religion itself. This category of effort embraces general quantitative assessments of the state of religion in America during particular periods (Carroll, 1912; Coe, Gillen, North, Walker, Riley, and Cutler, 1910; Fry, 1930a, 1930b; Fry and Jessup, 1933; Hart, 1942; A. E. Holt, 1929; Landis, 1935; Pearl, 1931), social historical works tracing the emergence and change over time of types of religious movements (e.g., "holiness" religion, fundamentalism, and sectarianism: Holt, 1940; Jones, 1974; Singleton, 1975; Stark and Bainbridge, 1981a), and economic and social class analyses of religious institutions and behavior in the United States (Azzi and Ehrenberg, 1975; Hoult, 1950, 1952). Daniel Rigney, Richard Machalek, and Jerry D. Goodman (1978), in one example, measured trends in Census church membership counts as a percentage of the national population. They compiled this and six other statistical series in an effort to test Robert Wuthnow's (1976) contention that secularization in America has not advanced as a strictly linear function of time. The internal structures of particular religious bodies (e.g., Christian Science: Pfautz, 1956, 1964; Wilson, 1961: 149–152) have been examined with the aid of Census data, and the relationships among these bodies, individually and as representatives of religious organizational types, have received the attention of historically minded sociologists.

This latter approach deserves elaboration here, because it is a mode of research employing Census religious statistics that is closely akin to the

empirical analyses which follow in this study. Specifically, this approach attempts to account for the development of religious groups in relation to one another, and thereby to evaluate the changing condition of what may be termed the intergroup religious environment. In other words, these studies adapt data from the censuses to ascertain the relative numerical balance or imbalance among religious bodies, and to estimate how that balance affects overall religious and social relations.

In two publications, Kenneth Westhues (1971a, 1971b) tested the hypothesis that the historical expansion of Catholic social service systems in the United States may be regarded as a defensive reaction to nativistic Protestant cultural dominance. In states where Catholics comprised a small proportion of the population, the Church's involvement in elementary education, Westhues (1971b: 287) discovered, was most intensive; this relation held at both 1926 and 1950. Similarly, the greater the degree to which Catholics were in a minority in a state in 1950, the more active they were in providing Church-sponsored hospital care for their members (Westhues, 1971a: 467).[26] The two findings for 1950, dealing with Catholic schools and hospitals, were sustained convincingly when controls for region of the country were imposed (Westhues, 1971a: 468).

The recent research of Rodney Stark and William Sims Bainbridge (1981b; cf. Stark and Bainbridge, 1980b, 1985) on the formation of cults in twentieth-century America provides one more straightforward illustration of group interaction in the larger religious environment. The relations of interest, however, are not those among denominations, but functional ones, between types of religious organization. Stark and Bainbridge present strong inverse correlations between the sizes of cult movements in states and major cities reported in the 1926 Census of Religious Bodies and total membership in the more conventional churches.[27] Cult formation, they conclude, is hardly a new occurrence, but is rather a long-term concomitant of the prevalence, in modern denominations, of "an increasingly vague and inactive conception of the supernatural," for "cults find room to grow only as the conventional faiths have created vacuums" (Stark and Bainbridge, 1981b: 372). Because cult movements are themselves innovative and religiously fertile, their activity is interpreted by Stark and Bainbridge as both a sign of a general secularizing trend and a leading indicator of its ultimate reversal. A relentless human demand for spiritual compensation for the finitude of this world, they insist (Stark and Bainbridge, 1979, 1980a, 1985, 1987), makes secularization a self-limiting process.

The foregoing summary testifies that, far from having been neglected totally, Census data on religion have proven consistently useful to students of religion and society, and quite versatile in the range of problems

to which they can be applied. Not all of the studies that employed the data did so with an adequate understanding of either their limitations or their possibilities: most ignored the former and slighted the latter. But ordered roughly chronologically, the studies described above may be seen slowly to approximate a model of explanatory social science research.

The initial citations to Census religious statistics in works of polemicists were followed by more detached historical treatments. The data seemed to win the notice of social scientists, though, primarily by another route: through their wide application in the realm of church policy research. On the borders of these two fields, interest in describing the prevailing religious environment coincided with a desire to test sociological theories about the role of religion in social groups; studies in the social ecology of churches ensued. At a somewhat later point, academic sociologists of religion became intrigued, and looked to the Census data to endow their quantitative work, long centered on surveys of attitudes and individual behaviors, with historical and organizational dimensions. Their hope was bolstered by the fact that Census religious statistics are keyed to a great wealth of aggregated social, administrative, and demographic data in the adjoining Censuses of Population and in special reports issued in years between full Censuses.

Now, the reacquaintance of sociologists of religion with these valuable data has made it possible to begin a broad reinterpretation of religion in American history. Historically focused studies of religious groups in social context are not simply feasible with these data, they possess special warrant, since it is only within some social environment that any history is enacted (Hays, 1960; Marty, 1974).

One salient aspect of a social environment is its degree of heterogeneity. In any culture, the diversity of religious affiliations would presumably be an important factor in determining dominance and subordination, conflict and cooperation among participating religious groups. The next chapter introduces diversity as an historical and sociological variable, and details the method utilized in this study to construct empirical indicators of religious diversity for turn-of-the-century American cities.

# "An Infinite Variety of Religions"

## The Meaning and Measurement of Religious Diversity

Diversity is the hallmark of religion in America. Indeed, America's was the first society not merely to tolerate some diversity in religious behavior, but to make voluntary church affiliation – and hence the maintenance of a pluralistic religious environment – the very basis of its church-state system (Hudson, 1953; Latourette, 1941: 425–426; Lipset, 1967: 182). Unlike their European ancestors, the new Americans steadfastly refused the establishment of a national church, both because the rationalists among them feared the imposition by government of any religious orthodoxy, and because the radically orthodox feared any authority not wholly and reliably scriptural (Mead, 1954a, 1954c, 1956: 333–334; Miller, 1935; Sperry, 1946: 44–58).

The result has been a proliferation of religious organizations through American history. Although the rate of innovation has not been constant, its accumulated products are everywhere evident along the American cultural landscape. This variety is duly represented in the Census's data on church membership. As Henry K. Carroll (1912: xiii-xiv) wrote in summarizing the returns from the Census of 1890:

The first impression one gets in studying the results of the census is that there is an infinite variety of religions in the United States. There are Churches small and Churches great, Churches white and Churches black, Churches high and low, orthodox and heterodox, Christian and pagan, Catholic and Protestant, Liberal and Conservative, Calvinistic and Arminian, native and foreign, Trinitarian and Unitarian. All phases of thought are represented by them, all possible theologies, all varieties of polity, ritual, usage, forms of worship . . . We seem to have about every variety known to other countries, with not a few peculiar to ourselves. Our native genius for invention has exerted itself in this direction also, and worked out some curious results. The American patent covers no less than two original

49

Bibles—the Mormon and Oahspe—and more brands of religion, so to speak, than are to be found, I believe, in any other country . . . One may be a pagan, a Jew, or a Christian, or each in turn. If he is a pagan, he may worship in one of the numerous temples devoted to Buddha; if a Jew, he may be of the Orthodox or Reformed variety; if a Christian, he may select any one of 125 or 130 different kinds, or join every one of them in turn. He may be six kinds of an Adventist, seven kinds of a Catholic, twelve kinds of a Menno-nite or Presbyterian, thirteen kinds of a Baptist, sixteen kinds of a Lutheran, or seventeen kinds of a Methodist. He may be a member of any one of 143 denominations, or all in succession. If none of these suit him, he still has a choice among 150 separate and independent congregations, which have no denominational name, creed, or connection.

This chapter will examine more closely the historical meaning of reli-gious diversity in the American context. An attempt is made here to trace briefly the multiple sources of sentiment for a society rid at last of coer-cion on questions of religion, and conditions forcing accommodation to one open from the first to the kind of proliferation of faiths, the "infinite variety of religions," which so amazed Carroll.[1]

Attention then turns to the difficult problem of measurement. Discus-sions in this and the first chapter testify to the importance of a recogni-tion of diversity for an adequate comprehension of religion through American history. The entire second chapter in turn was devoted to a lengthy analysis of the validity and utility of the largest single body of historical statistics on American religion. In the present chapter, the insights of theory and the technology of research finally begin to meet, as two different measures of religious diversity in American cities are devel-oped from existing methods and are explained with illustrations from turn-of-the-century data.

## Historical Meaning of American Religious Diversity

"Congress shall make no law respecting an establishment of religion, or prohibiting the free exercise thereof . . ." So promises the First Amend-ment to the Constitution of the United States, a simple litany of protec-tions for personal expression appended to the body of the main docu-ment in 1791. Simple in form though these provisions may appear, they in fact comprise a complex whole: part acknowledgment of the past and part hope for the future, part necessity and part virtue. They are first and most enduringly law, but they suggest an unreported scrutiny of Ameri-can life as much as they convey a widely spoken faith in it; for the "religion clauses" of the First Amendment required of their authors a

realistic survey of divisions in the new American society, and joined the understanding so derived with their resolute commitment to its success.

By placing these sixteen words at the head of a terse declaration of the liberties to be enjoyed by citizens of the new nation, the founders both tacitly recognized a diversity of religions across the land at the end of the eighteenth century and set up the legal and political grounds for the preservation of that diversity. The clauses, preventing on the one hand the designation and support of a state church, but barring on the other any official interference with voluntary religious practice, were designed at once to keep civil peace in a pluralistic religious environment and, equally importantly, to make from that peace a useful basis for purposeful living. The "establishment" clause and its partner, the "free exercise" clause, thus represent two imperatives in American thought about the public status of belief (cf. Kurland, 1962). Together they exhibit a tension so tightly wound, a conflict so compact as nearly to be obscured.

How free should government be from the particular dictates of a religious creed? Yet, how far dares government stray from the moral underpinnings of the society it administers? For their part, how immune should churches be to control by legitimate secular authority? Yet, how far ought churches to move from the political actors who look to them for guidance and inspiration? The dilemmas here are obvious; solutions to them are not. Nevertheless, these tensions hint at the competing historical influences, both ideological and practical, that made freedom of religious affiliation the only feasible course for the infant government of the United States to permit, and the best course for the already numerous churches of this country to follow. These influences are considered more fully in the next section of this chapter.

## Social Sources of Religious Liberty

To some early Americans, of course, religious diversity was an absolute abomination. These people sought continuously to maintain standing orders of establishment in the former colonies, or to assert a pervasive cultural control as state sponsorship for religion crumbled. To others, however, religious liberty was a welcome development, either because they believed that any condition short of complete freedom of thought was an infringement on their natural rights, or because they had for so long been deprived of any rights to free worship that a negotiated truce with the state looked as good as anything they could recall.

Still others, if they did not actively celebrate religious toleration, at least tolerated it. Some drew comfort from the assurance that distinctions between churches were "denominational" (that is, differences in name only), and were therefore ultimately unimportant in the eyes of their

Creator, who was, after all, everyone's Creator. Less lofty, a remaining group thought the whole issue unimportant—to God or to anyone else. The vast mass of Americans, if statistics are to be relied upon (see Gaustad, 1976; but cf. Bonomi, 1986; Bonomi and Eisenstadt, 1982; Sweet, 1976), had neither the time nor the temperament for the heavy demands of church membership in the first years of the new republic. Though their lives were unquestionably informed by the grand themes of the Bible, they probably met the effects of the First Amendment's "establishment" clause more with relief than they did those of the "free exercise" clause with joy.

A new philosophy of rights for the unfettered mind, reaction against colonial experiences of religious persecution, the precursors of ecumenical spirit, an American pattern of preference for work over contemplation, and, not least of all, the sheer social practicality of religious freedom in a land where one's neighbor was not always of like mind and where community had to be secured just the same amid a constantly shifting population—all of these factors contributed to acceptance over time of the guarantees of the Constitution, and to the diversity in religion that they allowed. But the path was never clear, and progress seldom easy.

One factor of certain influence was the Enlightenment, a European philosophical movement that was embraced by many of the early leaders of America (Commager, 1977), and whose tenets about natural rights permeated much of their thinking on religion (Brauer, 1966: 48–56). John Locke, the English philosopher, put down an early foundation for the eighteenth-century theorists of church and state in America. To compel religious action by law was improper, Locke reasoned, because the force involved was unjustified and because genuine salvation demanded a submission to religious discipline that was voluntary. The church could not legitimately wield the power to coerce choices which were by nature to be free. When it did, it ironically destroyed a necessary condition for the validity of such commitments (Sweet, 1935: 54–55). Religion thus could not gain so long as it was state religion.

As can be seen in Locke, the opposition of Enlightenment thinkers to an established religion was premised on a theory of natural rights which exalted the powers of individual reason and tamed the reach of the state into articles of conviction. The men of the Enlightenment perceived order in the physical world, and they believed in the capacity of human beings to apprehend and understand that order. In this process, humans affirmed their continuity with nature, and thereby claimed possession of a range of rights imparted to them from that source.

Natural rights were both universal and unalienable. They were equally available to all, and they could not be surrendered or taken away. Such rights defied the burdens of history and transcended the pressures of the

present moment. They provided stability for the future. No government could violate these rights without at the same time undermining the ultimate authority by which it purported to rule. Furthermore, no God imaginable would wish to revoke these rights because God was the original source of the reality from whose harmony they flowed (Brauer, 1966: 49–52; cf. Jefferson, 1964: 152).

Chief among the rights which came from nature to humanity by virtue of their common subjection to universal law was freedom of religion. "If religion had proved to be one of the bulwarks of ignorance and superstition, then," in the minds of the natural rights theorists, "it had to be stripped of all powers of coercion and manipulation over mankind." Church historian Jerald C. Brauer (1966: 53) continues, "Man had to be set free from the bondage of religious coercion in order to exercise his true humanity." Nowhere is the resolve to achieve this end more evident than in the political writing of Thomas Jefferson.

"Almighty God hath created the mind free," announced Jefferson in the opening phrases of the "Statute of Religious Liberty" (1786) that he wrote for Virginia.[2] How then could earthly rulers frustrate divine intention by imposing restrictions of their own on theology and worship? Such "impious presumption," according to Jefferson, leads directly to "habits of hypocrisy and meanness," tendencies so displeasing to the Lord that the coercion which produced them must be classed as "sinful and tyrannical" (Jefferson, 1963: 125). By natural law, Jefferson contended, our rights as citizens "have no dependence on our religious opinions, any more than our opinions in physics or geometry."

Truth is great and will prevail if left to herself . . . she is the proper and sufficient antagonist to error, and has nothing to fear from the conflict, unless by human interposition disarmed of her natural weapons, free argument and debate, errors ceasing to be dangerous when it is permitted freely to contradict them. [Jefferson, 1963: 126]

Elsewhere, in his *Notes on the State of Virginia* (1785), Jefferson reiterated his confidence in liberty of the mind as the natural protector of religious truth:

Reason and free inquiry are the only effectual agents against error. Give a loose to them, they will support the true religion by bringing every false one to their tribunal, to the test of their investigation. They are the natural enemies of error, and of error only . . . It is error alone which needs the support of government. Truth can stand by itself. [Jefferson, 1964: 152–153]

However, one would be mistaken to think that the articulation of a new and more liberal philosophy was alone sufficient to pry religious believers away from the security of an establishment. Enlightenment theories did not appeal to all Americans; many found rationalism and the rejection of tradition to be dangerous. There were, however, other grounds on which to stand in arguing for religious liberty, and Jefferson did not neglect these, either.

There was, to start, the recent and graphic memory of religious persecution under colonial establishments. Especially victimized under these systems were the churches of the so-called "left wing" of the Protestant Reformation. Their habitual defiance of state power, in America as in Europe before, made championing religious freedom an essential strategy for their survival. Again in his *Notes on Virginia,* Jefferson (1964: 150) wrote movingly of "the poor Quakers," who had left England and had "cast their eyes on these new countries as asylums of civil and religious freedom." Yet the Quakers were not tolerated in their New World points of destination; rather, "they found them free only for the reigning sect." Indeed, Jefferson noted, if the authorities in Virginia had not succeeded in executing any Quakers (as had happened in New England), "it was not owing to the moderation of the church, or spirit of the legislature, as may be inferred from the law itself; but to historical circumstances which have not been handed down to us" (Jefferson, 1964: 150).

Jefferson may in fact have been wrong on at least two counts: the influence on later generations of the gentle Quaker example in opposing religious intolerance, and the actual causes of their comparatively lenient treatment in the Virginia colony. As the historian Perry Miller has pointed out (Jefferson's testimony notwithstanding),

the Quakers were only one, and a relatively small, group; nobody could seriously argue that the fathers of the Constitution and framers of state constitutions had arrived at the conclusion of religious liberty by studying Quaker precedents. [Miller, 1954: 14]

Perhaps Quakers were saved from death at the hands of officialdom in colonial Virginia by another product of well-entrenched establishments which alternates predictably with persecution: a kind of institutionalized lethargy about most matters religious. If religion is to be the province of the state, it becomes possible for clerical custodians of religion to adopt the attitudes of passionless bureaucrats, and its adherents the passivity that is widespread even in formally participatory systems. In Virginia, by Jefferson's own account, "the great care of the government to support" the Anglican church had "begotten an equal degree of indolence in its

clergy," and any previous zeal for exclusivity eventually "subsided into moderation" (Jefferson, 1964: 150).

The support of the government for the state church with time inevitably lessened the intensity of whatever popular support it might have enjoyed. Thus was it possible for others, including some favored Anglicans, to endorse without concern—though for less principled reasons—Jefferson's (1964: 152) remark that the government had no business regulating harmless, if varying, expressions of religious commitment: ". . . it does me no injury for my neighbor to say there are twenty gods, or no God. It neither picks my pocket nor breaks my leg." In the face of competing demands, many in the new nation were frankly indifferent to religion, or at least unwilling to press old sectarian conflicts if they damaged current interests (Mead, 1956: 320–322). They were content personally to cede to those who sought it the opportunity to worship independently, regardless of whether the state withheld legal status from such independence (cf. Sweet, 1935: 54).

Yet even among those who remained conventionally religious, there were principled rationales for wanting to broaden the scope of religious liberty, rationales not dependent, like Jefferson's, on reputedly suspect trends in continental philosophy, or fashioned, like the minority churches', out of self-interest (Sweet, 1935: 50–51). Baptist groups, for example, preached religious tolerance unceasingly, and went so far as to found a settlement (Rhode Island) on that preaching, though it was to be held up to ridicule by more acceptable bodies.

Along other lines, Winthrop S. Hudson (1955a) has speculated that the true inspiration for denominational cooperation as it evolved in the United States lies back in the seventeenth century, in the struggles over government in the Church of England waged by Independent clergy. Specifically, the labors of factions like the Dissenting Brethren resulted, according to Hudson, in the view that church affiliations were merely nominal classifications, below which existed a wider realm of agreement.

No denomination claims to represent the whole church of Christ. No denomination claims that all other churches are false churches. No denomination claims that all members of society should be incorporated within its own membership. No denomination claims that the whole of society and the state should submit to its ecclesiastical regulations. Yet all denominations recognize their responsibility for the whole of society and they expect to cooperate in freedom and mutual respect with other denominations in discharging that responsibility. [Hudson, 1955a: 32]

These convictions powerfully inclined the churches which accepted them toward a tolerance of religious diversity. "So thoroughly was the

victory won," Hudson (1955a: 47) contends, "that the leaders of the Evangelical Revival in England and America could take the denominational conception of the church largely for granted."

Indeed, evangelicals did take the denominational conception for granted. By the time that pietistic and revivalistic religion swept over America in the eighteenth and again in the nineteenth century, its proponents, in their sermons and tracts, could diminish the importance of maintaining a strict homogeneity in religious affiliation. More crucial to salvation than the church of one's birth was the rebirth of one's spirit (Mead, 1956: 328–333). Since conversion had to be voluntary in order to be deemed effective, any emphasis on the condition of an individual's soul also stressed, if inadvertently, the freedom of individuals to choose to be religious or not. Hence, "during the clash between traditionalists and revivalists," Sidney E. Mead (1956: 332) has observed, "the latter were thrown willy-nilly – but somewhat incidentally – on the side of greater toleration and freedom."

More crucial to the acceptance in America of religious freedom than any ideological drift, however, were social conditions prevailing in the new nation, particularly the distribution of its people over the land (see Mead, 1954b, 1956: 322–326) and their division already into numerous religious bodies. What Timothy L. Smith (1968: 160) has called the need "for personal identity, for recognition and response, in a threatening wilderness" motivated the European immigrants to early America whom he studied to place concerns about the viability of their tiny congregations over expectations of religious orthodoxy. In a social world where people came and went quickly as new migrants arrived and new land opened up, it was vital for congregations to seek members where they could and to notice what common features there were among them. Legislation and legalism could not bridge the gaps gouged between people by heterogeneous origins and an expanding country. Voluntarism and fellowship would have to suffice to start church communities and to keep them intact, "to knit erstwhile strangers into units of belonging" (Smith, 1968: 160). Fortunately, they did suffice, and so well, Smith finds, that the techniques of voluntarism supplied in later years the bases for building new churches and organizing them into denominational associations.

Legislation would not have worked anyway to create spiritual solidarity, for the New World was already religiously quite diverse (Parsons, 1960: 299, 305–306; Smith, 1968: 176). Not every group was represented in every location; religious bodies tended to be concentrated regionally. Furthermore, when the odd group did appear in a locality, its members may not have had much to do with the wider community. Nonetheless, the heterogeneity of religions in the colonies, though modest by the standards of the 200 years to follow (see especially Chapter 7),

was pronounced enough in enough places to dash lingering hopes for achieving uniformity by decree. For example, "even if there had been a desire on the part of the later proprietors to establish a state church" in cosmopolitan Pennsylvania, W. W. Sweet (1935: 51) estimated that "the very nature of the population would have made it impossible." Instead, diversity was advertised as a virtue in itself, and liberty was recommended as an asset in argumentation. "Let us reflect," Thomas Jefferson suggested, that the earth

is inhabited by a thousand millions of people. That these profess probably a thousand different systems of religion. That ours is but one of that thousand. That if there be but one right, and ours that one, we should wish to see the nine hundred and ninety-nine wandering sects gathered into the fold of truth. But against such a majority we cannot effect this by force. Reason and persuasion are the only practicable instruments. To make way for these, free inquiry must be indulged; and how can we wish others to indulge it while we refuse it ourselves. [Jefferson, 1964: 153]

Jefferson's numbers were certainly round, but his logic was sharpened to a pragmatic point: not only was uniformity of religion unnatural and undesirable, it was practically impossible. Moreover, those who might venture to challenge religious diversity could do so only with the aid of free expression, a weapon which, if it may be used against the unorthodox, is equally placed at their disposal.

The unavoidable fact of religious diversity, above any ideological commandment, dictated the necessity of toleration, here and now and most likely forever. And the perpetuation of toleration removed official impediments to greater levels of diversity. Sociologist Talcott Parsons correctly realized that the process is reciprocal:

If no human agency has a right to claim a monopoly of religious legitimacy and enforce it by coercion, then there is no basis on which to deny the legitimacy of plural competing claims at least to the point that many groups may have enough access to the truth to justify their adherents in each "worshiping God in their own way." [Parsons, 1960: 313]

Perry Miller offers a succinct, if blunt, summary:

The point is, to put it baldly, that both in education and in religion, we didn't aspire to freedom, we didn't march steadily toward it, we didn't unfold the inevitable propulsion of our hidden nature: we stumbled into it. We got a variety of sects as we got a college catalogue: the denominations and the sciences multiplied until there was nothing anybody could

do about them. Wherefore we gave them permission to exist, and called the result freedom of the mind. Then we found, to our vast delight, that by thus negatively surrendering we could congratulate ourselves on a positive and heroic activity. So we stuck the feather in our cap and called it Yankee Doodle. [Miller, 1954: 15–16]

The degree of religious diversity that pertained in colonial times reduced to zero the possibility of commanding a strict uniformity of affiliations at the outset of American history. The best chance for an official national establishment passed unrealized. Although the voluntary system of church membership and support was lamented by many, it quickly became an undeniable fact of life, for it was "more the product of conditions of pluralism which no one sect had the power to overcome as of an abstract belief in the value of pluralism" (Moore, 1986: 205). Dominant churches, bodies given preference during the periods of establishment, for the most part would have liked to continue their anointed state, but demographic circumstances had outraced political desires, and all now had to live with religious competition. Previously ardent defenders of state-sponsored piety saw the wave of the future and stretched to ride its crest lest it swamp them totally.

Lyman Beecher was one who caught the wave following the withdrawal by Connecticut of its government's endorsement of Congregationalism. "It was as dark a day as ever I saw," the great preacher at first confessed. "The odium thrown upon the ministry was inconceivable. The injury done to the cause of Christ, as we then supposed, was irreparable" (Beecher, 1864: 344). Beecher's son Charles remembered encountering his father, on the day after the electoral defeat that would decide the church's status, slumped in a chair, "his head drooping on his breast, and his arms hanging down." The elder Beecher was, he said, mourning a blow dealt to a thing no less sacred than "THE CHURCH OF GOD" (quoted in Beecher, 1864: 344).

Yet, before very long the Protestant patriarch had deftly adopted a new attitude, labeling disestablishment *"the best thing that ever happened to the State of Connecticut,"* because it forced the churches to rely "wholly on their own resources and on God" (Beecher, 1864: 344). The activism that the requirements of a disestablished church actually stimulated gave to religion more, not less, influence in the affairs of citizens, Beecher concluded.

## Establishments Formal and Informal

Part of the explanation for the relative ease with which Protestant churches in America made the transition to a policy of church-state

separation, a plan contrary to that under which a privileged few groups had grown comfortable, points beyond the indubitable necessity of the policy and beyond its grudgingly conceded practicality. True, there was no stomach for eradicating religious dissent, so diversity had to be tolerated. It was also true that the young system of voluntarism yielded for religious minorities a kind of freedom from external threat. For them, the system bore the seal of approval most valuable to Americans: *it worked.*

Yet there was security to be found in voluntarism for the more powerful groups as well. As examples in Chapters 8 and 9 will indicate, the larger and more stable denominations could, within a voluntary system, coordinate their work in ways that exerted their control over culture well past the time at which government backing for it was removed. "Though Protestantism was denominationally divided," notes Robert T. Handy (1966b: 134), "by mutual efforts and by cooperative participation in common causes it was anticipated that the Protestant tone and influence could be maintained."

Protestant churches learned that sometimes superior to a monopoly, with all the resentment and opposition that its imposition generates, is an oligopoly which is able still to sustain the semblance of a free-market environment. So long as both product loyalty and the cooperative spirit hold up, effective market control is guaranteed; so long as entry into the market remains open and successes are occasionally permitted to marginal firms, freedom seems to prevail and the continuing participation of the dominant coalition is thus legitimated. In the case of religion, the only motion to "bust" this trust comes from smaller and more unpopular sects, whose challenges not simply to orthodoxy but to cultural propriety are usually too poorly funded, too sporadic, and too brief to be taken seriously. As typically American as competition is considered to be, it is also expensive, redundant, and potentially lethal to the firm. No wonder, then, that the desire to quell competitive fervor is nearly as characteristic of Americans who have much to lose.

The subtle changes in the practice of religious liberty that Protestant churches initiated during the nineteenth century entailed, as a consequence, the reconception of the religious diversity that accompanied it. That one was legally free to affiliate with any religious body one chose was *not* a directive to anyone to do just that. All churches were equal, but some were more equal than others, and those that to the widening Protestant consciousness were more exotic, such as the Roman Catholics and the Mormons, were well nigh disreputable. It was not until the first part of this century that Catholics, Jews, and other "outsiders" (Moore, 1986) in the religious marketplace were skilled sufficiently in its mechanisms to solidify their own positions in American society, "a society made up," Martin E. Marty (1961: 73) recounts, "of large minorities, rather than a

monolithic one which merely tolerates minorities." From their improved positions, the newer denominations were poised to begin dismantling the informal Protestant establishment that persisted well after the legal one had been repealed. Handy, along with Marty (1961), quite rightly understands that

Voluntarism proved to be an open door for any group large enough and vigorous enough to push it open. All this meant that American religious pluralism gradually became something different from the days when Protestantism had dominated the culture and could afford to be tolerant of the minorities which were concerned chiefly with their own survival. It became instead "pluralism in its more fully realized sense." [Handy, 1966b: 138; the words between quotation marks are Marty's]

Clearly, if the analyses in this book are to treat the topic of religious diversity in American society adequately, some reliable measures of the phenomenon are necessary. Moreover, more than one index is necessary because, as we have seen above, the meaning of religious diversity itself, and not merely its absolute level, changes over time. The condition first looms importantly at the moment when the former colonies break with the past and declare themselves a new republic, with legal protections for the religious beliefs and practices of all citizens. But at this time there was yet a wide ground of agreement on religious questions (Handy, 1966b: 129), and compelling motivations, practical as well as principled, to overlook the differences that did manage to separate believers. With time, this stance was increasingly difficult to hold.

Toleration was legislated in a period of tolerable diversity; by the end of the nineteenth century, the religious situation had changed. "A wholly new factor appeared on the American scene," according to Marty: "the immigration and urban concentration of large minorities of non-Protestant groups who found themselves in a nation that was legally and explicitly *pluralistic* but which morally and implicitly favored its specifically Protestant memory" (Marty, 1961: 73; cf. Moore, 1986: 9). Nonevangelical groups were multiplying and non-Protestant groups were growing in size, so that "pluralism is no longer predominantly a 'Protestant pluralism' but one which shows fairly clear lines of demarcation between the major religious traditions" (Handy, 1966b: 129). Measures of trends both among Protestants and across the entire religious spectrum are therefore needed in order to describe diversity in the appropriate historical context, and to track accurately the response to it as the United States entered a new century.

## Measurement of Religious Diversity

The heavy reliance on diversity as a trait with which to characterize American statistics of religious affiliation, and more generally, as a principle around which to organize historical discussion of religion in the United States (cf. Ahlstrom, 1975a; Albanese, 1981; Commager, 1950: 183–189; Harrell, 1985; Latourette, 1941: 424–456; Stark and Bainbridge, 1985: 41–48) has not in sociological analyses been met with an equal interest in religious diversity as an explanatory variable.[3] This lacuna is puzzling because, for almost as long as quantitative data on church membership in the United States have been available, social commentators have wanted to know what those data indicated about trends in the heterogeneity of American religious life (see, e.g., Coe et al., 1910: 812–813). For example, Franklin H. Giddings, one of the founders of American sociology, used the 1890 and 1906 Census religious data, in an article published in 1910 in the *American Journal of Sociology,* to illustrate a scaling technique he had developed. In the process, Giddings (1910: 740) computed national religious diversity scores for these two years, and discovered that "in religious persuasion," the American people "are still becoming slightly more heterogeneous."

References to religious diversity in subsequent quantitative social research are scant. There could be located just two social historical studies of American community life wherein the author sought to measure quantitatively the diversity of religious affiliations among persons in those communities. The first is Inverarity's (1976) aforementioned analysis of Populism and lynching in Louisiana; the second is Gregory H. Singleton's (1979) history of religious institutions in urbanizing Los Angeles. The concept of religious diversity has most frequently been operationalized, surprisingly, in studies by cultural geographers, who have speculated— accurately, it turns out—that "low religious diversity is important in creating a religious landscape" (Shortridge, 1976: 428), that is, an environment in which material culture is discernibly altered in accordance with predominant religious values and dictates (cf. Shortridge, 1977; Stump, 1984; Zelinsky, 1961).

This study treats religious diversity as a "social fact" (cf. Johnson, 1978: 10–13). Emile Durkheim defined "social facts" (see Durkheim, 1982: 52, 59) as ways of acting which are external to the individual and which exert a coercive force over his or her behavior. To view a regularity in human behavior as a social fact is to make the claim that it is a "thing" in its own right; it is a pattern which proceeds from an array of individual (and perhaps eccentric) motivations and choices, but which nevertheless congeals into its distinctive shape (in philosophical language, "emerges") on

the collective level. Thus, a social fact, though the product of individuals, can be explained only by appeal to collective, or social structural traits.

In the coming analyses, religious diversity is regarded as a prominent structural characteristic of the urban social environment. While indicators of diversity are, by empirical definition, complex aggregations of individual affiliations, the concept of diversity is itself something else again. It reaches beyond the quantities of *aggregates* to refer to a *structure*. Peter M. Blau, one of the foremost American theorists of social structure, describes the difference:

> social structure refers to those properties of an aggregate that are emergent and that consequently do not characterize the separate elements composing the aggregate. In any structure, we can distinguish the elements composing it and the aggregate they compose, but analytically, we must also distinguish the aggregate from the structure. The aggregate is merely the sum of the elements, but the structure depends on their relationships . . . [Blau, 1981: 9]

Throughout this study, emphasis is placed on structure in preference to aggregate, a course which is traditional for sociologists, though perhaps not for social psychologists or historians. Such a focus is, however, appropriate, for the ultimate aim of this research is to explain the causes and consequences of the structure of American religious life at the turn of the century, and not primarily to determine how individual Americans living at that time participated in that structure.

Any historical work which, like this one, employs an authentically sociological framework is nevertheless susceptible to certain misinterpretations. Sequences of events about which one may wish to generalize are always and necessarily composed of specific incidents or situations — occasions or conditions which have their own special antecedents and their peculiar consequences. "All macrosociology is flawed," writes Arthur L. Stinchcombe (1985: 573), "by trying to wrest generality from instances that have obvious, causally crucial, historical particularity."

The uniqueness of the case or period ought, in any good historical account, to receive its due. Yet, because sociological explanations push beyond a recapitulation of history, into a discussion of structures and their relationships, they lie open to replacement by alternative narratives which, because they hover more closely over the data, seem to possess greater plausibility (if less scope). The sociologist is thus placed at a disadvantage in constructing his or her argument. This difficulty notwithstanding, to imagine that a description of an historical case or period, however exactly accurate, may pass as well as an explanation for it is,

from the sociologist's point of view, to fall victim to the lay belief that history is simply "one damn thing after another." Therefore, measures of key concepts in historical sociology must be formulated so that, in addition to serving adequately as descriptive devices, they can be said empirically to embody enduring or recurring features of collective life.

Since there exist few examples of sociological research on the correlates of religious diversity to imitate, it is necessary for this study to borrow methods from areas where population diversity has been a more prominent topic of analysis. The index of religious diversity used in this study is modeled after a type of Gini index (see Allison, 1978) adapted from linguistics (Greenberg, 1956) by Stanley Lieberson (1964, 1965: 13, 1969, 1970: 31–33; Lieberson and Hansen, 1974: 524) for his research on language pluralism.[4]

A city's score on the index is calculated by squaring, successively, the relative proportions of church membership reported for each relevant religious group, summing these quantities across all such groups represented in the city, and subtracting this total from one. The number thus arrived at may range from zero to one. It is zero when all church members in a given city are concentrated in one denomination; it approaches unity when church membership is distributed uniformly across a large number of categories. The diversity score may be interpreted substantively as the probability that any two church members in the city, chosen at random, will have *different* religious affiliations. To repeat, high religious diversity is indicated by scores on the index approaching unity. Scores closer to zero indicate, on the other hand, relatively homogeneous religious environments.

The index was calculated for each city for both years in two different ways. First, an overall index, measuring diversity among the broad American religious subcommunities – Protestantism, Catholicism, Judaism, and others – was computed. In addition, a more restricted index of diversity, gauging heterogeneity among the major denominations of American Protestantism, was created.[5]

These religious diversity indexes, then, measure the variety in a city's population of church members in major denominations. They are relatively insensitive, all the same, to the radical diversity embodied in sect and cult movements positioned along a population's social perimeter. Not only are these groups normally too small to influence aggregate statistics very greatly, but the system of classification employed here is not sufficiently broad to accord each sect or cult group individual handling. Nevertheless, the form of diversity the indexes successfully capture is arguably the most crucial to a city's religious environment, because it manages to implicate nearly all of its church-affiliated population.

Table 3.1. *Means and standard deviations of religious diversity measures, 1890 and 1906, and mean change in diversity, 1890–1906, for principal American cities*

| Diversity measure | Mean, 1890 | Mean, 1906 | Mean change, 1890–1906 |
|---|---|---|---|
| *Protestant-Catholic-Jewish-Other* | | | |
| *diversity index* | .461 | .418 | −.043 |
| Standard | | | |
| deviation = | .080 | .089 | |
| N = | (122) | (119)[a] | |
| *Diversity among Protestants* | | | |
| *index* | .818 | .841 | +.023 |
| Standard | | | |
| deviation = | .060 | .046 | |
| N = | (122) | (122) | |

[a]Data on Roman Catholic Church membership in 1906 are not reported separately for Auburn, Elmira, and Rochester, New York, making the calculation of a 1906 Protestant-Catholic-Jewish-Other diversity index for these cities impossible.

The means for both diversity measures at both time points, and their change over this period, are reported in Table 3.1. Overall religious diversity in 1890 ranged from a low score of .169 in heavily Protestant Atlanta to a high of .587 in Oakland; the mean level of diversity was .461. These numbers indicate that there would be roughly just a 17 percent chance of picking two persons with different religious affiliations from the pool of Atlanta church members in 1890, while the odds on failing to match a pair in Oakland in that year were about six in ten. By 1906, Atlanta was still the least heterogeneous city, with a diversity score of .178, but the distinction of most religiously diverse city shifted, within California, to Sacramento (.535).[6] Mean diversity among the principal religious communities dropped to .418 in 1906.

Protestant diversity, however, increased in this period: Table 3.1 shows it rising from a mean of .818 in 1890 to .841 in 1906. The least diversity among Protestants in 1890 prevailed in Richmond, Virginia (.484), where more than two-thirds of the Protestants belonged to Regular Baptist churches. Cleveland boasted the highest Protestant diversity level in 1890: .892. Milwaukee, where Lutherans dominated among Protestants, was least diverse in 1906 (.607); St. Joseph, Missouri (.906) was most heterogeneous.

The value of Census religious data and the utility of these diversity indicators lies, above all, not in the exactitude they lend to historical

descriptions of organized religion in the United States, but rather in the opportunities they afford for quantitative analyses of the structuring of religious environments in response to urbanization, immigration, industrialization, and attendant cultural change in the turn-of-the-century American city. These issues will be examined in the chapters ahead.

# "A Motley of Peoples and Cultures"

## Urban Populations and Religious Diversity

The urbanization of the United States, depicted in statistics in Chapter 1, may be identified with an assortment of social and historical changes. Certainly the most obvious of these changes is an increase, during the late nineteenth and early twentieth centuries, in the populations of existing urban places. United States Census data reported in Chapter 1 indicated that the populations of many American cities more than doubled in the short period bounding the turn of the century. More importantly, the same factors that produced such substantial increments in urban population also brought about qualitative changes within the growing populations of individual cities. These changes left cities not simply with more inhabitants, but with a class of residents whose presence signaled a newly diversified urban environment.

Many cities in the Northeast and Middle West were points of destination for widening streams of foreign immigration. Others, located in the South and in Border States, proved inhospitable to the foreign-born, but harbored large communities of black Americans. In either case, turn-of-the-century cities constituted a type of settlement different, in terms of both the scale and the composition of their populations, from what had prevailed in America at any previous point in its history.

Louis Wirth realized as much in 1938, when he commented that

never before have such large masses of people of diverse traits as we find in our cities been thrown together into such close physical contact as in the great cities of America. Cities generally, and American cities in particular, comprise a motley of peoples and cultures, of highly differentiated modes of life between which there often is only the faintest communication, the greatest indifference and the broadest tolerance, occasionally bitter strife, but always the sharpest contrast. [Wirth, 1938: 20]

Some of the consequences for organized religion of the changes in size and diversity which Wirth perceived in American cities are discussed in this chapter. This chapter, in particular, seeks to discover what causes of urban religious diversity may reside in historical characteristics of American city populations—their size, growth, and composition at the turn of the century. At issue is whether levels of religious diversity were greater, as urban theory would predict, both in places maintaining or achieving large scale, and within cities which were already diverse with respect to the race and nativity of their inhabitants.

Historians (e.g., Handlin, 1951; Schlesinger, 1933) have written extensively on how urban social life was changed by increases in Catholic and Jewish immigration at the close of the nineteenth century. Little is known, however, about the generic relationship between urbanization and religious diversity; indeed, it is not known if such a relationship exists at all. Similarly, there is no evidence that religious diversity may not be composed differently in different cities, by varying proportions of the same ethnic and racial groups. Diversity's meaning as a sociological concept is regrettably obscured by standard historical description.

A primary reason for pursuing this part of the study, then, is to determine if—and if so, how—structural changes representing the process of urbanization altered the character of religious affiliation and shaped its patterns under modern social conditions. "Much of the character of modern belief (secularization, variety, transitoriness, and so on)," James T. Borhek and Richard F. Curtis (1975: 144) assert, "is to be explained as a direct consequence of the single dominant social context of belief in industrial countries, namely urban social organization." This chapter is a limited attempt to assess the validity of this general assertion, using urban church membership data from the turn of the century.

The section that follows examines sociological theory and research on the relations connecting urban population, social organization, and social heterogeneity. Three particular theories that are cited all assume that a greater differentiation of social institutions and a wider diversity of social affiliations and practices will of course develop as urban populations grow larger and become otherwise more varied. Whether it results from the pressures of competition, from influences diffused by migration, or from the achievement of a critical cultural mass, these theories conclude in the expectation that with larger and more varied populations comes a more heterogeneous social life.

The chapter presents several operationalizations of the theories and evaluates them through a number of quantitative tests. First, a series of correlation and regression analyses assesses the impact of city size on religious diversity in both 1890 and 1906; the lagged effect of popula-

tion's dimensions in 1890 on diversity in 1906 is gauged as well. In addition, the influence of population growth over the sixteen-year period between 1890 and 1906 is estimated. The second part of the data analysis treats the effects of the proportions of foreign stock, foreign-born, and nonwhite persons in a city's population on that city's level of religious diversity. The extent of these relations is measured both cross-sectionally, with data for 1890, and over a lag period, from 1890 to 1906.

## Urbanization and Social Differentiation

This section summarizes several of the most prominent sociological explanations for the presumption of a relationship between urbanization and various forms of social differentiation. Such explanations are the logical starting point in the attempt made by this study to understand how religious diversity came to be a common structural aspect of the American urban environment.

Three theories – one from the classical European sociological tradition (Durkheim, 1933), another a seminal statement from the storied years of American sociology (Wirth, 1938), and the third the product of recent urban research (Fischer, esp. 1975b) – are addressed. Each theory places a distinct emphasis on a particular category of variables as causes of the heterogeneity of city dwellers and the institutions they establish. These emphases are identified and briefly elaborated. All the same, none of the explanations clearly excludes the social processes stressed by the others. Rather, the methods by which different social forces may have acted in concert to produce historic changes in urban populations and social structures in the United States at the turn of the century are suggested. A limited body of evidence from statistical tests of the effects of urbanization on diversity is reviewed, although little of this research has dealt directly with religious organizations. Lastly, a new analysis of urbanization and religious diversity is proposed, an analysis using the data and indicators that were described at length in the previous chapters.

Emile Durkheim, in his work on *The Division of Labor in Society* (1933), linked the key components of the process of urbanization – the size and density of population, and the resulting acceleration of the pace of interaction – with an increase in differentiation among and within social institutions. Durkheim posited that "cities always result from the need of individuals to put themselves in very intimate contact with others"; he noted further that "the division of labor develops as there are more individuals sufficiently in contact to be able to act and react upon one another" (Durkheim, 1933: 258 and 257; cf. 345–346). Indeed, "the

growth and condensation of societies . . . *necessitate* a greater division of labor" (Durkheim, 1933: 262; cf. Simmel, 1950: 420).

This necessity occurs, Durkheim indicated, because an increased volume and density of human activity leads to an intimacy of contact, and with it, a more "acute" and intense competition for existence. A potential for conflict and mutual injury thus arises which can be obviated only by functional specialization. Hence "all condensation of the social mass, especially if it is accompanied by an increase in population, necessarily determines advances in the division of labor" (Durkheim, 1933: 266–268; quotation at 268; cf. Durkheim, 1969: 26).[1]

Louis Wirth took a more psychological approach to this question in his famous analysis of "Urbanism as a Way of Life" (1938). Wirth (1938: 23) there emphasized the notion of the "urban personality," a stress-fractured and personally disorganized psychological consequence of the unique structure of life in the city. Yet he concurred in Durkheim's judgment about the effects of size and density on diversity, and additionally offered some explanations of his own for the connection.

First, the city grows by migration to it: large numbers are achieved by an inundation of people from outlying areas and distant nations. "The city has thus historically been the melting-pot of races, peoples, and cultures, and a most favorable breeding-ground of new biological and cultural hybrids" (Wirth, 1938: 10). Large numbers, Wirth continued, support a large market, which allows occupational specialization and thus a complex division of labor. At a higher level, a large market, with the interdependence of urban places, encourages the functional differentiation of city economies (Wirth, 1938: 13).

Large size increases diversity through enlarging the original stock of different traits in the population, and aids in the production of still greater diversity by furnishing more raw material for the permutations and combinations of interaction of which urban life is composed (Wirth, 1938: 11). The differentiation of social groups by urban life itself is solidified by virtue of urbanization's psychological consequences. Because urban life, according to Wirth (1938: 22), results in the loss of an individual's sense of efficacy, the city dweller seeks to recapture community by participation "in the enormous multiplication of voluntary organizations directed toward as great a variety of objectives as there are human needs and interests."

Claude S. Fischer (1975b; cf. Fischer, 1972: 220–224, 1975a, 1976: 35–38) combines the ecological and psychological themes[2] of these two theories in his own theory of urban diversity based on subcultures. His theory is ecological in that it acknowledges the importance of variables like community size and population density in spawning cultural

heterogeneity, but Fischer does not think such variables are themselves determinate. Rather, these forces conduce to subcultural development, and it is within and through subcultures, he claims, that city life is characteristically enacted. More explicitly, Fischer maintains that city size is important in that it facilitates the formation of distinctive urban networks, which are in turn psychologically vital because they provide structure, support, and familiarity, and stave off the alienation that Wirth feared inhered in urban life-styles. In addition, the subcultural theory does not neglect migration to the city as a means for new influences to gain a cultural foothold in a growing environment (Fischer, 1975b: 1325–1326).

To summarize, differentiation of social institutions and heterogeneity of social forms are companions to population growth as a result of at least three related processes: ecological, demographic, and cultural. On the ecological level, increasing size heightens competition for scarce resources, forcing actors and institutions to become specialized if they are to survive. Second, populations grow through demographic phenomena such as migration, and such movements of people, because they are also movements of habits and ideas, introduce new influences to the city. Third, migrants and natives alike, together in a growing environment, can combine and recombine to form subcultural constituencies of sufficient size to support specialized – even eccentric – cultural institutions, associations, and services, which are impossible to sustain in smaller locales.

The thesis relating urbanization and institutional differentiation has been tested with national economic data by several sociologists. Jack P. Gibbs and Walter T. Martin (1962: 673–674) found a high positive rank-order correlation between the proportion of the population in metropolitan areas and the degree of industrial diversification in forty-five countries. Sanford Labovitz and Gibbs (1964: 8–9) likewise discovered a strong positive relationship between the percentage of the population in urban places and occupational specialization in the United States over the first half of the twentieth century (cf. Clemente and Sturgis, 1972). Other analysts (Abrahamson, 1974; Keyes, 1958) correlated city size with the availability of specialized services and public facilities.

However, little research has been directed to the possible effects of urbanization on the specialization and differentiation of noneconomic institutions like religion (Fischer, 1975b: 1324).[3] This is in spite of Durkheim's (1933: 270) assertion that although he had taken most of his examples of differentiation from the economic sphere, "this explanation applies to all social functions indiscriminately." Instead, the neglect of religious organizations in analyses of the effects of urbanization is a case in proof of the general charge that "the relation between size of population and organization," as Amos H. Hawley (1950: 122) puts it, "appar-

ently ... has been so taken for granted that it has not been thought worthy of careful investigation."

William Fielding Ogburn and Otis Dudley Duncan (1964: 141–142), in a rare exception, did investigate the relationship between city size and religious diversity (measured crudely by the average number of separate denominations represented in cities of varying sizes in one part of the United States in the year 1936).[4] The finding they reported is a positive one: more denominations were represented in the larger cities. Similar results emerged from Gregory H. Singleton's (1979: 29, 70, 120, 227) examination of population size and religious diversity in Los Angeles between 1850 and 1930. The composition of church membership in Los Angeles, he discovered, was consistently more varied from decade to decade as the number of inhabitants of that city grew.[5] Furthermore, his comparative analysis, at several time points, of classes of American cities stratified by size (Singleton, 1979: 217–221) revealed a strong relationship between city size and the average number of denominations represented.

As a wide range of groups came together in the turn-of-the-century city, one would expect, on the basis of this discussion, that religious competition was intensified and that different forms of specialization – theological, organizational, and programmatic – ensued. The forces of immigration and rural-to-urban migration can be regarded as supplementing the broadening in place of the religious variety of the cities. This added effect is to be expected, for, as Fischer (1975b: 1325) notes, "given the cityward direction of migration, the consequence is that a large settlement will draw migrants from a greater variety of subcultures than will a small one." In this chapter, the hypothesis that population size and growth would have encouraged religious diversity is tested using Census data on urban growth. Religious diversity is measured in these tests with the pair of indexes based on Census church membership totals which were discussed in Chapter 3.

## City Size, Urban Growth, and Religious Diversity

The first step in the analysis is to examine the correlations between city size and religious diversity at each time point. As the results in Table 4.1 show, urbanization has little discernible effect on diversity. The bivariate correlation coefficients for the relationships between city size in 1890 and in 1906 and overall religious diversity in the corresponding years are positive, but are quite small, and are not statistically significant at the .05 level.[6] Slightly larger and positive correlations are produced from a parallel analysis, shown in the lower half of Table 4.1, of city size and diversity among Protestants. But an identical pattern holds there: in each instance,

Table 4.1. *Bivariate correlation coefficients (Pearson's "r") for the relationship between population size and religious diversity in American cities, 1890–1906*

| Diversity measure | Total population, 1890 | Total population, 1906 |
|---|---|---|
| *Protestant-Catholic-Jewish-Other diversity* | | |
| 1890 | .071[a] | — |
| N = | (122) | |
| 1906 | .023[b] | .022[c] |
| N = | (119) | (117) |
| *Diversity among Protestants* | | |
| 1890 | .121[d] | — |
| N = | (122) | |
| 1906 | .117[e] | .107[f] |
| N = | (122) | (120) |

[a]$p = .437$.
[b]$p = .807$; partial $r$, controlling for Protestant-Catholic-Jewish-Other diversity in 1890, is $-.037$ ($N = 119; p = .694$).
[c]$p = .811$.    [d]$p = .184$.
[e]$p = .199$; partial $r$, controlling for diversity among Protestants in 1890, is $.039$ ($N = 122; p = .668$).    [f]$p = .245$.
*Note:* All levels of statistical significance are gauged with two-tailed tests.

the magnitude of the coefficient is small, and both fail to achieve statistical significance.[7]

Population in 1890, considered as a lagged variable, hardly fares better in predicting religious diversity. The simple correlations between 1890 population and the 1906 diversity measures, presented in Table 4.1, are lower and less significant than their weak cross-sectional counterparts for 1890. The partial correlation coefficients included in footnotes *b* and *e* to Table 4.1 suggest the virtual absence of a relationship between total population in 1890 and either indicator of diversity in 1906, once the influence of diversity at 1890 is removed. The sign of the partial correlation between 1890 population and 1906 Protestant-Catholic-Jewish-Other diversity, controlling for Protestant-Catholic-Jewish-Other diversity in 1890, is in fact negative. The value of the partial correlation between total population in 1890 and diversity among Protestants in 1906 (with its 1890 version accounted for), unlike the other partial, is greater than zero, but still rather small and far from statistical significance. The absolute size of a city (above

Table 4.2. *Results of bivariate regression analyses of the effects of city size on religious diversity, 1890–1906 (unstandardized coefficients)*

| Dependent variable | Constant | Total population (in millions), 1890 | Total population (in millions), 1906 | $R^2$ | $N$ |
|---|---|---|---|---|---|
| Protestant-Catholic-Jewish-Other diversity | | | | | |
| 1890 | +.458 | +.0224[a] | — | .005 | 122 |
| 1906 | +.417 | +.0078[b] | — | .001 | 119 |
| 1906 | +.417 | — | +.0045[c] | .001 | 117 |
| Diversity among Protestants | | | | | |
| 1890 | +.814 | +.0283[d] | — | .015 | 122 |
| 1906 | +.838 | +.0213[e] | — | .014 | 122 |
| 1906 | +.838 | — | +.0113[f] | .011 | 120 |

[a]$t = 0.780; p > .40.$   [b]$t = 0.245; p > .80.$   [c]$t = 0.241; p > .80.$
[d]$t = 1.336; .10 < p < .20.$   [e]$t = 1.293; .10 < p < .20.$   [f]$t = 1.168; .20 < p < .30.$
*Note:* All levels of statistical significance are gauged with two-tailed tests.

a minimum of 25,000 inhabitants)[8] makes little difference, it seems, in the amount of religious diversity it harbors.

Although these results from zero-order and partial correlations appear to be conclusive, "when the researcher is interested in the establishment of a causal law for a given population, he is better advised to use the unstandardized regression coefficient" (Bohrnstedt, 1969: 122; cf. 128). Table 4.2 therefore reports bivariate ordinary least squares (OLS) regression analyses of these same data. The different diversity measures serve successively as the dependent variables in these models, and the population totals, current and lagged, are the independent variables. The initial conclusion, drawn from the correlation analyses, is confirmed: there appears to be little association between city size and religious diversity. At neither of the two time points does total population explain more than a miniscule 1½ percent of the variance in any type of diversity. Furthermore, while all of the population coefficients estimated in the six equations described in Table 4.2 are positive, none approaches statistical significance.

One reason for these null findings may possibly be that the size of a population does little by itself to generate diversity, but that population

*growth,* with the social upheaval that it implies, is the more relevant predictor. With this elaboration in mind, the multiple regression analyses summarized in Table 4.3 introduce the variable of population change. The hypothesis that a positive change in population increases religious diversity is investigated in two ways. Equations 4.3a and 4.3b estimate the 1906 overall and 1906 Protestant diversity indexes, respectively. Variables in the left-hand columns control for conditions extant in 1890, whereas the direction and magnitude of the coefficient for population in 1906 constitute the test of the idea that population change (here *change* because the population at the previous time point is already accounted for) promotes religious diversity (Land and Felson, 1976: 580–585). However, as Table 4.3 reveals, both coefficients are negative, and neither is statistically significant. The findings of the earlier analyses are thus sustained.

It is admittedly possible that there may exist some threshold of diversity, a cultural "saturation point," which the larger cities in the sample may have already exceeded. Such a limit may depress the statistical relationship between population growth and religious diversity. Substantial growth in smaller cities may in fact have had the predicted effect, but this effect may be obscured by a lack of a relationship in the cases of the larger cities. This notion is tested in Equations 4.3c and 4.3d. In these two models, population change is measured directly and an interaction term is inserted to ascertain whether the change carries a greater or lesser impact on diversity, depending upon the city's size before its most recent spell of growth began.

For both the population change variable and for the interaction term, though, no effect is detected; this is true for overall religious diversity as well as for diversity among Protestants. All four of the coefficients in the lower right-hand corner of Table 4.3 are negative, and all are statistically insignificant.[9] The first of the hypotheses to be tested in this chapter, then, may be safely rejected. City size and increasing population appear to have been unrelated to levels of religious diversity. If there *is* a threshold of population beyond which the range of cultural diversity is exhausted, it lies below the 25,000 mark.

## Foreign and Nonwhite Populations and Religious Diversity

One of the few works to search for the causes of the differentiation of religion in America in the diversity of its population is H. Richard Niebuhr's *The Social Sources of Denominationalism* (1954).[10] Niebuhr saw the development in the United States of a great variety of sects as the natural consequence of a process of accommodation to social conditions by normally more universal churches. The fellowship of these churches,

Table 4.3. Results of ordinary least squares (OLS) analyses of the effects of city size and urban population growth on 1906 religious diversity (unstandardized regression coefficients)

| Equation number | Dependent variable | Control variables | | | | Measures of population | | | $R^2$ | N |
|---|---|---|---|---|---|---|---|---|---|---|
| | | Constant | Protestant Catholic-Jewish-Other diversity, 1890 | Diversity among Protestants, 1890 | Total population (in millions), 1890 | Total population (in millions), 1906 | Population change, 1890–1906 | Interaction: Population, 1890 × Change, 1890–1906 | | |
| 4.3a | Protestant Catholic-Jewish-Other diversity, 1906 | +.085 | +.721 | — | +.221 | −.134[a] | — | — | .44 | 117 |
| 4.3b | Diversity among Protestants, 1906 | +.365 | — | +.579 | +.048 | −.025[b] | — | — | .57 | 120 |
| 4.3c | Protestant Catholic-Jewish-Other diversity, 1906 | +.087 | +.709 | — | +.076 | — | −.0055[c] | −.0568[d] | .45 | 117 |
| 4.3d | Diversity among Protestants, 1906 | +.366 | — | +.578 | +.021 | — | −.0068[e] | −.0082[f] | .57 | 120 |

[a] t = 1.091; .20 < p < .30.   [b] t = 0.454; .60 < p < .70.   [c] t = 0.032; p > .90.   [d] t = 1.089; .20 < p < .30.
[e] t = 0.084; p > .90.   [f] t = 0.345; .70 < p < .80.

Niebuhr charged, had receded, eventually approximating the boundaries of narrow social groups and thereby excluding many of the sincerely faithful from communion. Sects arose then as vehicles for the religious sentiments of disaffected segments of society.

Diversity, in Niebuhr's view, was a brand of entropy, an accelerating disarray into which religion fell when existing social distinctions became qualifications for church membership, and the excluded organized in response.

For the denominations, churches, sects, are sociological groups whose principle of differentiation is to be sought in their conformity to the order of social classes and castes. It would not be true to affirm that denominations are not religious groups with religious purposes, but it is true that they represent the accommodation of religion to the caste system. They are emblems, therefore, of the victory of the world over the church, of the secularization of Christianity, of the church's sanction of that divisiveness which the church's gospel condemns. [Niebuhr, 1954: 25]

Although Niebuhr singled out class-based divisions in Christianity for especially intense scrutiny and attack, he did not overlook the influences on religious diversity in America of a large foreign immigrant population and a separate caste of black citizens:

Among the factors which have been responsible for the continued division of European proletarian, bourgeois, and nationalist Christianity in America, for the development of new types of conflict between them, and for the rise of wholly American schisms, sectionalism, the heterogeneity of an immigrant population, and the presence of two distinct races are of primary importance. [Niebuhr, 1954: 135]

A new generation of social historians has come likewise to emphasize population diversity as a theme underlying accounts of social change in America. Measures of the nativity and racial backgrounds of city dwellers in America are among the variables that "lie at the center of both the nation's history and the process of urbanization" (Warner and Fleisch, 1977: 16; cf. Warner and Fleisch, 1976). The United States was urbanized, and its cities' institutions and histories determined, in no small part in coincidence with great migrations of people, both from foreign continents and from the rural South. Yet, the meaning of these changes for religious diversity in America has not been adequately understood. The second set of analyses in this chapter, accordingly, is concerned not with the overall size of urban populations, but with their composition. The analyses explore how varying proportions of foreign stock, foreign-born,

Table 4.4. *Results of weighted least squares (WLS) analyses of the effects of population composition on Protestant-Catholic-Jewish-Other diversity, 1890; all 122 cities (unstandardized regression coefficients)*

| Equation number | Constant | Total population, 1890 | 1890 population composition (in millions of inhabitants) | | |
|---|---|---|---|---|---|
| | | | Foreign stock | Foreign born | Nonwhite |
| 4.4a | +.451 | −1.317 | +2.663[a] | — | — |
| 4.4b | +.445 | −0.497 | — | +2.823[b] | — |
| 4.4c | +.443 | +0.693 | — | — | −5.651[c] |
| 4.4d | +.441 | +0.948 | −0.374[d] | — | −6.042[e] |
| 4.4e | +.438 | +1.611 | — | −2.829[f] | −7.169[g] |

[a]$t = 3.178; .001 < p < .01.$  [b]$t = 1.878; .05 < p < .10.$  [c]$t = 4.930; p < .001.$
[d]$t = 0.322; .70 < p < .80.$  [e]$t = 3.619; p < .001.$
[f]$t = 1.555; .10 < p < .20.$  [g]$t = 4.779; p < .001.$

and nonwhite persons affected levels of religious diversity in American cities at the turn of the century.[11]

Table 4.4 presents results computed from data on all 122 cities in the study. Equations 4.4a through 4.4c estimate the net effects of individual aspects of the composition of urban populations in 1890 on Protestant-Catholic-Jewish-Other diversity in that same year. Three demographic characteristics of cities are employed as independent variables. Two of these measure foreign presence in the cities: a Census count of the foreign-born population, and a figure, also from the 1890 Census, for the more inclusive group of inhabitants derived from foreign stock (i.e., foreign-born persons and persons born in the United States of foreign parents). This latter variable serves as an indicator of the foreign presence in a city's population in broader terms, encompassing as it does immigrants and urbanites who were second-generation Americans. The third population-composition variable employed here is the city's total of nonwhite[12] residents. In each equation, total population in 1890 is entered as an explicit control, a step that renders the analyses of diversity tests for the influence of *proportions* of nonnative or nonwhite persons, and not their aggregate numbers.

The findings in Table 4.4, on first inspection, appear to be plain and at the same time powerful. Diversity across major religious groupings (Protestantism, Catholicism, Judaism, and others) was to be found prominently in 1890 in city populations featuring large proportions of persons of foreign stock or foreign birth. The population-composition coefficients in Equations 4.4a and 4.4b are both positive; furthermore, the coefficient

for foreign stock population is highly significant statistically, and the one for foreign-born population falls just short of the .05 standard. The impact of nonwhite population, gauged in Equation 4.4c, is even more statistically unmistakable, though it draws diversity in the opposite direction. Large nonwhite populations, it seems, were common in cities of low religious diversity.

Such a simple impression of the countervailing effects of foreign and nonwhite populations on religious diversity is complicated somewhat by an examination of Equations 4.4d and 4.4e, in which indicators of the relative sizes of both minorities appear jointly. In these models, the size of the nonwhite segment of a city's population still exerts a marked negative influence on that city's prevailing degree of diversity. However, the signs of the two variables representing foreign elements in the population reverse themselves in conjunction with nonwhite population, and assume its negative direction. In addition, the achieved significance levels of the coefficients for the foreign stock and foreign-born populations are reduced when they are entered as coregressors with nonwhite population. The statistical implication of this change is that the effect on diversity of the relative size of the foreign population—measured in either manner—is confounded with that of the size of the nonwhite population.

In fact, the proportion of a city's population that is nonwhite correlates at −.716 with its proportion descended from foreign stock, and at −.647 with its proportion born abroad. Admittedly, the reciprocal nature of this relation may have been determined in part by the technique of ratio measurement. As any proportion declines, at least one among the remaining ones must increase, because the whole set always sums to one. Even conceding this mutual dependence, a separate regression analysis (the results of which are not exhibited) showed foreign stock and foreign-born population (when accompanied by a total population control) each to be an extremely powerful negative predictor of nonwhite population levels. The relationship was symmetrical, with nonwhite population, controlled for total population, functioning as a strong inverse indicator of both measures of foreign population. These statistics suggest that in cities where immigrants and their children comprised a sizable fraction of the population in 1890, nonwhites were correspondingly fewer (and vice versa).

Some familiar historical facts may be assembled to justify the existence of this relationship. As the opening section of this chapter made clear, the "new" immigrants of the turn-of-the-century period converged in great numbers on northern and north central manufacturing cities; the cities of the South, on the other hand, were unattractive to the foreigner. Southern cities, rather, contained in 1890 large numbers of blacks who would soon migrate to the North, where they were to compete with whites of

Table 4.5. *Results of weighted least squares (WLS) analyses of the effects of population composition on Protestant-Catholic-Jewish-Other diversity, 1890, by region (unstandardized regression coefficients)*

| Eq. no. | Region | Constant | Total population, 1890 | Foreign stock | Foreign born | Nonwhite | N |
|---|---|---|---|---|---|---|---|
| | | | | 1890 population composition (in millions of inhabitants) | | | |
| 4.5a | Non-South | +.444 | +0.911 | $-0.763^a$ | — | — | 100 |
| 4.5b | South | +.432 | −3.670 | $+10.914^b$ | — | — | 22 |
| 4.5c | Non-South | +.441 | +1.256 | — | $-2.663^c$ | — | 100 |
| 4.5d | South | +.419 | −3.648 | — | $+31.019^d$ | — | 22 |
| 4.5e | Non-South | +.449 | +0.224 | — | — | $+5.474^e$ | 100 |
| 4.5f | South | +.432 | +2.438 | — | — | $-9.785^f$ | 22 |
| 4.5g | Non-South | +.448 | +0.392 | $-0.226^g$ | — | $+4.929^b$ | 100 |
| 4.5h | South | +.430 | −4.983 | $+12.910^i$ | — | $+2.461^j$ | 22 |
| 4.5i | Non-South | +.443 | +1.061 | — | $-2.290^k$ | $+2.306^l$ | 100 |
| 4.5j | South | +.414 | −5.280 | — | $+37.762^m$ | $+3.179^n$ | 22 |

$^a t = 0.755; .40 < p < .50.$  $^b t = 4.388; p < .001.$  $^c t = 1.657; p < .10.$
$^d t = 4.942; p < .001.$  $^e t = 1.156; .20 < p < .30.$  $^f t = 3.169; p < .01.$
$^g t = 0.192; .80 < p < .90.$  $^h t = 0.889; .30 < p < .40.$  $^i t = 2.440; p < .02.$
$^j t = 0.430; .60 < p < .70.$  $^k t = 1.251; p < .30.$  $^l t = 0.430; .60 < p < .70.$
$^m t = 3.088; p < .01.$  $^n t = 0.647; p < .60.$

European ancestry for a share of the fruits of America's industrial growth.[13] Thus, relatively large nonwhite populations, and a relative paucity of foreigners, distinguished southern cities in 1890, while the opposite distribution characterized cities elsewhere in the United States.

This difference is addressed in the analyses reported in Table 4.5. For this table, each of the analyses of the effects of population composition on interfaith diversity has been repeated, with the cases in the study split now into two separate groups: nonsouthern and southern[14] cities. By dividing the cities according to region, the confusion of population effects by their social contexts which was implied in Table 4.4 is avoided, and the pattern of results is consequently refined.

The sizes of the foreign stock and foreign-born populations in cities outside the South, Table 4.5 suggests, are inversely related to diversity across the major religious faiths represented in those cities. This regularity constitutes a reversal of the general finding reported in Table 4.4.

However, in none of the equations in which a variable measuring foreign presence is inserted (Equations 4.5a, 4.5c, 4.5g, and 4.5i) does its coefficient reach the .05 level of statistical significance. Equally consistent, but far more striking, are the estimates of foreign population's effects on religious diversity in southern cities. There, the relative size of the foreign population is associated with higher levels of diversity. The coefficients for foreign stock and foreign-born population in Equations 4.5b, 4.5d, 4.5h, and 4.5j are, without exception, positive, and all meet or surpass the .05 significance level.

In a second departure from Table 4.4's results, which pertained to all 122 cities, the higher the nonwhite proportion of the 1890 population of a city located outside the South, the greater was its religious diversity. This finding recurs in all three tests in Table 4.5, although the coefficients for nonwhite population in Equations 4.5e, 4.5g, and 4.5i are not statistically significant. Nonwhite population's association with Protestant-Catholic-Jewish-Other diversity in the South is unfortunately more mixed. By itself, nonwhite population in a southern city, as indicated in Equation 4.5f, exhibits a strong negative relation. When coupled with either variable representing foreign population, however, the estimate of the influence of nonwhites in the population on a southern city's broadest form of religious diversity is weakened statistically (see the notes to Equations 4.5h and 4.5j) and its sign changes to positive.

This much describes the effects of the composition of the urban population on diversity across the major categories of religious affiliation. Do these same effects pertain within Protestantism alone? In the case of American Protestantism, much of the religious influence of immigration would be removed from consideration. However, the relationship between religion and race ought to compensate by moving into greater analytical prominence.

Analyses that are identical in form and execution to the two sets discussed above, but which invoke diversity among Protestants in 1890 as their dependent variable, are detailed in Tables 4.6 and 4.7. The analyses of data from all 122 cities summarized in Table 4.6 reveal that both measures of foreign population are related directly to diversity among Protestants, although not to a statistically significant degree. The single population-composition coefficients in Equations 4.6a and 4.6b, as well as the estimates for the contributions of foreign populations to Protestant diversity in Equations 4.6d and 4.6e, are positive, though their corresponding t-ratios — especially in the final pair of models — are not very large. Throughout the analyses described in Table 4.6, the effect, where it is measured, of the size of the nonwhite population is negative. Only, however, when it stands apart from other population-composition variables, as in Equation 4.6c, does it achieve statistical significance.

Table 4.6. *Results of weighted least squares (WLS) analyses of the effects of population composition on diversity among Protestants, 1890; all 122 cities (unstandardized regression coefficients)*

| Equation number | Constant | Total population, 1890 | 1890 population composition (in millions of inhabitants) | | |
| --- | --- | --- | --- | --- | --- |
| | | | Foreign stock | Foreign born | Nonwhite |
| 4.6a | +.813 | −0.500 | +0.982[a] | — | — |
| 4.6b | +.813 | −0.427 | — | +1.834[b] | — |
| 4.6c | +.810 | +0.230 | — | — | −1.925[c] |
| 4.6d | +.810 | +0.209 | +0.031[d] | — | −1.893[e] |
| 4.6e | +.811 | +0.053 | — | +0.548[f] | −1.631[g] |

[a]$t = 1.631; .10 < p < .20.$   [b]$t = 1.745; .05 < p < .10.$   [c]$t = 2.239; .02 < p < .05.$
[d]$t = 0.032; p > .90.$   [e]$t = 1.511; .10 < p < .20.$
[f]$t = 0.397; .60 < p < .70.$   [g]$t = 1.436; .10 < p < .20.$

The five models from Table 4.6 were estimated a second time, on the group of cities dichotomized again by region. The recalculated results are reported in Table 4.7. From inspection of this table, it is evident that the most pronounced effects of foreign population on Protestant diversity occurred in southern cities, and not outside the South. The coefficients in Equations 4.7a and 4.7c are inconsistent in sign and insignificant statistically. Meanwhile, the two statistics which measure the relationship of foreign population to Protestant diversity in the South (in Equations 4.7b and 4.7d) are positive, and one meets while the other approaches the .05 level of statistical significance. Even so, the foreign population variables, in response to the strong effects of nonwhite population, slip to statistical insignificance in the four equations at the bottom of Table 4.7 (4.7g through 4.7j).

Indeed, a city's nonwhite population emerges in Table 4.7 as its clearest demographic predictor of Protestant diversity, and its effects are enhanced in the division of the cities under examination by region. Outside the South, a large nonwhite population has an unfailingly positive association with diversity among Protestants. The coefficients for nonwhite population in Equations 4.7e, 4.7g, and 4.7i, moreover, are all highly significant. Among cities in the South, the outcome with nonwhite population is consistently the opposite, though this is not as easily discernible with statistics, perhaps because of the small number of cities so situated. Again, only where nonwhite population appears unaccompanied by another population-composition variable (i.e., in Equation 4.7f) does it reach statistical significance.

Table 4.7. *Results of weighted least squares (WLS) analyses of the effects of population composition on diversity among Protestants, 1890, by region (unstandardized regression coefficients)*

| Eq. no. | Region | Constant | Total population, 1890 | 1890 population composition (in millions of inhabitants) | | | N |
| --- | --- | --- | --- | --- | --- | --- | --- |
| | | | | Foreign stock | Foreign born | Nonwhite | |
| 4.7a | Non-South | +.805 | +0.395 | $-0.228^a$ | — | — | 100 |
| 4.7b | South | +.833 | −1.989 | $+4.432^b$ | — | — | 22 |
| 4.7c | Non-South | +.806 | +0.190 | — | $+0.164^c$ | — | 100 |
| 4.7d | South | +.828 | −2.224 | — | $+14.944^d$ | — | 22 |
| 4.7e | Non-South | +.807 | −0.041 | — | — | $+8.646^e$ | 100 |
| 4.7f | South | +.836 | +1.067 | — | — | $-5.939^f$ | 22 |
| 4.7g | Non-South | +.812 | −0.762 | $+0.967^g$ | — | $+10.979^h$ | 100 |
| 4.7h | South | +.837 | +2.018 | $-1.654^i$ | — | $-7.508^j$ | 22 |
| 4.7i | Non-South | +.813 | −0.775 | — | $+2.008^k$ | $+11.423^l$ | 100 |
| 4.7j | South | +.832 | −0.699 | — | $+8.640^m$ | $-2.973^n$ | 22 |

$^a t = 0.330; .70 < p < .80.$   $^b t = 1.666; p < .10.$   $^c t = 0.148; p < .90.$
$^d t = 2.182; .02 < p < .05.$   $^e t = 2.749; p < .01.$   $^f t = 2.149; p < .05.$
$^g t = 1.247; .20 < p < .30.$   $^h t = 3.006; p < .01.$   $^i t = 0.303; p < .80.$
$^j t = 1.274; .20 < p < .30.$   $^k t = 1.662; p < .10.$   $^l t = 3.230; p < .01.$
$^m t = 0.646; .50 < p < .60.$   $^n t = 0.552; .50 < p < .60.$

The relations examined up to this point have been entirely cross-sectional: that is, regression models have been constructed to estimate prevailing levels of two types of religious diversity in 1890 by use of data on nativity and race from the Census of that same year. The results of these analyses are assessments of the magnitude of the net covariation between religious diversity and aspects of the composition of urban populations. Such covariation, however, is conceived in measurements taken simultaneously, and hence it is temporally static. It simply quantifies the associations among different variables at one point in time. Its discovery points up neither the causes of any relationship between urban population and religious diversity nor its likely future course. Yet, these are important considerations, both practically and substantively. Cities in the process of rapid development may not, at a given moment, have acquired the population proportions which may be necessary to achieve a certain degree of religious diversity, but charted over time, population character-

Table 4.8. *Results of weighted least squares (WLS) analyses of the effects of population composition in 1890 on Protestant-Catholic-Jewish-Other diversity in 1906; 119 cities (unstandardized regression coefficients)*

| Equation number | Constant | Control variables | | 1890 population composition (in millions of inhabitants) | | |
|---|---|---|---|---|---|---|
| | | Protestant-Catholic-Jewish-Other diversity 1890 | Total population (in millions), 1890 | Foreign stock | Foreign born | Nonwhite |
| 4.8a | +.116 | +.643 | −0.51 | +.252[a] | — | — |
| 4.8b | +.113 | +.649 | +.060 | — | +.141[b] | — |
| 4.8c | +.106 | +.664 | +.066 | — | — | +0.446[c] |
| 4.8d | +.108 | +.665 | −.540 | +.887[d] | — | +1.383[e] |
| 4.8e | +.105 | +.669 | −.197 | — | +.800[f] | +0.908[g] |

[a]$t = 0.288; .70 < p < .80.$    [b]$t = 0.095; p > .90.$    [c]$t = 0.366; .70 < p < .80.$
[d]$t = 0.725; .40 < p < .50.$    [e]$t = 0.746; .40 < p < .50.$
[f]$t = 0.409; .60 < p < .70.$    [g]$t = 0.520; .60 < p < .70.$

istics may be followed eventually by discernible alterations in the religious environment of a city.

This possibility is accommodated by the analyses reported in Tables 4.8 through 4.11. The equations arranged in these exhibits retain as predictors the three 1890 population-composition variables that have appeared in the earlier analyses; however, substituted for the dependent variables from 1890 are measures of religious diversity in 1906. In addition, another independent variable has been inserted in these models; its purpose is to control for diversity levels in 1890. Regression coefficients computed in these analyses thus indicate the lagged effects of foreign and nonwhite populations on shifts in religious diversity realized after nearly two decades. They thereby provide a better historical view of urban population and attendant religious change across the turn-of-the-century period.

Tables 4.8 and 4.9 summarize the influences of the relative numbers of foreign stock, foreign-born, and nonwhite urban residents in 1890 on Protestant-Catholic-Jewish-Other diversity in 1906 (with a city's 1890 score on that diversity index controlled). The tables are informative only in that they convey two simple outcomes: the predominantly positive contributions of nonnative and nonwhite groups in 1890 to increases in interfaith diversity over the subsequent sixteen years, and the universal failure of any of the *t*-ratios calculated for these effects to approximate even remotely the preestablished standard of statistical significance.

Table 4.9. *Results of weighted least squares (WLS) analyses of the effects of population composition in 1890 on Protestant-Catholic-Jewish-Other diversity in 1906, by region (unstandardized regression coefficients)*

| Equation number | Region | Constant | Control variables | | 1890 population composition (in millions of inhabitants) | | | N |
| | | | Protestant-Catholic-Jewish-Other diversity, 1890 | Total population, 1890 | Foreign stock | Foreign born | Nonwhite | |
| --- | --- | --- | --- | --- | --- | --- | --- | --- |
| 4.9a | Non-South | +.074 | +.715 | +0.006 | +0.374$^a$ | — | — | 97 |
| 4.9b | South | +.265 | +.400 | −2.142 | +4.506$^b$ | — | — | 22 |
| 4.9c | Non-South | +.073 | +.716 | +0.124 | — | +0.409$^c$ | — | 97 |
| 4.9d | South | +.264 | +.392 | −2.045 | — | +11.925$^d$ | — | 22 |
| 4.9e | Non-South | +.078 | +.705 | +0.173 | — | — | +2.594$^e$ | 97 |
| 4.9f | South | +.226 | +.492 | +0.196 | — | — | −3.277$^f$ | 22 |
| 4.9g | Non-South | +.081 | +.706 | −0.484 | +0.881$^g$ | — | +4.714$^h$ | 97 |
| 4.9h | South | +.266 | +.399 | −2.375 | +4.870$^i$ | — | +0.425$^i$ | 22 |
| 4.9i | Non-South | +.077 | +.712 | −0.215 | — | +1.054$^k$ | +4.030$^l$ | 97 |
| 4.9j | South | +.263 | +.396 | −1.709 | — | +10.464$^m$ | −0.624$^n$ | 22 |

$^a$ $t = 0.366$; $.70 < p < .80$.   $^b$ $t = 1.103$; $.20 < p < .30$.   $^c$ $t = 0.226$; $.80 < p < .90$.   $^d$ $t = 1.014$; $.30 < p < .40$.
$^e$ $t = 0.493$; $.60 < p < .70$.   $^f$ $t = 0.840$; $.40 < p < .50$.   $^g$ $t = 0.680$; $.40 < p < .50$.   $^h$ $t = 0.769$; $.40 < p < .50$.
$^i$ $t = 0.685$; $.40 < p < .50$.   $^j$ $t = 0.063$; $p > .90$.   $^k$ $t = 0.515$; $.60 < p < .70$.
$^l$ $t = 0.675$; $.50 < p < .60$.   $^m$ $t = 0.551$; $.50 < p < .60$.   $^n$ $t = 0.100$; $p > .90$.

Table 4.10. *Results of weighted least squares (WLS) analyses of the effects of population composition in 1890 on diversity among Protestants in 1906; all 122 cities (unstandardized regression coefficients)*

| Equation number | Constant | Control variables | | 1890 population composition (in millions of inhabitants) | | |
| | | Diversity among Protestants, 1890 | Total population (in millions), 1890 | Foreign stock | Foreign born | Nonwhite |
|---|---|---|---|---|---|---|
| 4.10a | +.283 | +.665 | +.871 | −1.177[a] | — | — |
| 4.10b | +.283 | +.665 | +.710 | — | −1.943[b] | — |
| 4.10c | +.277 | +.677 | +.028 | — | — | +1.810[c] |
| 4.10d | +.275 | +.677 | +.428 | −0.586[d] | — | +1.199[e] |
| 4.10e | +.273 | +.679 | +.330 | — | −0.931[f] | +1.315[g] |

[a] $t = 3.706; p < .001.$  [b] $t = 3.473; p < .001.$  [c] $t = 3.944; p < .001.$
[d] $t = 1.298; .10 < p < .20.$  [e] $t = 1.825; .05 < p < .10.$
[f] $t = 1.301; .10 < p < .20.$  [g] $t = 2.210; .02 < p < .05.$

Diversity among Protestants in 1906, the dependent variable in the analyses summarized in Tables 4.10 and 4.11, proves more amenable to statistical prediction with population-composition indicators. Table 4.10 depicts a pattern of results, however, which is the opposite of that in the cross-sectional analyses of Table 4.6. Foreign representation in the population, which in 1890 seemed to be associated with diversity among Protestants, actually depressed the magnitude of the change in that index between 1890 and 1906. The coefficients for foreign stock and foreign-born population are all negative in Table 4.10, and the ones (in Equations 4.10a and 4.10b) which are estimated for foreign population as the sole population-composition variable are highly significant statistically. Also in a pattern opposite to the earlier cross-sectional analyses, Equations 4.10c through 4.10e find that by 1906, Protestant diversity increased in cities with substantial nonwhite populations in 1890. All three coefficients in the last column in Table 4.10 are positive, and two meet—while the third approaches—statistical significance.

Table 4.11 presents minor adjustments of these results, with the cases in the study disaggregated by region. The measures of foreign population in 1890 are negatively related, and consistently so, to growth in diversity among Protestants by 1906. Nonwhite population, in contrast, exhibits varying effects depending on whether it is situated in a southern city or not. The size of the nonwhite segment as a proportion of a city's total population in 1890 is directly related to increases in Protestant diversity in places outside the South. The estimates in Equations 4.11e, 4.11g, and

Table 4.11. *Results of weighted least squares (WLS) analyses of the effects of population composition in 1890 on diversity among Protestants in 1906, by region (unstandardized regression coefficients)*

| Equation number | Region | Constant | Control variables | | 1890 population composition (in millions of inhabitants) | | | N |
| --- | --- | --- | --- | --- | --- | --- | --- | --- |
| | | | Diversity among Protestants, 1890 | Total population, 1890 | Foreign stock | Foreign born | Nonwhite | |
| 4.11a | Non-South | +.174 | +.795 | +0.680 | $-0.816^a$ | — | — | 100 |
| 4.11b | South | +.471 | +.467 | +0.054 | $-0.015^b$ | — | — | 22 |
| 4.11c | Non-South | +.170 | +.801 | +0.534 | — | $-1.248^c$ | — | 100 |
| 4.11d | South | +.469 | +.469 | +0.077 | — | $-0.244^d$ | — | 22 |
| 4.11e | Non-South | +.206 | +.760 | -0.007 | — | — | $+4.613^e$ | 100 |
| 4.11f | South | +.500 | +.434 | +0.315 | — | — | $-0.980^f$ | 22 |
| 4.11g | Non-South | +.198 | +.768 | +0.324 | $-0.444^g$ | — | $+3.479^h$ | 100 |
| 4.11h | South | +.508 | +.425 | +1.988 | $-2.894^i$ | — | $-3.778^j$ | 22 |
| 4.11i | Non-South | +.197 | +.769 | +0.234 | — | $-0.658^k$ | $+3.624^l$ | 100 |
| 4.11j | South | +.488 | +.452 | +1.674 | — | $-6.744^m$ | $-3.191^n$ | 22 |

[a] $t = 2.018$; $.02 < p < .05$.　[b] $t < 0.001$; $p > .90$.　[c] $t = 1.915$; $.05 < p < .10$.　[d] $t = 0.095$; $p > .90$.　[e] $t = 2.352$; $p < .02$.

[f] $t = 0.949$; $.30 < p < .40$.　[g] $t = 0.941$; $.30 < p < .40$.　[h] $t = 1.511$; $.10 < p < .20$.　[i] $t = 1.704$; $.05 < p < .10$.　[j] $t = 1.975$; $p < .05$.

[k] $t = 0.844$; $.30 < p < .40$.　[l] $t = 1.603$; $.10 < p < .20$.　[m] $t = 1.571$; $.10 < p < .20$.　[n] $t = 1.853$; $.05 < p < .10$.

4.11i are positive in direction. Within the southern region, large numbers of nonwhites in 1890 apparently inhibited the diversification of Protestant church affiliations through 1906. The three remaining coefficients in the rightmost column of Table 4.11 (in Equations 4.11f, 4.11h, and 4.11j) are all negative.

## Conclusion

Neither a city's absolute size nor the composition of its population, it seems from these analyses, exerts an effect on religious diversity that is always uniform in direction, substantial in magnitude, and discernible with even advanced statistical techniques. City size and urban growth simply did not yield the predicted increases in religious diversity, and exactly how the foreign stock, foreign-born, and nonwhite proportions of a city's population affected its distribution of religious membership is contingent upon which group is being examined, when and how diversity is measured, and where the city in question is located. Nevertheless, a few regularities can be culled from the extensive results reported in this chapter.

To begin, the impact of foreign populations on religious diversity in the South is worthy of note. The relative numbers of both foreign stock and foreign-born persons were positively and significantly associated with Protestant-Catholic-Jewish-Other diversity in southern cities in 1890. In addition, foreign-born population had a similarly positive relation to diversity among southern Protestants. An inference to be drawn from this pair of findings is that the southern cities which in the decade before the turn of the century possessed populations of heterogeneous origins supported an atypically high degree of religious diversity. While this conclusion is not in itself surprising, it is interesting that the effect of foreign population extended to categories of religious membership (i.e., Protestant denominations) with which few foreigners of that period were directly affiliated.

Nonwhites, these analyses further suggest, performed the same role outside the South as foreigners did within the region: their presence in a city's population was linked significantly to diversity among those church members whose affiliations (in this instance, with Protestant denominations) were closest to their own. In either case, the cross-sectional analyses strongly imply that large concentrations of people of a type comparatively uncommon in a certain region were a concomitant of broad religious diversity.

Change in Protestant-Catholic-Jewish-Other diversity between 1890 and 1906 appeared to be associated with no distinctive population configuration in 1890, although several relations between population composi-

tion and shifts over the period in levels of diversity among Protestants were uncovered. Specifically, greater numbers of nonwhite persons augmented Protestant diversity outside the South, while for sixteen years depressing it within that region. Furthermore, both indicators of foreign population restrained growth in Protestant diversity in turn-of-the-century cities. Especially salient was the power of persons of foreign stock to induce greater homogeneity among Protestants in cities outside the South, where foreigners were in fact concentrated.[15]

The statistical analyses in this chapter suggest, in sum, that religious diversity was not a consequence of urban population growth itself, but that instead it can be attributed in part to blocs of city dwellers with distinctive religious ties, and their movements in the years bridging the two centuries. In the largest sense, results scattered through this chapter, when viewed together, reflect historic movements of rural peoples and their religious cultures into late-nineteenth-century cities. For example, a few foreigners found that the most tolerant and least homogeneous southern cities would also tolerate them and their religion. Also, nonwhites streaming north before the First World War established urban communities organized around race and racial churches, or expanded such communities as already existed (Frazier, 1964: 47–67; Mays and Nicholson, 1933: 32–33, 94–113; Woodson, 1945: 296–297). In both cases, migration functioned to diversify the religious environments of American cities.

# CHAPTER V

# "A New Society"

## Industrialization and Religious Diversity

The demographic development which was the subject of the last chapter, the massive growth of the American population in the latter half of the nineteenth century, had historic consequences for the national economy. In the fifty years from 1860 to 1910, the population of the United States nearly tripled, and so did the size of the market for goods and services which it supported. One particular component of growth in this period – a great increase, by immigration, in numbers of young adult males – led to an expansion of the country's labor force which more than matched the enormous increments in total population. Together with advances in technologies of production and transportation, and increases in capital investment and personal income, these structural changes in American society made possible the realization, by the outbreak of the First World War, of a trend which had begun in the decades before the Civil War, a trend toward an economy based predominantly in manufacturing (North, 1965: 693–700; cf. Diamond, 1963; Hays, 1957: 4–17; Ross, 1968: 25–37).

"Judged by the total volume of its industrial output," one economic historian (North, 1965: 702) writes, "the United States was, by 1914, the most industrialized nation in the world." A sociologist illuminates the more far-reaching, if intermediary, steps in the process by which industrial supremacy was achieved:

A new society – an industrial society – was being created, and its creation involved the uprooting and transplanting of millions of people, the raising of new groups to power and the decline of the once-powerful, the learning of new routines and habits and disciplines, the sloughing off of old ideas. Nothing was left untouched – the state itself in its relation to its citizens, the churches, the family; all were altered because the circumstances of life itself were being altered. [Diamond, 1963: 6]

89

How did the industrialization of the United States affect religion? A number of historical narratives (e.g., Abell, 1943; Hopkins, 1940; May, 1949; Reimers, 1968) have already proposed an answer to this question. These respected works agree in asserting that leaders of institutional religion in the late nineteenth and early twentieth centuries perceived industrialism to be both a social and a religious problem of some proportion. The two dimensions of their concern were furthermore closely connected, for some socially conscious churchmen felt, at the very least, that the future of religion as an influential force in America was threatened if it could not speak to the problems of the present society. "Direct experience with the impact of industrialism on individuals and on society," notes Samuel P. Hays (1957: 72), "convinced many religious leaders that the new conditions were more a menace than a boon to spiritual values." This conviction, while perhaps originating in organizational commitments, prompted in much religious thought and writing of the day a distinct emphasis on the seemingly opposing tasks of individual sanctification and social betterment.

Industrialism was regarded in liberal church circles as an incentive for the creation of a new system of social ethics, and not exclusively as an assault on the maintenance of religious traditions. A new emphasis on tradition, on the unambiguous articulation of doctrinal "fundamentals," alternately gained control in conservative religion, where it legitimated a more general rejection of "an industrialized civilization in which the acceptance of change as a primary law of life was encouraged by the dynamic and changing character of the social process, especially in the economic sphere" (Niebuhr, 1931: 527). Unlike proponents of the Social Gospel, who engaged the rising industrial order so as to "Christianize" it, fundamentalists betrayed a deep distrust of an "industrialized culture with its rational and artificial methods of production and its immediate urban environment, all largely subject to human control" (Niebuhr, 1931: 527).[1]

Fittingly, the liberal churches' responses to industrial change, some of which were outlined in this study in Chapter 1, were incorporated into a more or less coordinated plan of social activism. The fundamentalists, for their part, launched grand crusades for religious revival and the evangelization of millions. The stories of these plans—their philosophies, leadership, and execution—today dominate historians' treatments of the relations between industrialization and religion. Indeed, much of the general historiography dealing with the years straddling the turn of the century (e.g., Faulkner, 1931; Hays, 1957; Schlesinger, 1933; Wish, 1952) has centered its attention on religious efforts at charity and on religiously inspired movements for personal piety and social reform. The bulk of the text usually is devoted to certain historical actors and their ideas; the

larger conditions to which they were exposed and which they presumably went on to influence are not as often addressed in their own right. Seldom, it follows, has there been any attempt in historical works actually to measure industrialization, or to discern—other than by tracing intellectual tendencies—its impact on features of the religious environment. The reaction of religion to industrialism rarely is cast in recognizably sociological terms, or subjected to quantitative analysis.

## Sociological Approaches to Industrialization and Religious Diversity

Yet, a sociological analysis seems warranted, for there are reasons to suppose that a change as momentous as the industrialization of the United States would have brought with it not simply a change in elite attitudes, but a profound rearrangement of the religious environment of the nation. Four sociological theories relating industrialization and religion are discussed in this section. Because they indicate different outcomes for religious diversity as a consequence of industrial development, the theories together present a confusing picture of how a changing economy may have affected the turn-of-the-century religious environment.

One rationale for a possible rearrangement in the religious environment is furnished by two of the earliest students of industrialism, Karl Marx and Friedrich Engels. "Empiric observation," they insisted in the opening of *The German Ideology* (Marx and Engels, 1964: 73), "must in every single case reveal the connection of the social and political organization with production, empirically and without any mystification or speculation." This sweeping declaration stemmed from the belief of Marx and Engels that social organization begins in the labor of men to sustain life for themselves, "under definite material limitations, provisions and conditions which do not depend on their free will" (Marx and Engels, 1964: 73). Thus,

the production of men's ideas, thinking, their spiritual intercourse, here appear as the direct efflux of the material condition. The same applies to spiritual production as represented in the language of politics, laws, morals, religion, metaphysics, etc. of a people. [Marx and Engels, 1964: 74]

A doctrinaire Marxian position would expect changes in religion, as well as changes in cognate areas of culture like politics, to correspond to trends in the underlying economic relations which are presumably their source. More specifically, a Marxian perspective would posit the eventual demise of religious diversity in the advance of industrialization. Class, Marx predicted, would become the paramount social division under in-

dustrial capitalism, and traits attaching to racial, ethnic, and national allegiances in turn would recede in importance. This development, along with the homogenizing influence of labor in large production units, would serve, then, to erode religious distinctions.

On the other hand, different tracts of Marx can be cited to support an opposite hypothesis, one which anticipates a progressive expansion of religious variety in industrial society. As religion gradually withdraws from its position as a legitimating force for the state, Marx elsewhere contended, it could be freed to reflect to a greater extent the influences of individual tastes. Religion, he charged, "is no longer the essence of *community,* but the essence of *differentiation*" (Marx, 1963: 15). In the private realm, "the religious consciousness runs riot in a wealth of contradictions and diversity" (Marx, 1963: 21), for religion, according to Marx,

is now only the abstract avowal of an individual folly, a private whim or caprice. The infinite fragmentation of religion in North America, for example, already gives it the *external* form of a strictly private affair. [Marx, 1963: 15]

Later research carried out in the Marxian tradition, however, seems to have confirmed the null hypothesis: that of no significant relation between industrialization and religious diversity. Michael Hechter's study of *Internal Colonialism* (1975) in the British Isles capably analyzes data from more than a century of marriage records to demonstrate how the industrialization of Britain's "Celtic fringe" (i.e., Ireland, Scotland, and Wales), though it promoted contact between the non-English "periphery" and the English "core," nevertheless failed to induce an expected convergence of religious affiliations.

Differences in the religious commitments of core and periphery populations persisted in Britain after industrialization, Hechter speculates, because the manufacturing system there was superimposed on a "cultural division of labor." This cultural pattern organized social stratification in the periphery, holding natives in subordinate positions under the supervision of representatives of the core culture. Cultural contact that followed the arrival of the factory in the colonial "fringe" was still premised on the cultural division of labor, and so it quite likely exaggerated differences in religion between the natives and the English managers and administrators, instead of removing such differences. Indeed, members of the supervisory class sometimes went as far as to convert in order to divest themselves of any preexisting ties which might unintentionally have bound them to the workers they directed. Thus, Hechter (1975: 191) concludes, "each of the peripheral lands maintained its religious distinctive-

ness from England despite the vast social disruptions of the nineteenth century."

Emile Durkheim's theory of *The Division of Labor in Society* (1933), which was tested in one of its aspects in Chapter 4, may be applied as well to the question of the effects of industrialization on religious diversity. Durkheim supposed that, under preindustrial, "mechanical" solidarity (a form of structural integration based on the similarity of social units and actors), there prevailed a "common conscience," consisting of a universal and homogeneous set of beliefs, values, and meanings which pervaded all social action. Industrialization and the division of labor posed a change, however, for they confined social interaction progressively to "occupational groups," so, in Durkheim's (1933: 170) assessment, there remained "a decreasing number of collective beliefs and sentiments which are both collective enough and strong enough to take on a religious character."

As societies become more voluminous and spread over vaster territories, their traditions and practices, in order to adapt to the diversity of situations and constantly changing circumstances, are compelled to maintain a state of plasticity and instability which no longer offers adequate resistance to individual variations. These latter, being less well contained, develop more freely and multiply in number; that is, everyone increasingly follows his own path. At the same time, as a consequence of a more advanced division of labour, each mind finds itself directed towards a different point on the horizon, reflects a different aspect of the world and, as a result, the contents of men's minds differ from one subject to another. One is thus gradually proceeding towards a state of affairs, now almost attained, in which the members of a single social group will no longer have anything in common other than their humanity, that is, characteristics which constitute the human person in general. [Durkheim, 1969: 26]

The common conscience, by this fact, "becomes enfeebled," and "it more and more comes to consist of very general and very indeterminate ways of thinking and feeling, which leave an open place for a growing multitude of individual differences" (Durkheim, 1933: 170, 172). Certainly prominent among these newly allowed differences are those with respect to religion. In this sense, Durkheim may be interpreted as having predicted an increase in religious diversity as a result of industrialization.

Because theory, both old and new, provides little clear guidance for research, the style of this chapter is unavoidably exploratory. Its aim is to probe the ways in which prominent aspects of the economic structure of American cities at the turn of the century affected levels of religious

diversity in those places. The American case is especially complicated, for although many historical writers have loosely associated the industrialization of the United States with religious diversity in the nineteenth century, they have for the most part neglected to specify the sociological mechanisms whereby this connection was to have been established. Ought these writers to refer, more exactly, to the economic growth which attracted waves of immigrants to American cities, or perhaps to burgeoning urban populations and the possibilities for religious differentiation which they appeared to create at the turn of the century? If so, industrialization may in fact explain much less than its reputation among historians might suggest.

To help to ascertain what industrialization does and does not explain, this chapter communicates the findings of several empirical analyses of the relationship between that process and religious diversity. The section immediately following is preliminary to the analysis, as it assesses historical Census data on manufacturing, and composes from the data quantitative indicators of industrialization. With the aid of these indicators, a series of regression analyses of diversity is performed. The analyses include estimation of cross-sectional models of religious diversity for 1890 and 1905–1906, as well as attempts to measure the lagged effects of industrialization and the effects of its progress over time on changes in religious diversity. The findings of these analyses are reported in detail, and a closing discussion elaborates several interpretations which are compatible with most of the statistical results.

## Measures of Industrialization, 1890–1905

Data for the analyses of manufacturing in this chapter were compiled from two publications of the United States Census (Census Office, 1894, and Bureau of the Census, 1907). The tabulations they contain summarize attempts by the federal government to depict, in statistics, industrialization in 1890 and 1905, respectively. Differences between the two Censuses in planning and methods are noted in this section, and the uses to which their data are put in this study are explained.

After concluding its count of the population, the Census of 1890 under took to enumerate, by means of personal visits from special agents, "every establishment of mechanical and manufacturing industry . . . having a product valued at $500 or more during the census year" (Census Office, 1894: 703). According to the instructions issued to Census agents, the survey was to encompass "the operations of all small establishments and the mechanical trades" as well as heavy industry (Census Office, 1894: 703).

Although the data which were assembled in 1890, and particularly the statistics on capital, were the object of some criticism from economists (see American Economic Association, 1899), the Census Office had obviously made special efforts to number completely trades involving the use of machinery, and to include in the canvass industries about which no census before had inquired. Omissions, consequently, were "with but few exceptions, unimportant," in that their correction would have had "but slight effect on the totals." In sum, the government's statisticians maintained "that the data constitute a substantially correct presentation of the manufacturing industries of the respective cities during the census year of 1890" (Census Office, 1894: 704).[2]

Through the latter part of the nineteenth century, statistics on manufacturing had been gathered in conjunction with the decennial censuses. In 1902, however, the same law which established the Census Bureau as a permanent agency of the federal government authorized it to carry out, in 1905 and in each succeeding decade, a special canvass "confined to manufacturing establishments conducted under what is known as the factory system, exclusive of the so-called neighborhood and mechanical industries" (quoted in Bureau of the Census, 1907: 1). By virtue of this definition, manual trades employing machinery to some minor extent (e.g., blacksmithing) were excluded for the first time from Census compilations on manufacturing. This difference in scope means that the totals on manufacturing activity in 1905 are not fully comparable with those from 1890. Even so, production which was basically manual, and hence deliberately not counted in 1905, was in all probability also small in scale and scattered across many locations. Its absence from the 1905 statistics, then, ought not to bias too greatly estimates of industrial change for any city.

From the two enumerations of manufacturing, five indicators of industrialization common to both sets of data were selected. The five are: the number of manufacturing establishments in a city, the number of persons employed in these establishments, the dollar value[3] of capital invested in these firms, the dollar value of their manufactured product, and "value added" in manufacturing.[4] In addition, a sixth indicator, the number of types of products manufactured in a city,[5] was coded for 1890 only.

The measures listed above range from the concrete to the abstract, and refer to different aspects of the manufacturing process and the social reality it constituted. For example, numbers of establishments and employees signify the embodiment of industrialization in organizations central to the lives of people. Statistics on the value of product and value added, on the other hand, suggest the consequences of that physical presence in economic terms: they emphasize the structural — as opposed to the human — scale of industrialization in American cities. Because the

Table 5.1. *Results of weighted least squares (WLS) analyses of the effects of industrialization in 1890 on religious diversity, 1890 and 1906 (unstandardized regression coefficients; t-statistics in parentheses)*

| | | | Protestant-Catholic-Jewish-Other diversity, 1890 | Diversity among Protestants, 1890 | Total population (in millions), 1890 | Measures of |
|---|---|---|---|---|---|---|
| Equation number | Dependent variable | Constant | | | | Number of manufacturing establishments (in millions) |
| 5.1a | Protestant-Catholic-Jewish-Other diversity, 1890 | +.330 | — | — | −.291 | −56.660 (1.163) |
| 5.1b | Diversity among Protestants, 1890 | +.776 | — | — | −.033 | −6.783 (0.187) |
| 5.1c | Protestant Catholic-Jewish-Other diversity, 1906 | +.151 | +.632 | — | +.998 | +23.404 (0.475) |
| 5.1d | Diversity among Protestants, 1906 | +.304 | — | +.643 | +.314 | +1.947 (0.100) |

various indicators of manufacturing chosen for this study are, in these and other ways, distinct in their meanings, they are employed as a group in the regression models which are estimated in the following section.[6]

## Manufacturing and Religious Diversity

The four equations shown in Table 5.1 estimate levels of interfaith diversity and diversity among Protestants for major American cities in 1890 and 1906, using a weighted least squares (WLS) regression procedure.[7] Six quantitative indicators of urban manufacturing activity from the Census of 1890, all measures of the historical scale and scope of industrialization in that year, are used as predictors. In each equation, total population in 1890

Table 5.1 *(cont.)*

| | | | | | |
|---|---|---|---|---|---|
| industrialization in 1890 | | | | | |
| Number of employees (in millions) | Number of types of manufactured products (in thousands) | Dollar value of invested capital (in billions) | Dollar value of manufactured product (in billions) | Value added in manufacturing (in billions of dollars) | N |
| −2.722 (0.727) | +2.157*** (3.603) | −3.673 (1.698) | +5.737** (2.671) | −3.220 (1.022) | 122 |
| −6.306* (2.270) | +0.660 (1.488) | +2.020 (1.259) | +1.373 (0.861) | −0.611 (0.261) | 122 |
| −3.429 (0.909) | −0.534 (0.834) | −2.997 (1.343) | +2.518 (1.120) | −1.929 (0.603) | 119 |
| +1.085 (0.705) | +0.046 (0.187) | −2.289** (2.616) | +0.725 (0.837) | −0.145 (0.114) | 122 |

*$p < .05$.   **$p < .01$.   ***$p < .001$.

appears as a control, removing the effects of size of place on manufacturing by effectively transforming the independent variables into per capita ratios, without inviting the statistical doubts which have been imputed to ratio variables (Schuessler, 1974; Uslaner, 1976; but cf. MacMillan and Daft, 1980). Unstandardized regression coefficients for each measure of industrialization are reported along the right side of Table 5.1, and corresponding $t$-statistics are positioned below the coefficients, in parentheses. Statistically significant coefficients are designated by asterisks (*).[8]

Equation 5.1a indicates that Protestant-Catholic-Jewish-Other diversity in a city in 1890 is positively and significantly associated with two aspects of its industry: the number of different types of manufactured goods the city was credited by the Census with producing in 1890, and

the total dollar value of those goods. The other four indicators of industrialization included in Equation 5.1a, without exception, are negatively
related to diversity, although none of these remaining coefficients
reaches the .05 level of statistical significance. The element of the economy which most discernibly coincided with diversity across the broad
faith communities in late nineteenth-century American cities, then, was
production – production of a wide variety of goods, and production of
these goods in large volume.

The situation was different, however, for diversity among Protestants
in 1890, as Equation 5.1b reveals. While five of the six coefficients for
aspects of manufacturing bear the same sign in this equation as they did
in the prediction of Protestant-Catholic-Jewish-Other diversity, just one
is statistically significant. The number of manufacturing employees in a
city in 1890 (controlling for city size and the number of industrial employers, among other factors) is negatively related, and significantly so, to
Protestant diversity in that same year. It may be inferred from this result
that a city in which industry was dispersed into small workshops was a
more likely environment for an array of Protestant groups of more or less
equal standing than was a large factory center or mill town. This finding is
in agreement with the outcome of Linda K. Pritchard's (1984: 253–261;
cf. Pritchard, 1980) research on economic development and religious
(largely Protestant) diversity in western New York and the rest of the
upper Ohio Valley in the middle of the nineteenth century. "Commercial
farming," Pritchard (1984: 262) writes, "accompanied an expanding organized religion, but industrial development coincided with a reduced and
more concentrated religious structure," as measured by both the number
of religious groups represented in a county and by the average number of
church seats per capita controlled by denominations other than eight
most dominant numerically.

On the whole, the coefficients calculated for Equations 5.1c and 5.1d,
which measure the effect of manufacturing activity in 1890 on changes
over the subsequent sixteen years in interfaith and in Protestant diversity,
respectively, are weaker than those computed in the two cross-sectional
models. In Equation 5.1c, none of the terms representing industrialization in 1890 contributes significantly to estimating shifts by 1906 in
Protestant-Catholic-Jewish-Other diversity. Furthermore, only one lagged
indicator of manufacturing activity (the dollar value of invested capital)
appears, from Equation 5.1d, to have affected the development of diversity among Protestants through the turn of the century. With the other
variables held constant, Protestant diversity was reduced by 1906 in
cities beginning the period with heavily capital-intensive industrial bases.
By implication, Protestantism achieved greater heterogeneity in places
which, conversely, seem to have been marked by the prior existence of

firms without the capital necessary for a thoroughgoing mechanization of job tasks.

Table 5.2 reports the results of regression analyses of religious diversity in 1906, with five measures of industrialization from the special Census survey of 1905, controlled for population, as the independent variables.[9] Unfortunately, the statistics are once more not very powerful. In the second equation in the table (Equation 5.2b), which seeks to explain diversity among Protestants in 1906, no manufacturing variable approaches statistical significance. The analysis in Equation 5.2a, above it, *does* yield a significant coefficient (that for number of employees), but its success in this model conflicts with the findings for 1890 contained in Table 5.1. There, the number of persons employed in manufacturing is significantly related not to overall diversity, as in Equation 5.2a, but to diversity among Protestants.

It is possible, of course, that the nature of the relationship between industrial employment and types of religious diversity could have changed with the centuries. If this is so, the change might be depicted more clearly in a genuine analysis of the temporal covariation of the two sets of measures, economic and religious. Such an analysis is described in Table 5.3. In the two WLS equations[10] (one for each type of religious diversity) computed for this table, the manufacturing indicators from both time points are paired and entered simultaneously. This conjunction is designed to control each indicator for its initial level in 1890, and thus to allow its 1905 version to represent any change in that variable which may have occurred from 1890 until 1905. The same treatment has been applied to the two religious diversity measures. Each is controlled for its value in 1890, thereby making the dependent variable, nominally from 1906, in actuality a measure of religious change across the interval (Land and Felson, 1976: 580–585).

The results in Table 5.3, however, do not go far toward clarifying quantitatively the connections between the process of industrialization and changes in levels of religious diversity in large American cities. In each equation reported in the table, just one of the measures of change in manufacturing activity (in the columns labeled "1905") is statistically significant, and in each instance, it is a variable which had not so proven itself in the earlier analyses. Heightened additions to value imparted by manufacturing brought like increases in Protestant-Catholic-Jewish-Other diversity across the turn of the century. Diversity among Protestants declined, however, in the face of growth in the number of manufacturing establishments. These findings reinforce a very general impression, drawn from the other analyses, of associations between heavy production and diversity across the major faiths, and between manufacturing on a smaller scale and diversity among Protestants. However, the analyses neither in-

Table 5.2. Results of weighted least squares (WLS) analyses of the effects of industrialization in 1905 on religious diversity in 1906 (unstandardized regression coefficients; t-statistics in parentheses)

| Equation number | Dependent variable | Constant | Total population (in millions), 1906 | Measures of industrialization in 1905 | | | | | N |
|---|---|---|---|---|---|---|---|---|---|
| | | | | Number of manufacturing establishments (in millions) | Number of employees (in millions) | Dollar value of invested capital (in billions) | Dollar value of manufactured product (in billions) | Value added in manufacturing (in billions of dollars) | |
| 5.2a | Protestant-Catholic-Jewish-Other diversity, 1906 | +.395 | +.337 | +201.742 (1.654) | −7.283* (2.100) | −2.330 (1.547) | +1.653 (1.279) | +1.420 (0.496) | 117 |
| 5.2b | Diversity among Protestants, 1906 | +.826 | +.342 | −40.530 (0.607) | −2.884 (1.499) | −0.069 (0.084) | +0.563 (0.786) | +0.893 (0.562) | 120 |

*$p < .05$.

form these relations to the point where they might be more easily interpretable, nor endow them with such consistency as to render them more fully trustworthy.

## Discussion

The results of the analyses presented in the preceding section are intriguing and suggestive, but they lack the kind of regularity that would invest them with more general social scientific import. In the absence of strong and consistent patterns in the regression coefficients, speculative, or at best tentative, explanations are all that can be offered for them.

On an abstract plane, one might, for example, rely wholly on the distinction between Protestantism and other faiths, and claim that the radical individualism promoted in various strains of Protestant ideology justified a clear affinity on the part of Protestants for employment in small businesses. Catholicism and Judaism were thought, by comparison, to inculcate values of group solidarity which, it might be said, afforded their practitioners greater adaptation to the collective organization of industrial labor. Because heavy industry could therefore recruit workers from a broader religious spectrum than could small-scale enterprise, it makes sense that indicators of scale in manufacturing would predict Protestant-Catholic-Jewish-Other diversity. Levels of diversity among Protestants, in turn, would match approximately the prevalence in a city's economy of individual, smaller workplaces.

Although such an argument is attractive for its parsimony and its range, it is weak from the standpoint of social history: it ignores the many social distinctions separating Protestants, Catholics, and Jews as these groups appeared in American history, and makes much theoretically out of what might well be a poorly specified empirical relationship. A more historically sensitive account would interpret these results differently.

To explain these results, a more historical approach would refer to differences in nativity and ethnicity distinguishing Protestants, Catholics, and Jews. Social historians (e.g., Greenberg, 1981; Hershberg, Katz, Blumin, Glasco, and Griffen, 1974; Hirsch, 1978: 107; Laurie, 1980: 3–30; Laurie, Hershberg, and Alter, 1975; Ward, 1975) have documented how, as immigration stoked industrialization with new workers, members of particular groups of foreign-born Americans came to predominate in the work forces of certain industries.[11] Many of the ethnic groups from which these immigrants were drawn were also relatively homogeneous with respect to religion, their members—here as abroad—being nearly universally Catholic, Jewish, or liturgical Protestant. Hence, it is not surprising that there would exist crude correlations between the scale and variety

Table 5.3. *Results of weighted least squares (WLS) analyses of the effects of changes in industrialization, 1890–1905, on changes in religious diversity, 1890–1906 (unstandardized regression coefficients; t-statistics in parentheses)*

| | | | | Measures of | | | |
|---|---|---|---|---|---|---|---|
| | | | | Total population (in millions) | | Number of manufacturing establishments (in millions) | |
| Equation number | Dependent variable | Constant | Diversity, 1890 | 1890 | 1906 | 1890 | 1905 |
| 5.3a | Protestant-Catholic-Jewish-Other diversity, 1906 | +.144 | +.583 | +.100 | +.624 | −38.222 (0.817) | −17.372 (0.138) |
| 5.3b | Diversity among Protestants, 1906 | +.302 | +.640 | +.398 | +.246 | +37.314 (1.921) | −114.781* (2.236) |

of the industries in which a city was engaged, and its level of diversity across the major religious faiths.

In contrast, native workers born of native parents, whether white or black, and regardless of industry, were typically Protestant. Protestant diversity's relationship to manufacturing, moreover, was not as obviously due to the salience of ethnicity. So, one is left to account for diversity among Protestants – or its lack – by the operation of group processes rather than by identification of groups themselves.

Assuming that whole families shared both in a specific brand of Protestantism and in labor for the same industrial firm, and assuming further that what denominational switching that took place was guided by the local religious culture (which was mirrored in the workplace and probably transmitted by personal ties established on the job), Protestant diversity would be linked not so strongly to a mix of different types of manufacturing, but more directly to the existence of small groups of employees gathered in relatively nonmechanized shops. Each shop, as the scene of daily, face-to-face interaction, could become a pocket of denominational uniformity which nevertheless served, with others, to diversify the larger Protestant environment. Protestantism could be diverse, this argument would hold, in places where economic life provided numerous small

Table 5.3 *(cont.)*

industrialization, 1890 and 1905

| Number of employees (in millions) | | Dollar value of invested capital (in billions) | | Dollar value of manufactured product (in billions) | | Value added in manufacturing (in billions of dollars) | | |
|---|---|---|---|---|---|---|---|---|
| 1890 | 1905 | 1890 | 1905 | 1890 | 1905 | 1890 | 1905 | N |
| +2.009 | −6.908 | −2.018 | −1.243 | +12.182* | −4.221 | −21.170** | +13.469* | 117 |
| (0.322) | (1.241) | (0.633) | (0.703) | (2.507) | (1.922) | (2.877) | (2.474) | |
| +1.576 | +1.238 | −2.762* | −0.189 | −2.004 | +0.721 | +2.260 | +0.062 | 120 |
| (0.604) | (0.542) | (2.067) | (0.253) | (1.009) | (0.792) | (0.775) | (0.032) | |

$*p < .05.$   $**p < .01.$

arenas for family continuity, unimpeded socialization, strong personal influence, and the conformity they all engender. Many different forms of religious belief and practice could find a haven in such cities, and the various churches representing these perspectives could claim a pool of potential members already joined in a primitive community. In this, Pritchard for one sees the beginnings of the American system of denominational pluralism. She regards as "plausible" that

the demands of a physically and economically expanding society led religious leaders to specialize and centralize their ministrations to American souls in ways similar to those employed by other large-scale enterprises. Eventually, monopolies coexisted with a broad spectrum of tiny entrepreneurial groups in settings as varied as business, politics, and religion. [Pritchard, 1984: 263]

To recapitulate the historical explanation for the economic correlates of religious diversity, immigrants — largely Catholics and Jews — congregated in urban economies by industries, where they were insulated by ethnic loyalties, while native Protestants were differentiated instead by small, religiously homogeneous work groups. Bruce Laurie, for example, notes in

his study of working class life in early nineteenth-century Philadelphia, that new migrants to that city often lacked the skills required for employment in any but the most mechanized of work settings. Though these shops were small in scale compared to the industrial establishments yet to be built, they were still places offering jobs "which relied more on brawn and dexterity than craft knowledge, and which enforced a rigorous work routine." This routine, he suggests, could well have "conditioned worker behavior along the lines expressed by the new Protestantism" (Laurie, 1980: 51), a revivalist cast stressing regular Sunday observance, temperance, and probity in personal affairs. "The incentive to endorse the new morality," Laurie (1980: 51) argues, "was the same for all in-migrants employed in modernizing plants: the need for greater self-discipline wrought by the unfolding of industrial capitalism."

Although Laurie does not mention this possibility explicitly, the new discipline of the industrial workplace may also have influenced, through the assumption of shared moral values and near-constant peer contact, a movement toward greater uniformity in religious backgrounds among workers in any single shop. Moreover, some historical research (e.g., Johnson, 1978: 124–128) points to a tendency on the part of evangelical Protestant employers to hire first for their firms journeymen who belonged to their own church congregations. An unyielding cultural defense waged by urban Catholics throughout the nineteenth century was also a force in homogenizing religion in the workplace. Laurie (1980: 149) tells of Philadelphia priests who warned parents in their parishes not to indenture sons to masters who were not Catholic, lest the solidity of the young men's faith be undermined.

It remains to be explained why the relation in 1890 between number of employees and Protestant diversity was not sustained across the turn of the century. Indeed, in Table 5.2, a city's number of manufacturing employees in 1905 is, in 1906, a significant negative predictor not of diversity within Protestantism, as it is in 1890, but of Protestant-Catholic-Jewish-Other diversity.

Contradictions like this one erode the confidence with which any explanation of these results can be regarded. How industrialization affected the development of religious diversity at the turn of the century, then, is a question whose resolution awaits more detailed analysis, possibly in the form of attention to specific historical cases.

# "No Fast Friend to Policy or Religion"

## Literacy and Religious Diversity

The turn of the twentieth century would not seem to offer a prime period in which to evaluate the effects of literacy on a major social institution like religion, for vast segments of the population of the United States were already literate, and school enrollments had long been high, particularly on the primary level, in rural areas, and in the northern states (Fishlow, 1966; Kaestle and Vinovskis, 1980; Soltow and Stevens, 1977). Yet, illiteracy had taken on the status of a social problem only when urbanization, industrialization, and population diversity coincidentally threatened traditional American culture and its presumably common bases. At that point, the organization of schooling on a wide scale was recommended to policy makers as a recourse by which social control could be reimposed (Graff, 1979: 22–23). Whereas previously education had been a popular movement (cf. Meyer et al., 1979), it now had become a bureaucratic imperative. Indeed, sweeping terms have been called upon to describe the subject of literacy in America in the latter two-thirds of the nineteenth century:

In much of the western world, and especially in Anglo-America, a new context for social life and social relations was forming; the role of schooling and literacy can be appreciated only in this context. New requirements and new demands resulted, to which institutions responded. These included the need to meet the perceived threats from crime, disorder, and poverty; the need to counteract cultural diversity; the need to prepare and discipline a work force; and the need to replace traditional popular culture with new values and habits. These problems, especially that of disciplining the work force and that of countering crime, disorder, and cultural heterogeneity, interacted with one another to heighten the need for action and to hasten the pace of institutional response. [Graff, 1979: 28]

105

Because the new social context for literacy was largely urban, the growing cities of the late nineteenth century are especially appropriate as cases for observing its institutional effects. Moreover, religion is a key institution, for crucial to the initial expansion of popular education was an emergent morality of Christian republicanism (see Handy, 1971), which stressed literacy as a minimum trait of Americans – individuals truly free from political and intellectual tyranny, yet bound together as a nation under God (Meyer et al., 1979: 599–601; cf. Smith, 1967; Soltow and Stevens, 1981: 48–49, 55–56; Tyack, 1966).

How a literacy that resulted from the Protestant-inspired common school might in turn have affected religion is a question which, unfortunately, has received less attention. Literacy attained the force of an independent cultural variable as one result of a deliberate religious initiative to advance education, but there were those who feared still that literacy carried a potentially secularizing capacity, too. Indeed, wide acquisition of the abilities to read and to write promised not only to depress levels of popular religiosity, as some felt, but to alter the very structure of religion itself. Literacy allowed a transition in the accepted sources of religious teaching, which became more open and more literal, and permitted a continuing and legitimate reinterpretation of those sources.

The purpose of this chapter is to consider the contribution of popular literacy to the construction of new religious environments in American cities at the turn of the century. This chapter continues with a description of rates of literacy in major American cities in 1890. Cities with highly literate and relatively illiterate populations are identified, and some comparisons of rates for populations classified by nativity and race are made as well. Next, noteworthy research on the historical relations between religion and literacy is summarized. This exposition leads to a discussion of literacy as a sociological variable. Quantitative tests of the effects of urban literacy in 1890 on religious diversity in that year and in 1906 are then presented. Finally, a concluding section explores the meaning of these results.

## Literacy in American Cities, 1890

Rates of literacy[1] varied widely across the most populous American cities in 1890, but a certain amount of that variation can be traced to the cities' different proportions of residents who were black, Asian, or American Indian. Statistics in Chapter 1 describing the units of analysis in this study indicated that nearly 99 percent of native whites ten years of age or older living in the 122 cities were literate. This is in contrast to a rate of just above 65 percent for nonwhites. Thus, the native white population of these cities was over 50 percent more literate than was the nonwhite group.

This difference is accentuated more acutely when particular cities are examined. Augusta, Georgia, for example, suffered the lowest level of literacy of any of the cities in the analysis, a rate of .677. Only about two of every three of Augusta's adult or adolescent inhabitants in 1890, this statistic testifies, could write. The city's condition, moreover, was the result of a combination of two more specific rates which were also among the lowest of their types recorded for principal cities by the Census. Augusta had the lowest incidence in the country of literacy among native whites born of native parents (.863), and the third lowest level of nonwhite literacy nationally (.446) among its sizable black population. Illiteracy was a trait of a clear majority of Augusta's nonwhite inhabitants at least ten years old.

New England cities, by way of comparison, were home to more highly skilled populations. Chelsea, Massachusetts could boast of being the only large city in America in 1890 with universal literacy among its native whites of native parentage. In New Haven, all but .03 percent of those born in the United States of foreign parents before 1881 could write. Furthermore, almost 95 percent of nonwhites in Waterbury, Connecticut in 1890 were literate by Census standards.

Sioux City, Iowa sustained the highest overall level of literacy in 1890: 98.4 percent. This distinction was in part due to the unusually high literacy of that city's foreign-born whites, less than 4 percent of whom were unable to write. Two Pennsylvania cities, Allentown and Scranton, anchored the other end of the foreign literacy scale. Allentown in 1890 had the worst record of literacy for white second-generation Americans, and Scranton the worst for immigrant whites. In the latter case, more than a quarter of the persons who were born abroad and who settled in Scranton lacked an ability to write in any language.[2]

Literacy varied from city to city at the turn of the century, and although a large fraction of the population of each of the cities in the analysis possessed skills required for engaging in written communication, important differences existed between cities and across their constituent populations. The next section of this chapter reviews historical analyses of literacy and religion. The review suggests some mechanisms whereby religion may have promoted the diffusion of literacy in the modern era, as well as ways in which literacy could thereupon have encouraged the differentiation of religious commitments.

## Historical Views of Religion and Literacy

A series of historical writings has identified religion, and specifically "religions of the book," as a powerful impetus to literacy (see Soltow and Stevens, 1981: 11–22). Much attention in this research is focused on

early Protestantism, both in England (Cressy, 1980: 1–6; Stone, 1969) and in North America (Lockridge, 1974, 1981). The Protestant Reformation, it is argued, introduced into Christianity a strong emphasis on the laity's gaining an understanding of the Bible (Soltow and Stevens, 1981: 28–29). This understanding, while expected to conform to a strict orthodoxy, was to be arrived at, in the new Protestant sects, through personal study and reflection. In contrast, the Catholic Church, whose functionaries toiled through the ages to ensure the survival of sacred scriptures and to preserve their integrity, nevertheless regarded Bible study by nonclerics as a suspect activity. The Word of God was open to varying interpretations; the discipline of Church authority was therefore required to reconcile these views, and in the process to shield the innocent faithful from harm by incipient heresy.

Protestantism officially differentiated itself from Catholicism on the basis of theological distinctions whose legitimacy was said to derive directly from the Bible. The achievement by large numbers of untutored people of an understanding of the Bible – and the achievement by them of the religious autonomy this understanding signified – were dependent, in turn, on spreading literacy. It was clear to Protestants, then, that their success would rely to a great extent on efforts to educate the common folk in the rudiments of literacy. Instruction in reading and writing, when motivated by this religious goal, took on an importance it had not until this time known. Even if instruction could not bring the common folk to the level where they could locate the textual roots of doctrine, a semblance of literacy enabled them at least to read through the Bible. This practice, a common form of Protestant piety, was thought to impart a moral tone to one's behavior, if not intellectual rigor to one's thinking on religion (Graff, 1979: 24).

Once literacy allowed persons to adopt and to justify the new religious ideologies spawned in the Reformation, religious pluralism served to induce still greater efforts at inculcating literacy. The abilities to read and to write were pressed into service as creeds conflicted; indeed, Lawrence Stone (1969: 81) asserts that "the rivalry of the various Christian churches and sects for control of men's minds did more to stimulate education in the West between 1550 and 1850 than any other single factor."[3] The immediate adversary of the Protestant sectarians was the Roman Catholic Church, but almost simultaneously their labors shifted to the pursuit of a Christian society. Protestantism thus inaugurated a modern tradition of social reform extending from Puritanism in England through the nineteenth-century campaigns of evangelicals in the United States against slavery and for temperance.

In America, more precisely, the Protestant motivation for education

came to be joined, in the nineteenth century, with a millennial vision of nationhood (see Tuveson, 1968). This perspective successfully fused "the outlook and interests of small entrepreneurs in a world market, evangelical Protestantism, and an individualistic conception of the polity" (Meyer et al., 1979: 592). In conjunction with this amalgamation, the responsibilities of individuals were extended, from saving their own souls to assuming the moral obligations of citizenship in a "redeemer nation." Literacy, nevertheless, would figure now as it had before. The common school was looked to as the institution that would save the citizens of this new polity from Old World corruption, consecrate their energies toward hard work and self-reliance, train them for widening yet more radically individuated forms of economic activity, and admonish them of the necessity for an ongoing defense of freedom and an unflagging faith in God's plan for His people.

Others were more wary of the effects of literacy on religion, however. They took the stance of Francis Osborne, a seventeenth-century English commentator. "A too universally dilated learning," insisted Osborne (quoted in Stone, 1969: 85), "hath bin found upon Trial in all Ages no fast friend to Policy or Religion; being no less ready to discover blemishes in the one then Incongruities in the other." Jack Goody and Ian Watt elaborated much later the social scientific basis for Osborne's apprehension:

Instead of the unobtrusive adaptation of past tradition to present needs, a great many individuals found in written records, where much of their traditional cultural repertoire had been given permanent form, so many inconsistencies in the beliefs and categories of understanding handed down to them that they were impelled to a much more conscious, comparative, and critical, attitude to the accepted world picture, and notably to the notions of God, the universe, and the past. [Goody and Watt, 1963: 325; cf. Furet and Ozouf, 1981: 221–227]

The discovery of incongruities in doctrine could lead people oriented to religion to throw over their faith, now judged flawed, for a new religious attachment, or to forge, under the banner of a new sect, a synthesis of heretofore disparate ideologies (Soltow and Stevens, 1981: 21–22, 60–61). Either event represents a demonstration of the likelihood that, in aggregate, religious affiliations in a highly literate society will lose mass and creep toward the widest permissible boundaries. In order to discover how literacy might historically have been associated with religious diversity, this chapter now turns to sociological theory on literacy and its operation in social life.

## Literacy as a Sociological Variable

Mass literacy is a development that figures centrally in accounts of modern historical change and in social scientific descriptions of the process of modernization (e.g., Inkeles and Smith, 1974). In some strains of modernization theory (e.g., Lerner, 1957, 1958, 1963), the attainment of a high rate of literacy is seen as a stage following closely the arrival of a society at a certain level of urbanization or industrialization. According to the claims of this literature, the growth of cities and the related creation of centers of dense population have, in the West and in other regions of the world, spurred education and the spread of literacy.[4]

Along a society's path to widespread literacy (though definitely not incidentally), a critical social change is said to take place: the consciousness of the society's members is simultaneously detached from tradition and broadened in scope. Pumped up from deep deposits of unquestioned commitment, consciousness is freed to spill out across the surface of commitment's full range (cf. Berger, Berger, and Kellner, 1974). This transformation happens because

with literacy, people acquire more than the simple skill of reading. They gain access, in the very act of achieving distance and control over a formal language, to the world of vicarious experience and the complicated mechanism of empathy which is needed to cope with it. [Lerner, 1957: 272; cf. McLeish, 1969: 171–175]

Some of the vicarious experiences to which persons, once literate, are newly exposed are located within the religious realm. With the mastery of a written language, individuals are equipped to evaluate their faith by reading and interpreting for themselves the holy books of its tradition. In doing so, they remove themselves from the center of their experience of religious knowledge, and standing aside, along the perimeter of belief, they subject that knowledge to examination under a harsh light. Literate individuals are able to appreciate writings by apologists for their religious position, but they can also encounter, perhaps for the first time, its critics. They inevitably learn of other beliefs, become potential consumers of their tracts, and are rendered susceptible to their appeals. "General literacy claimed two victims," Francois Furet and Jacques Ozouf (1981: 225–226) contend: "the parish priest and old people, by robbing the former of the secret of his prestige and the latter of the utility of his memory."

Of course, all literate individuals in a society need not pass through a period of personal spiritual turbulence for literacy to have an impact on religious culture. Rather, change in religious belief and practice (and change in how they are organized) may occur slowly, entering the inter-

stices between generations silently and extending over decades. Literacy's effects on religion may, in fact, be confined entirely to the level of social institutions and processes, and not much disturb the continuity of the biography of any single individual. Literacy can operate structurally, for example, by duplicating carriers of new human knowledge, through them multiplying the number of possible life experiences, undermining the seriousness with which choices among experiences are approached, and thereby reducing the efficacy of customary modes of socialization. Thus may the written word and its understanding eventually lead a people into a world they never intended, and one which they could not, even with their newly acquired educations, have anticipated.

The historical Census data on religious diversity assembled for this study afford an opportunity to assess the hypothesis that literacy fosters a broadening of popular commitments, with religious affiliation as the test. If, through literacy, people are acquainted with the previously unimagined, are loosened from traditional attachments, and are inducted into new worlds of thought and experience, religion should be affected as least as much as any social institution based in tradition but open to intellectual challenge. Specifically, one would predict the existence of a positive relationship between rates of literacy and levels of religious diversity across cities in the United States at the turn of the century. The statistical analyses described in the section that follows are designed to determine whether such a diversification of affiliations occurred within urban religion in turn-of-the-century America.

### Illiteracy and Religious Diversity

The regression models displayed in Table 6.1 employ illiteracy[5] as the principal independent variable in estimating levels of religious diversity. Illiteracy is measured by the raw number of illiterate persons recorded for each city by the Census of 1890. Also entered in these equations is a control for the total population in 1890, aged ten and older, whose abilities were at issue. Illiteracy is effectively represented, then, as that segment of a city's adult and adolescent populations which is comprised of people who could not write. The rows of coefficients in Table 6.1, as in each table in this chapter, are sets of weighted least squares (WLS)[6] estimates for the effects of population and illiteracy in 1890 on Protestant-Catholic-Jewish-Other diversity and on diversity among Protestants, in 1890 and in 1906.

Equations 6.1a and 6.1b gauge the cross-sectional relationship between illiteracy and religious diversity. In both models, the coefficients for illiteracy are negative and are statistically significant at or beyond the .01 level. What is clear from these results is that cities in which great proportions of the population (aside from young children) were unable to write

Table 6.1. Results of weighted least squares (WLS) analyses of the effects of illiteracy in 1890 on religious diversity, 1890 and 1906 (unstandardized regression coefficients)

| Equation number | Dependent variable | Constant | Control variables | | | | N |
| --- | --- | --- | --- | --- | --- | --- | --- |
| | | | Protestant-Catholic-Jewish-Other diversity, 1890 | Diversity among Protestants, 1890 | Total population age 10 and older, 1890 (in millions) | Illiterate population, 1890 (in millions) | |
| 6.1a | Protestant-Catholic-Jewish-Other diversity, 1890 | +.445 | — | — | +1.672 | −18.828[a] | 122 |
| 6.1b | Diversity among Protestants, 1890 | +.811 | — | — | +0.643 | −7.501[b] | 122 |
| 6.1c | Protestant-Catholic-Jewish-Other diversity, 1906 | +.123 | +.623 | — | +0.276 | −1.521[c] | 119 |
| 6.1d | Diversity among Protestants, 1906 | +.265 | — | +.691 | −0.083 | +4.057[d] | 122 |

[a] $t = 6.074$; $p < .001$.  [b] $t = 3.157$; $p < .01$.  [c] $t = 0.387$; $.60 < p < .70$.  [d] $t = 2.953$; $p < .01$.

had relatively homogeneous religious environments. Conversely, a varied formal religious life, these results imply, was supported in cities where high degrees of popular literacy prevailed. This regularity obtained with respect to both diversity within Protestantism and diversity across the major faiths.

The results in Equations 6.1c and 6.1d are inconsistent, however. Equation 6.1c measures the lagged effect of illiteracy in 1890 on Protestant-Catholic-Jewish-Other diversity in 1906. Because the model includes a term for the same diversity indicator in 1890, it may be said more accurately to estimate the change in diversity over the sixteen-year period between 1890 and 1906 that is attributable to a city's original state of literacy (Land and Felson, 1976: 580–585). If literacy is a tool for life, both individual and collective, and if illiteracy is an enduring handicap, not only for a person but for his culture, the effects associated with how the two traits are balanced in a given population should extend over time and be continually reinforced. Yet, the lag coefficient for illiterate population in Equation 6.1c – though negative like the two coefficients above it – is far from statistical significance. The negative effect of illiteracy on diversity, strong in place, appears not to be transmitted intact through time. Indeed, Equation 6.1d suggests that the relationship even changes direction over the lag interval. The effect of 1890 illiteracy on change in diversity among Protestants between 1890 and 1906 is positive, surprisingly, and it is statistically significant as well.

That this aberrant finding arises in an analysis of Protestants hints at one possible explanation for it. As the description of literacy rates provided in an earlier section of this chapter pointed out, cities with large nonwhite populations (in most localities, large numbers of blacks) were burdened with the highest overall incidences of illiteracy. A disproportionately large growth in black population, such as that which continued in a number of these cities through this period, could also diversify the composition of Protestantism there, for most black church members were Protestants, and they were concentrated in a few primarily racially defined paradenominations, which were segregated from the main Protestant bodies whose traditions they shared. The interference of a population trend could have generated an artificially positive relationship between Protestant diversity and the lagged illiteracy measure. This possibility suggests that religious diversity ought to be analyzed with illiteracy classified within categories of race. In this manner, the confounding of illiteracy with the relative size of a city's black population would be ended, and illiteracy's actual effects on religious diversity would be depicted more clearly.

Accordingly, Table 6.2 repeats the cross-sectional and lag analyses of Table 6.1, with the counts of illiterates and of the potentially literate population divided by race. Of the eight equations in Table 6.2, just one

Table 6.2. Results of weighted least squares (WLS) analyses of the effects of illiteracy, by race, in 1890 on religious diversity, 1890 and 1906 (unstandardized regression coefficients)

| Equation number | Dependent variable | Constant | Control variables | | | Population age 10 and older, 1890 (in millions) | | Illiterate population, 1890 (in millions) | | N |
| --- | --- | --- | --- | --- | --- | --- | --- | --- | --- | --- |
| | | | Protestant-Catholic-Jewish-Other diversity, 1890 | Diversity among Protestants, 1890 | White | Nonwhite | White | Nonwhite | |
| 6.2a | Protestant-Catholic-Jewish-Other diversity, 1890 | +.391 | — | — | +2.591 | — | $-20.736^a$ | — | 122 |
| 6.2b | Diversity among Protestants, 1890 | +.354 | — | — | — | +378.001 | — | $-711.818^b$ | 122 |
| 6.2c | Protestant-Catholic-Jewish-Other diversity, 1890 | +.792 | — | — | +0.706 | — | $-3.738^c$ | — | 122 |
| 6.2d | Diversity among Protestants, 1890 | +.779 | — | — | — | +73.863 | — | $-79.376^d$ | 122 |
| 6.2e | Protestant-Catholic-Jewish-Other diversity, 1906 | +.139 | +.600 | — | +1.006 | — | $-20.927^e$ | — | 119 |
| 6.2f | Protestant-Catholic-Jewish-Other diversity, 1906 | +.052 | +.736 | — | — | +26.635 | — | $+17.349^f$ | 119 |
| 6.2g | Diversity among Protestants, 1906 | +.383 | — | +0.562 | +0.252 | — | $-7.062^g$ | — | 122 |
| 6.2h | Diversity among Protestants, 1906 | -.123 | — | +1.152 | — | +45.533 | — | $-68.096^b$ | 122 |

[a] $t = 1.953$; $.05 < p < .10$.  [b] $t = 1.750$; $.05 < p < .10$.  [c] $t = 0.459$; $.60 < p < .70$.  [d] $t = 0.415$; $.60 < p < .70$.
[e] $t = 2.118$; $.02 < p < .05$.  [g] $t = 1.831$; $.05 < p < .10$.  [f] $t = 0.063$; $p > .90$.  [b] $t = 0.574$; $.50 < p < .60$.

(Equation 6.2f) produces a coefficient for illiteracy that is positive. The other seven, arrayed down the right-hand columns of the table, are negative, confirming the hypothesis. The $t$-ratio associated with the sole exception to this pattern, moreover, is so small as to make the statistic to which it refers negligible.

More specifically, the model relating literacy to diversity appears, in its cross-sectional formulation, to hold for both whites and nonwhites when Protestant-Catholic-Jewish-Other diversity is predicted (Equations 6.2a and 6.2b). It performs worse, again for both groups, with diversity among Protestants as the dependent variable (Equations 6.2c and 6.2d). In the second four equations in Table 6.2 (6.2e through 6.2h), which measure the lagged effects of illiteracy, only the indicator for illiteracy among whites bears up over time. Together, the results from these more refined analyses affirm the idea that literacy and religious diversity (and especially diversity across the major faiths) were companion conditions in American cities in 1890. They add the further impression that the effects on religion of illiteracy among whites persisted for some time.

Finally, Table 6.3 combines the white and nonwhite illiteracy measures in one set of equations, estimating both types of diversity at both time points. The signs of the coefficients for illiteracy in these equations are not consistent, but the results nonetheless reinforce the observations already drawn, more than they detract from them.

Equations 6.3a and 6.3b assess the 1890 cross-sectional relationships between illiteracy and Protestant-Catholic-Jewish-Other diversity and diversity among Protestants, respectively. White and nonwhite illiteracy, when entered jointly in the model with appropriate population controls, both maintain their negative associations with diversity across the major faiths. In fact, white illiteracy does so to a statistically significant degree. Nonwhite illiteracy, for its part, was a powerful inhibitor of diversity among Protestants in 1890, as Equation 6.3b reveals. This finding makes sense, for more nonwhites were Protestants than held any other religious affiliation, so the effects of levels of illiteracy among them should be felt most severely in the Protestant churches. The positive coefficient for illiteracy among whites in this same equation, in contrast, does not even approach statistical significance.

Three of the four illiteracy coefficients in Equations 6.3c and 6.3d are likewise not significant. The two with positive signs, disconfirming the hypothesis, fall short of the standard by some distance. The pair of coefficients for the lagged effects of white illiteracy on changes in diversity between 1890 and 1906 are negative, however, and the first, in Equation 6.3c, is statistically significant. On the whole, the most striking results in Table 6.3 are those which sustain the hypothesis that illiteracy depresses levels of religious diversity. In particular, white illiteracy appears to affect

Table 6.3. *Results of weighted least squares (WLS) analyses of the effects of illiteracy in 1890, by both racial groups jointly, on religious diversity, 1890 and 1906 (unstandardized regression coefficients)*

| Equation number | Dependent variable | Control variables | | | | | | | N |
|---|---|---|---|---|---|---|---|---|---|
| | | Constant | Protestant-Catholic-Jewish-Other Diversity, 1890 | Diversity among Protestants, 1890 | Population age 10 and older, 1890 (in millions) | | Illiterate population, 1890 (in millions) | | |
| | | | | | White | Nonwhite | White | Nonwhite | |
| 6.3a | Protestant-Catholic-Jewish-Other diversity, 1890 | +.441 | — | — | +2.151 | −0.809 | −25.176[a] | −13.754[b] | 122 |
| 6.3b | Diversity among Protestants, 1890 | +.829 | — | — | −0.511 | +23.540 | +1.486[c] | −59.137[d] | 122 |
| 6.3c | Protestant-Catholic-Jewish-Other diversity, 1906 | +.147 | +.585 | — | +1.149 | −3.159 | −22.553[e] | +5.829[f] | 119 |
| 6.3d | Diversity among Protestants, 1906 | +.326 | — | +.621 | +0.302 | +0.258 | −5.859[g] | +2.781[b] | 122 |

[a] $t = 2.714$; $p < .01$.  [b] $t = 1.183$; $.20 < p < .30$.  [c] $t = 0.224$; $.80 < p < .90$.  [d] $t = 7.099$; $p < .001$.  [e] $t = 2.186$; $.02 < p < .05$.
[f] $t = 0.463$; $.60 < p < .70$.  [g] $t = 1.542$; $.10 < p < .20$.  [h] $t = 0.489$; $.60 < p < .70$.

diversity over all the major faiths most sharply, while the effect of non-white illiteracy is concentrated in diversity among Protestants.

## Conclusion

The results of this analysis lend support to the thesis that literacy promotes, and illiteracy hampers, religious diversity. Data from turn-of-the-century American cities yield moderate inverse relations between illiteracy among the population of a city and the level of religious diversity it maintained. When illiteracy is computed by racial groups, a negative relationship between it and either of the two diversity measures in this study is frequently evident; the effect of white illiteracy travels a sixteen-year lag period as well.

Literacy, it seems, may have made innovation in religion more likely and more frequent in the modern world, and may still work to produce religious differentiation. In turn, much of the inclusiveness of modern education can be credited to religiously based movements for spiritual and social transformation through mass literacy. Yet in this historical reciprocity lies a pronounced irony. Religious activists were forerunners in the drive to expand schooling in the United States and to place it under public auspices. They thus helped to spread literacy among the American people before the bureaucratization of their educational system. Literacy, however, may have contributed to weakening and ultimately to undermining the very ideological bases from which the early activists proceeded.

In seizing the written word as the vehicle by which the message of God was to reach His people, and in then equipping the people to grasp it, religious bodies were, in a sense, investing in the marginally greater truth they perceived in their own variant of that message. They relied, further, on the supposed readiness of their audiences and the presumed appeal of their arguments. Although the birth of new variants of belief in fact added to religious diversity, each group assumed it was to be the last contender for men's souls, and that subsequent literacy would only solidify its position. What many did not adequately appreciate was the prospect that in the ensuing competition, no version of the message might resoundingly silence the others. They did not foresee the evolution, instead, of a sometimes tense, sometimes lethargic religious pluralism. How this pluralism, as it took shape in American cities at the turn of the twentieth century, affected the fortunes of all religious groups in that period is the subject of the next chapter.

# "God's Bible at the Devil's Girdle"

## Religious Diversity and Urban Secularization

Walter Rauschenbusch, the individual most responsible for the formulation of a theological rationale for the Social Gospel movement of the early
1900s (see Ahlstrom, 1975b: 268–270), was, at the turn of the century,
ending more than a decade as a German Baptist pastor in New York City.
In the pastoral role, Rauschenbusch was perhaps typical of clergymen of
his time in his beliefs about the impact of city life on organized religion.
Departing New York in 1897, en route to a seminary post, he confessed in
the pages of the fledgling *American Journal of Sociology* that

I am sure that there is no great city in which modern industrialism has set
up its smoking and flaring altars of Mammon in which religion is not
struggling for its life like a flower among the cobble stones of the street.
The larger our cities grow, the less hold does religion seem to have over
the multitude of men and the general life. [Rauschenbusch, 1897: 29–30]

Church responses to the spread of urbanism in the turn-of-the-century
period were not identical, as illustrations in Chapter 1 demonstrated.
What all had in common, however, was the conviction that America's
religious status quo could not withstand the fury of what one writer
called *Christianity's Storm Centre* (Stelzle, 1907)—the modern city.

By the time the federal government had determined —after the 1920
Census—that the majority of its citizens resided in places it classified as
"urban,"[1] social scientists had belatedly joined churchmen in identifying
urbanization as a cause of secularity. Pitirim Sorokin, for example, delivered his assessment of the effects of city life on traditional religious
practice in a massive textbook he coauthored with Carle C. Zimmerman
on differences between rural and urban social patterns. "The real menace
to historical Christianity, once an urban (Roman) development," he concluded, "is this same urbanization of society" (Sorokin and Zimmerman,

118

1929: 442).[2] Sorokin was not to be alone in this view; one modern religious historian (Gilbert, 1980: 83) points out that many analysts have come to "regard as inescapable the conclusion that the city itself, in its basic structures and essential social configurations, is a potent agent in the secularization of consciousness" (cf. Borhek and Curtis, 1975: 150, 168–175, 180–181).

An "essential social configuration" of urban life with special meaning for religion is its high degree of diversity. The analyses in Chapter 4 indicated that religious diversity did not occur in cities at the turn of the century as a linear function of population size, and that growth in cities' sizes (above a minimum of 25,000 inhabitants) did not independently broaden variation in the affiliations of their church members. Nevertheless, a reasonable historical proposition would still be that cities in general have sustained greater levels of diversity at any one time than have smaller settlements like towns and rural villages (cf. Turner, 1940). The modest resources and the physical isolation of rural settlements especially, combined with the broad homogeneity if not the sheer sparseness of their populations, probably set a low practical ceiling to the degree of religious diversity any could support. Toleration of this religious diversity, though incorporated as a founding principle of the United States, and later a fact of everyday life in its larger cities, was, like the city itself, thought at numerous points in American history to pose a threat to collective religiosity. Possibly the earliest expression of this fear of toleration was broadcast from within a culture of village life, in the days predating the American republic.

Nathaniel Ward, Puritan divine of Ipswich, Massachusetts, was a man of achievement, a Christian with a curiously cosmopolitan background, and a perceptive religious thinker. Ward came to North America in the 1600s as a founder of the Massachusetts Bay Company. A lawyer in Britain before entering the ministry, he helped to formulate the legal code of the New England colony the company sponsored. As a clergyman, he had traveled on the European continent and had observed different systems of relations between church and state. In addition, Ward published in 1647 a popular commentary from afar on the affairs of the mother country, *The Simple Cobler of Aggawam in America* (see Ward, 1969).

Writing under a pseudonym, Ward accused Satan of motivating sentiment in favor of religious toleration. "Tolerations in things tolerable, exquisitely drawn out by the lines of Scripture" may be approved, Ward (1969: 7) volunteered, but "laxe Tolerations" were the design of the devil, "the next subtle Stratagem he will spread to distate the Truth of God and supplant the peace of the Churches." Ward and, according to Ward (1969: 6), God as well, supported religious liberty of a sole, peculiar type, a type embodied in the provision that dissenters "shall have free

Liberty to keepe away from us." The alternative was altogether unthinkable; "poly-piety," charged Ward (1969: 8), "is the greatest impiety in the world."

He that is willing to tolerate any Religion, or discrepant way of Religion, besides his own, unlesse it be in matters merely indifferent, either doubts of his own, or is not sincere in it. He that is willing to tolerate any unsound Opinion, that his own may also be tolerated, though never so sound, will for a need hang Gods Bible at the Devills girdle. [Ward, 1969: 10]

A nation that accommodated religious independence, Ward (1969: 13) insisted, was an environment equivalent to "Hell above ground." Toleration invited error and its idiocy; it betrayed the Almighty, threatened heresy and schism, and ultimately imperiled the continuation of God's work on this earth. More concretely, religious toleration presented a possibility for the decay of the state's civil conduct. The components of religious belief were pervaded by a single spirit of truth, Ward believed, and were thereby made interdependent:

the least Truth of Gods Kingdome, doth in its place, uphold the whole Kingdome of his Truths; Take away the least *vericulum* out of the world, and it unworlds all, potentially, and may unravell the whole texture actually, if it be not conserved by an Arme of superiordinary power. [Ward, 1969: 22]

More than three centuries after Ward composed these words, social scientists would come to endorse the bristling Puritan's approach to the dynamics of religious belief and unbelief (if not his antipathy toward religious freedom).[3] Moreover, they would trace the impetus of modern secularization not to the conflicts of a religiously divided British Parliament, but rather to forces seemingly above any interest or intent and beyond any legislation: among them, in societies permitting religious freedom, the onset of urbanization and the subsequent development of a distinctive form of social life in cities. A diversity of religions in cities and their mutual toleration there, social scientists were to conclude, were, at the same time, preconditions to church growth and, paradoxically, signals of its limited prospects. A variety of formally equal religious choices prompted the city dweller to "doubt of his own" religion; diversity further stimulated doubt to gain cultural standing and to "unravell the whole texture actually."

Not all social scientists, of course, believe that recent centuries are remarkable in this respect. Some reject the idea that secularization has

occurred in any real sense through time (e.g., Greeley, 1972), and they instead speak more neutrally of "religious change" (e.g., Yinger, 1963: 67–74). Others, less scornful, at least doubt that secularization can accurately be conceived as a relentless historical development, a trend forward in motion, linear in course, and ever upward in trajectory (see, e.g., Stark and Bainbridge, 1980b, 1981b, 1985). Indeed, few social scientists have managed to agree on precisely what empirical conditions and historical changes constitute the widely announced disenchantment of the modern world.[4] Rather than to assume to clarify this clouded body of issues, this chapter instead selects a single theme from the theory of secularization—that of religious subjectivization—and relates it to diversity within religion in American society. This more modest approach seems promising, for as Meredith B. McGuire (1981: 224) notes, "If a theory specifies level of analysis, justifies its indicators of religion, and clarifies its time frame, it can be a useful interpretation of religious change."

The presumed causal connection between religious diversity and secularization is tested with statistics on religious membership from turn-of-the-century American cities. The presentation begins by explaining how moral communities were sundered and cultural opportunities multiplied in the process of urbanization. Parallel changes which took place in the religious realm are described, and their presumed effects on religious institutions are elaborated. The statistical analyses conducted for this chapter do not, however, provide clear support for the secularization hypothesis. Although increases in diversity across major religious divisions (Protestantism, Catholicism, Judaism, and others) contributed to lower overall levels of church membership in American cities between 1890 and 1906, differentiation within Protestantism was associated, surprisingly, with a strengthening of the Protestant churches' position within a sluggishly expanding pool of potential urban adherents. A concluding section summons into consideration some peculiarities of the case of American religion to better account for the mixed results.

## The Urban Moral Order and Religion

Cities have long been regarded as centers of diversity of all sorts, and, just as importantly, as havens of tolerance for that diversity (Borhek and Curtis, 1975: 138–142, 148–149; Karp, Stone, and Yoels, 1977: 131–163). "The industrial city well exemplifies the sociological principle that as social organization becomes more complex, individuals necessarily have more opportunity for development" (Turner, 1940: 239). The cultures that cities spawn are minutely differentiated, the theories discussed in Chapter 4 were in agreement. So their inhabitants must routinely pass

among others who occupy different urban life-worlds. The continuous merging of subcultural traffic in cities is not, however, without its effects on urban inhabitants. Among "the psychological conditions which the metropolis creates," Georg Simmel (1950: 410) lists "the rapid crowding of changing images, the sharp discontinuity in the grasp of a single glance, and the unexpectedness of onrushing impressions." To these perceptions may be added the realization that those others who are observed in the city dweller's regular glimpses of cultural tumult possess peculiar sets of ideas and varying expectations about behavior. "In this segmentation of culture we find the essence of urbanization," noted H. Paul Douglass (1938: 515), "and, as well, the substitution of multiple moral standards for a single communal standard." The causes of this latter event, and how they are associated with urbanization, require greater attention.

Alasdair MacIntyre (1967: 12), writing of the modern decline of religion in Great Britain, cites three social products of urbanization as factors which conspired to destroy venerable moral communities: first, the demise of a sense that worldly activity is set before an immutable and universal natural order; second, a disruption by social change of the continuity and timeless order of human affairs; and third, an increasingly fractionalized allegiance to traditional norms. "When the working class were gathered from the countryside into the industrial cities," MacIntyre recounts,

they were finally torn from a form of community in which it could be intelligibly and credibly claimed that the norms which govern social life had universal and cosmic significance, and were God-given. They were planted instead in a form of community in which the officially endorsed norms so clearly are of utility only to certain partial and partisan human interests that it is impossible to clothe them with universal and cosmic significance. [MacIntyre, 1967: 14–15]

A traditional orientation toward the world, MacIntyre suggests, relies for its maintenance and support on communities within which some beliefs, however few in number, are unambiguously articulated and unconditionally accepted. If such communities break down in urban areas, and leave behind a proliferation of belief systems, an ominous situation for religion develops. What ensues in the place of communal harmony is a polyphony of religious "music" and an open competition for the ears — and minds — of potential believers. This competition of creeds has historically had the effect, some assert, of amplifying the forces which had first brought it about. It encouraged the further differentiation of religious organizations and ideologies, and this heightened the confusion of moral

claims on the individual behavior of city dwellers. Religion certainly was drawn against its interests into the vortex of urban social change:

> Denominational diversity, however, has in itself promoted a process of secularization, in providing for the uncommitted a diversity of religious choice, in creating institutionalized expression of social differences and divisions, and in the very circumstance which, in extending choice, allows some to make no choice at all. The divergence of belief systems and of ethical codes in society, short of creating a persistent state of tension, is likely to reduce the effectiveness of the religious agencies of social control. [Wilson, 1966: 30; cf. Wilson, 1982: 36–37, 44, 129]

The polyvalent urban moral order "confronts organized religion with the task of integrating and disciplining its components—a task, the like of which it never had before" (Douglass, 1938: 515). The purpose of the next part of this study is to indicate in more detail how religious diversity presumably contributed to "softening" or weakening the already otherwise weak moral order of the city, and how especially the American pattern of religious pluralism predisposed urban religious institutions to this role. Some consequences which could be anticipated for religious institutions at their own hands as the urban moral order deteriorated are also explored.

## Religious Diversity and Religious Subjectivization

The implications of urban religious diversity for a stable moral order, and hence for traditional church involvement, can be elaborated readily. As populations expand and different peoples meet, old ideas are exchanged and are thus made new, new ideas are generated when the old ones will not suffice, and all ideas are compared and contrasted. In the course of this mixing, juxtaposing, and coexisting, the persuasiveness of all ideas and ideologies, including those which form the basis of social continuity, is seen to be reduced (Wirth, 1938: 15). Soon, as the anthropologist Clyde Kluckhohn (1973: 78) describes it, "the moral order becomes for the first time a genuine problem."

The urban moral order is rendered problematic not by challenges to it, or by unconventionality per se. Such challenges are ubiquitous and they often serve the important function of clarifying norms (Dentler and Erikson, 1959; Erikson, 1966). Rather, it is presumably the toleration of diversity—the inability or refusal to identify a challenge to normality as such—which both prevails in urban environments (Karp et al., 1977: 131–163) and weakens any moral or religious code (cf. Lenski, 1961: 9). Explaining how, in cities, a softening of normative expectations follows

on the toleration of religious diversity requires reference to the social functions of religious belief.

Religion's power lies in its ability to explain and interpret events of the world to persons in a manner that is authoritative and cogent. Its accounts are constructed from a comprehensive set of symbols simultaneously conveying the deepest meanings of human experience and transcending that experience altogether. Any religion loses influence when the social-psychological roots by which it is anchored in the everyday lives of its adherents—a unanimous though implicit assent to belief and the assumed community so achieved—are disrupted. Without these moorings—what Peter L. Berger (1967, 1969: 42–48) calls "plausibility structures"—the religious interpretation of the world loses its overwhelming authenticity, its "facticity." Religious belief denied these underpinnings becomes subjective, and its truth value becomes relative.

One way to disrupt religious plausibility is to introduce religious pluralism (and the competition it engenders) to a society. As Walter Lippmann wrote in his *A Preface to Morals* (1929):

The existence of rival sects, the visible demonstration that none has a monopoly, the habit of neutrality, cannot but dispose men against an unquestioning acceptance of the authority of one sect. So many faiths, so many loyalties, are offered to the modern man that at last none seems to him wholly inevitable and fixed in the order of the universe. The existence of many churches in one community weakens the foundation of all of them. [Lippmann, 1929: 76]

Berger and Thomas Luckmann (1966: 81) have more recently rephrased this understanding in sociological language:

Religious pluralism, to wit, entails religious subjectivization. This means that the old religious contents lose their status of objective facticity in individual consciousness. This change is already given in the reflective attitude that the consumer comes to take as he is presented with a multiplicity of products. He must choose between them, is thereby forced to hesitate, to compare, to deliberately evaluate. In this process, the traditional religious affirmations about the nature of reality lose their taken-for-granted quality. They cease to be objective truth and become matters of subjective choice, belief, preference. Other meaning systems take the place of objective facticity previously occupied by the religious traditions. Thus it makes no sense for a contemporary individual to say that he has a personal preference for the germ theory of disease. On the other hand, he may have any number of religious preferences. Strictly speaking, every religion in the pluralistic situation is a *heresy* —that is, a

*hairesis,* or *choice.* [cf. Berger, 1967: 145, 150–151, 1969: 53–56; Berger et al., 1974: 79–82]

Berger's theory is especially applicable to the United States, for, as Will Herberg (1955: 99) observed, "pluralism of religions and churches is something quite axiomatic to the American." The legitimacy of religious pluralism in America was successfully sustained through the early years of nationhood, in the face of various challenges. Most of the time, an odd alliance of pietists and secularists in the interest of religious freedom prevailed (Mead, 1954a, 1954c; Miller, 1986; Sperry, 1946: 44–58). Yet, God's New Israel was not a religious Tower of Babel. The country itself, to be sure, was religiously heterogeneous from the start (Alger, 1974: 327–328; Harrell, 1985). It claimed Congregationalists, Baptists, Quakers, Reformed, a few Catholics, and members of many other groups.[5] The bounded, sealed social worlds in which individuals moved, however, were normally not diverse (Bender, 1982: 67–71, 97; Lipset, 1967: 159–160).[6]

At the end of the eighteenth century, Congregationalism was legally established in Massachusetts, whereas the Baptists had long before fled to Rhode Island. Quakers had taken refuge in Pennsylvania and western New Jersey; Dutch Reformed influence was centered in New York City and extended up through the Hudson Valley. Catholics were isolated in Maryland, and so forth (Gaustad, 1976, 1985). In fact, it was not until about a half-century after the federal Constitution (containing a Bill of Rights guaranteeing religious freedom) had begun to be ratified that Congregationalism lost its status as the state religion of Massachusetts.

Thus a formal kind of diversity distinguished religion in the first decades of the new nation, but its implications for American society were not immediately evident. "The terrible indictments drawn up in a Mississippi village against the Pope in Rome, the Russian nation, the vices of Paris, and the enormities of New York are in the main quite lyrical," remarked Lippmann back in 1929. "The Pope may never even know what the Mississippi preacher thinks of him and New York continues to go to, but never apparently to reach, hell" (Lippmann, 1929: 270–271). It instead took a trend of increasing urbanization over the nineteenth century to erode partially the insularity and localized domination of the denominations and to draw out the secularizing propensities of religious pluralism in America (cf. Finke, 1984: 168–170).[7] Cities were where this change began to happen; the city was potentially the supreme secular environment, for, as Sorokin and Zimmerman noted in 1929:

Cities are the centers of interaction of several, and often different, religions. The city man rarely may avoid this fact and the silent or open struggle and rivalry of various religious and philosophical systems. This

rivalry leads to a mutual criticism; and the mutual criticism leads to a weakening of the sacredness and infallibility of each of the fighting religions. As a result, the city man is inculcated with the ideas of not one but of several religions; he is robbed of the infallible sacredness of his professed religion; he is shown its shortcomings by the rivals; he has an opportunity to see and, at the same time, to learn the positive traits of other beliefs; he often hears or reads the most radical criticism of all religious ideas; he witnesses the most sophisticated discussions of various theological dogmas; all this stimulates his doubts of the infallibility of his traditional religion. It calls forth his own thinking about religious ideas, and leads to analytical criticism. Under such circumstances, it becomes difficult to believe "naively" the complete righteousness of one set of ideas; religious relativism and syncretism become rather inevitable; criticism, skepticism, sophistication, and sometimes "freedom from any religion" have greater chances of development. Instead of the rural monopolistic, unsophisticated, and naive, but quite firm, religious convictions, soft, critical, rationalized, syncretic, often mutually tolerant, and highly sophisticated ideologies begin to blossom in the city. [Sorokin and Zimmerman, 1929: 441; cf. Berger et al., 1974: 66–67; Sorokin, 1928: 237–238]

The following section reports the results of several quantitative analyses of the assumption that the very fact of religious diversity made evident will, over time, induce a decline in collective religious commitment and create a more generally secularized religious environment. The hypothesis is tested with respect to overall religious membership in turn-of-the-century American cities and, more narrowly, in relation to church affiliation by Protestants in those settings. In addition, an effect on secularization of Protestant-Catholic religious competition is suggested.

## Religious Diversity and Secularization

The hypothesis predicts a positive association between a city's level of religious diversity and its degree of secularization at a later time point. Table 7.1 presents the results of statistical tests of this hypothesis, relying on a weighted least squares (WLS) procedure.[8] Totals for aggregate church membership and Protestant church membership are used as measures of citywide secularization in 1906. Low levels of church membership are taken to denote a secularized environment.

The 1906 total and Protestant church membership figures are controlled for their values in 1890 and for the sizes of the populations in 1890 and 1906 from which churches in general, and Protestants in particular, could potentially draw members. The first controls allow an estimation of actual *changes* in church membership (Land and Felson, 1976:

Table 7.1. *Results of weighted least squares (WLS) analyses of the effects of religious diversity on secularization, 1890–1906 (unstandardized regression coefficients)*

| Equation number: | 7.1a | 7.1b | 7.1c |
|---|---|---|---|
| Dependent variable: | Total church membership, 1906 | Protestant church membership, 1906 | Protestant church membership, 1906 |
| *Constant* | +2422.764 | −5000.461 | +2588.362 |
| *Control variables* | | | |
| Total church membership, 1890 | +1.141 | — | — |
| Protestant church membership, 1890 | — | +1.316 | +1.190 |
| Total population, 1890 | −.237 | — | — |
| Total population, 1906 | +.341 | — | — |
| Population "at risk" to Protestantism, 1890 | — | −.125 | −.097 |
| Population "at risk" to Protestantism, 1906 | — | +.156 | +.143 |
| *Religious diversity measures* | | | |
| Protestant-Catholic-Jewish-Other diversity, 1890 | −5009.524[a] | — | — |
| Diversity among Protestants, 1890 | — | +6444.370[b] | — |
| Proportion of population Catholic, 1890 | — | — | −8261.049[c] |
| *N* = | 117 | 117 | 117 |

[a]$t = 0.729; .40 < p < .50.$    [b]$t = 1.362; .10 < p < .20.$    [c]$t = 4.279; p < .01.$

580–585). The second set serves the function of casting these changes in terms of proportions rather than in aggregate numbers. Populations grew rapidly between 1890 and 1906 (as was described in Chapter 1), so an increase in the raw number of church members in this period would be expected even if religious affiliation itself were not a relatively more common trait. Equation 7.1a therefore compensates by entering total population in 1890 and 1906 as controls in the prediction of total church membership in 1906.

However, if the resort to total population as a control were continued in analyses of Protestantism's fortunes over this period, measurements would be artificially depressed by the effects of massive Catholic immigration to urban America. What this study seeks to determine from these

statistics is *not* the change in the proportion of the urban population which is Protestant (it is negative), but rather how successful Protestantism was within its own sphere of influence, among a constituency which at the turn of the century was admittedly shrinking in relative size. For this reason, in Equations 7.1b and 7.1c, which predict Protestant membership in 1906, the control employed is the population then "at risk" to Protestantism. This variable is defined as a city's total population, minus its reported numbers of Catholic, Eastern Orthodox, and Mormon church members, Jews or Jewish families,[9] and adherents of numerically smaller churches or sects not affiliated with larger ecclesiastical bodies. Those who remain are persons who were either claimed as members of a Protestant denomination or who could conceivably have become Protestants had conditions been favorable to that choice.

The religious diversity measures for 1890 are arrayed across the bottom of Table 7.1. To the two discussed previously has been added another: the proportion of the 1890 population of each city reported as Catholic Church members. High levels on this measure reflect a challenge of sorts to Protestant cultural dominance in cities in which Catholics may already have been the major religious group numerically.

Equation 7.1a, which extends down the first column in the table, uncovers the effect of a tradition of religious diversity on the change in the proportion of the urban population counted as members of any church. Although the coefficient for the diversity score is not statistically significant, its sign is negative, a result in keeping with theoretically derived expectations. Religious diversity may, it seems, hamper church membership sixteen years later. Diversity's effects diverge, however, in Equations 7.1b and 7.1c, which gauge Protestantism's growth relative to its constituency. This divergence will be the subject of further explanation.

The added indicator of citywide diversity in 1890, the proportion of the population Catholic, has a powerful negative effect, as shown in Equation 7.1c, on the ability of Protestantism to expand subsequently among those whose ethnicity or current religious affiliation did not shield them from its appeals. However, a precedent of diversity within Protestantism in a city does *not* have an analogous negative effect. Instead, diversity seems to have augmented Protestantism's support at the later time point. The sign of the coefficient for the diversity variable in Equation 7.1b is positive, contrary to the theory.

The pattern of effects for the three indicators of religious diversity in 1890, then, is not fully consistent with the outcomes for church membership rates that would have been predicted by the theory of secularization outlined at the beginning of this chapter. Rather, diversity seems to influence the religious environments of American cities over time in different

ways, depending on how diversity is measured and on which of the American faith communities is specified as the subject of the analysis.

High Protestant-Catholic-Jewish-Other diversity in 1890 apparently impeded the advance of organized religion in cities over the decade and one-half that followed, although the coefficient estimated for this variable in Equation 7.1a does not approach statistical significance. Substantial Catholic Church membership in turn-of-the-century cities quite convincingly weakened the later numerical strength of Protestants, even considering that Equation 7.1c measures that change in relation to the diminishing size of Protestantism's own cultural constituency. Strong Protestant-Catholic religious competition, this finding implies, was a powerful secularizing force in urban America in the period spanning the two centuries.

Protestant diversity is an exception to the pattern of these results, however. The coefficient for diversity among Protestants in 1890, like that computed for overall diversity, is not statistically significant. In contrast to both the others, though, it is positive. The sign of the diversity coefficient in Equation 7.1b indicates that the Protestant denominations may have grown *in conjunction with,* and not in spite of, increases in internal differentiation. This finding is confirmed by Roger Kent Finke's (1984: 173–180) analysis of the empirical connection between religious diversity and church membership in America. Across much of the twentieth century, the relationship between diversity and the rate of adherents "is weak and inconsistent" (Finke, 1984: 175). Yet when church memberships are controlled for their Catholic and Latter-day Saint (i.e., non-Protestant) components, a positive relationship emerges. "These results," reflects Finke (1984: 176), "would suggest that the Catholics and L.D.S. have effectively dominated the local religious markets in some areas, but the religious involvement in most local markets increases as the religious diversity increases." Discussion in the final section of this chapter proposes two reasons for this effect, based on the work of Berger (1963) and Herberg (1955).

## Discussion

What factors allowed the Protestant denominations to respond to internal diversity anomalously, by increasing their membership relative to their base of likely support? One answer may lie in a consideration of the ideology of American religious pluralism, a system to which reference was made earlier, in phrasing the argument that such pluralism would cause secularization. Even if, as Berger (1967: 145) theorizes, religious affiliation has been relegated to the realm of personal preference or choice, and has become a matter of taste or fashion, it is still conceivable

that, under specific circumstances, a wider variety of denominations (such as that offered by Protestantism) could better serve, and so embrace, a broad segment of the population.

Berger, in fact, has compared the conduct of Protestant denominations in the United States with that of retail firms by drawing an analogy between church affiliation and the choices that consumers make in a market economy (Berger, 1963: 79). Actions of denominations (here, vendors of a religious product) are partly dependent upon, and therefore respond more or less directly to, "consumer patterns" (Berger, 1963: 88), or the expectations that individuals have about how well their needs will be met by initial or continued patronage of a church. Churches as firms plan strategies to sell the benefits of membership to persons who have other uses for their money and time. These sales strategies are designed to gain for churches maximum consumer support and allegiance while incurring minimum costs. The temptation to seize the savings that come with strategic planning rather than expose the firm to the risks that accompany innovation is especially inviting when other forces have rendered differences within the target population for the firm's product so small that little advantage may be achieved by conscious specialization.

At the same time, Berger notes, firms in such a system are prone to cooperate so that the market for their products can be stabilized. Stability is a condition that, in religion as in business, promotes managerial continuity and control. Market stability in addition makes discharging managerial responsibilities easier, because it discounts the importance of monitoring information concerning future trends, while it reduces in the near term the pressures for abrupt changes in policy. To reach stability in the market, producers are persuaded to standardize their products. Differentiation between versions is limited to accessory features, and advertising resists formulating invidious comparisons among the various models for sale (Berger, 1963: 88).

What in the marketplace is condemned as collusion, as a restraint of trade, is in religious circles, on the other hand, applauded as a manifestation of "the ecumenical spirit." Yet from a market standpoint, it is fundamentally the same thing: a knowing check on free competition in the interest of preserving the market shares of the best-known brands. It is, to put it another way, the religious equivalent of a cartel. Business analogies need not stop here, however. Failing the achievement of a cooperative posture with respect to rivals in the marketplace, there remains the possibility of a takeover or merger as a means to quell the turbulence of competition. Again, denominations have from time to time "acquired" the membership assets of the smaller and most proximate churches operating in the same fields of mission (market niches) as they do.

The critical circumstance which must pertain in the religious cartel is

that church leaders and members avoid drawing certain kinds of distinctions, and refrain from emphasizing distinctions where they may already exist. Such a concession to silence, some feel, adequately describes interorganizational relations within American Protestantism. Denominational affiliations in the United States, and the loyalties attaching to them, Herberg (1955: 52) wrote in his landmark work, *Protestant-Catholic-Jew*, "are not necessarily denied, or even depreciated, but they are held to be distinctly secondary." What is more, this attitude of interdenominational tolerance is hardly new. Schlesinger, in describing the structure of urban religion in the late nineteenth century, took due notice of the startling diversity of churches. "Differences within Protestantdom, however," he added, "had lost their ancient fierceness" (Schlesinger, 1933: 320). Organizational rivalry within Protestantism today survives not in the interstices between denominations, but along the edges of a chasm separating the mainline churches from the smaller though more staunchly separatist and autonomous fundamentalist bodies (Ahlstrom, 1978: 336).

By not according great merit to certain divisions among their denominations, Protestants have—in their own house—averted, for the most part, the conflict of creeds which is thought to bring on secularization outside. Instead of agreeing to disagree, a virtual recipe for secularization, Protestants have agreed that on basic points, there has occurred no defensible disagreement. Therefore, "it is no paradox," according to another commentator on church affairs (Bass, 1929: 69) writing more than fifty years ago, "to say that the very points which have forced chasms in the general Protestant landscape have now come to be indirectly the bridges which span those chasms and lead to a spirit of understanding and forbearance." Religious disputes of previous eras (predestinarianism vs. Arminianism; salvation by grace or by works, etc.) were, in the main body of American Protestantism, allocated to the class of—to return to the words of Nathaniel Ward (1969: 10)—"matters merely indifferent." The prominent religious differences instead came to be those which separated Protestants, Catholics, Jews, and others. As Herberg (1955: 100) observed:

Denominations are felt to be somehow a matter of individual preference, and movement between denominations is not uncommon; the religious community, on the other hand, is taken as something more objective and given, something in which, by and large, one is born, lives, and dies . . . [10]

Why, in view of these natural pressures, has religion in America not been thoroughly homogenized over time? Indeed, what may account for the notably high level of diversity evident in the roster of American churches, and particularly in the forms of American Protestantism? The sociological answer to this question inheres in an irony pointed out by

Berger. Conventional churches must cooperate in order to have any life at all, but they must not be so extremely cooperative that the need for their very existence is questioned. Protestant churches as firms must sell *something;* this product must be distinctive enough to be defended in its own right, but not so exotic in its appeal that the church which purveys it places itself outside the main religious marketplace. In Berger's (1963: 89–90) words, "religious organizations must de-emphasize denominational rivalry for the sake of rationalizing the rules of the competitive game; but they must simultaneously re-emphasize denominational identity in order to remain in this game at all."

Thus, while the surface of denominationalism in American Protestantism is overlooked, it retains functional importance. Affiliation with one of the major religious communities in America, such as Protestantism, "identifies and defines one's position in American society" (Herberg, 1955: 100–101). Participation in religion as a Protestant, though (like participation in many other American institutions), demands that participants adopt a more restricted identity first. It is only through this more narrow self-definition – "Baptist," "Methodist," etc. – that one is given access to the synthetic label of "Protestant."

In summary, if Protestant differences have declined in visibility and have diminished in importance, nominally specialized Protestant churches can appeal to more persons (Berger, 1963: 88–90; cf. Hammond, 1986: 149–151; Harrison and Lazerwitz, 1982: 372–373) without simultaneously competing head-to-head and confusing them. Furthermore, churches can establish denominational membership as a prerequisite to entry into the religious category ("Protestant") which American society at large recognizes as salient. These are two reasons why diversity among Protestants might lose its implications of disorientation and actually spur more intensive membership concentration in those churches. After all, as Archer B. Bass, a Baptist clergyman and himself a proponent of interdenominational cooperation, explained in 1929, "Christianity has to be presented to people on the plane where they live; and the large majority of people do not live in the broad fields of Christian expansiveness, but in the limited spheres of particularized Christian views" (Bass, 1929: 74).

By the dual processes of accommodation and specialization, Protestantism appears to have exempted itself from the effects of diversity within its own ranks. Such diversity did not pull Protestants away from the faith so much as it seems to have provided them with a spectrum of means whereby their religious sentiments and attachments could conveniently be continued. The same cannot be said for diversity across wider religious boundaries, however. These boundaries, the analyses in this chapter suggest, mark the religious divisions regarded as salient in the twentieth century. To cross them is an idea not readily entertained, even today;

to be aware that familiar others stand opposite one, across these lines, is a realization not readily dismissed. This extensive brand of diversity erodes levels of commitment within many religious groups as it assails the community which thrives when varying forms of belief are isolated. It further sets the cultural stage for interreligious conflict and the religious change which is its historical by-product. These events are taken up in Chapter 8.

# "If the Religion of Rome Becomes Ours"

## Religious Diversity, Subcultural Conflict, and Denominational Realignment

Analyses of historical Census data reported in the previous chapter revealed that a highly differentiated urban moral order, as indicated by religious diversity, acted under certain circumstances to reduce levels of church membership over time in turn-of-the-century American cities. The rise of the city, and the role it acquired as a magnet for and haven to diverse groups, presumably weakened (in the religious realm at least) what is thought by some to constitute the source of social integration for any smaller population: namely, a consensus of its members on basic values and ultimate commitments.

Recent writing on urbanism has challenged the view that cities are integrated in the same manner as are social collectivities of smaller scale—by value consensus—and that, in the absence of such consensus, order is maintained solely by the unstinting application of legitimate coercion. Claude S. Fischer (1975b: 1337), for example, disputes the notion that city dwellers are unified either by "sharing a common 'social world' " or "by the formal instruments of an anomic 'mass society.' " Rather, his research on public opinion data (e.g., Fischer, 1975a) shows that there is, in fact, relatively little normative restraint enforced in urban environments. He suspects, instead, that "the integration which does exist is . . . based on exchange, negotiation, and conflict among the various subcultures of the city."

This chapter transfers Fischer's supposition from the area of sociological theory to that of historical research on religion, and there supplies it with its first real substantiation. The chapter examines how conflict between Protestant and Catholic religious subcultures in the largest American cities in the late 1800s consolidated the faiths into competing factions, and in the process integrated urban religious life and shaped a relatively stable form of denominationalism which was to persist well into the next century. "The urban age," one of the first American sociolo-

134

gists of religion, H. Paul Douglass (1934: 41), observed, "is marked by the change of trend in organized religion from division to integration." The historical and statistical analyses in this chapter attempt to account for the integration of Protestantism, and for the resulting tripartite structure of religious denominationalism in the United States, by describing the nature and consequences of the intense religious conflict that occurred in the turn-of-the-century period.

This chapter argues that evangelical Protestants, in organizing in the late nineteenth century to meet the growing "Romanist peril" (Strong, 1891), contributed decisively to the construction of what church historian Sidney E. Mead (1954c: 318) identifies as "the general traditional ethos of the large families, Protestant, Catholic, and Jewish." Mead closed his famous essay of three decades ago, "Denominationalism: The Shape of Protestantism in America" (1954c: 318), with the prediction that "so far as Protestants are concerned, in the long run the competition between groups inherent in the system of separation of church and state, which served to divide them, may work to their greater unity."

The results in this chapter suggest that while Mead's causal claim is correct, his assertion of a kind of Protestant unity flowing from religious diversity applies most accurately not to the "long run" future—as glimpsed from the 1950s—nor to the present, but to the past. Thus could Max Weber (1946: 307), after a visit to the United States in 1904, write of church affiliation in this country that "Today, the kind of denomination is rather irrelevant. It does not matter whether one be a Freemason, Christian Scientist, Adventist, Quaker, or what not." And the Lynds, in the sequel to their pioneering community study, *Middletown,* could identify as components of "The Middletown Spirit" —defined as "intellectual and emotional shorthands of understanding and agreement among a large share of the people" of a typical American town in the Depression years (Lynd and Lynd, 1937: 402)—the convictions "that there isn't much difference any longer between the different Protestant denominations," and that, anyway, "what you believe is not so important as the kind of person you are." So long, that is, as that person is not Catholic, for respectable Middletowners agreed as well "that Protestantism is superior to Catholicism" (Lynd and Lynd, 1937: 416).

Unity did not arrive when ideological boundaries separating the denominations crumbled, a deterioration by which, Mead (1954c: 301) thinks, Protestantism acquired "a sense of irrelevance." Protestant consolidation appeared, rather, as social boundaries stiffened—that is, when evangelical Christianity coalesced to confront foreign religions, the implications of whose presence in American society were unacceptable to Protestants. In 1929, Protestant ethicist Arthur E. Holt predicted this outcome. "Unity, if it ever comes, will be an achievement built out of a

conflict situation by those who have social imagination," he hypothesized. "Protestantism will always be ragged behind and in front. It is more likely to achieve standardization through competition than through overhead manipulation" (A. E. Holt, 1929: 1116). A "haunting" spiritual demoralization was, contrary to the belief of Mead and others (e.g., Hudson, 1961: 128–176), a result and not a premise of this modern religious alignment.

"The separation of church and state provided the conditions not only for free assimilation of the culture and so for synthesis," wrote H. Richard Niebuhr (1954: 221) in the late 1920s, "but also for conflict with other religious organizations." Niebuhr located that conflict not on theological grounds but across racial, ethnic, and class divisions. "In many of the cities of America," he complained, "the opposition of a Protestant, Nordic, middle-class party to a Catholic, south-European, proletarian group is the basis of political battles; and the political cleavage in turn reinforces the religious conflict" (Niebuhr, 1954: 221).

Mead's view of the modern relations of religious bodies in the United States is thus subject to correction by Niebuhr's social realism. However, Mead's interpretive approach to religious organization, this chapter makes clear, may be combined with Niebuhr's sociological sensitivity to compose a description of the historical outcome of the conflict of subcultures which parallels the maintenance of religious pluralism in American society (cf. Moore, 1986).

## The Historical Setting for Religious Conflict

American Protestantism sought adjustment to urbanization in the latter part of the nineteenth century, historian Aaron I. Abell (1943: 11) has pointed out, by way of concerted activity toward three related objectives. "Thought and action," he wrote, "centered around, first, systematic plans for urban missionary endeavor . . . secondly, agitation for the unification of Protestant forces; and thirdly, an adequate solution of the industrial problem."

The first two of these efforts to address the problems of the city – urban missions and Protestant unity – shared a single nonspiritual motivation, a "purpose . . . of a social rather than a religious nature" (Abel, 1933: 3). Their common stimulus lay in the rapid expansion of the memberships of non-Protestant churches in the nation's cities as urban populations grew,[1] a change which was charted by the statistics in Chapter 1. Widening perception of this change prompted Protestants to act, and to act together. Among the collective responses of Protestants to the tide of Catholic immigration in the decades immediately prior to the turn of the century, as Abell noted above, was a missionary movement designed to

encounter and embrace the foreigners in urban communities, to break their ages-old habits of belief and action, and ultimately to Americanize the values and behavior of these newcomers from southern and eastern Europe.

However, the cultural obstacles to the hoped-for assimilation of the immigrants into American life were many, and the number of these drawbacks imparted to them specifically by their Catholicism was, by Protestant count, nearly as great. Samuel Lane Loomis, a Congregational pastor, recited a veritable litany of examples in his 1887 book, *Modern Cities and Their Religious Problems:*

The religion of Rome is far better than none, and we may well believe that many humble souls under the leadings of the Spirit have found their way through tangled meshes of falsehood with which she has covered it, down to the eternal truths on which her venerable faith is based. The influence of the Catholic Church, on the whole, is doubtless conservative, and will, probably, become more and more so. The Romanism of America is likely to be better than that of Europe. Yet Romanism is not the religion we wish for our fellow-citizens. It conceals the fatherhood of God behind the motherhood of the Church, and the brotherhood of Christ behind the motherhood of the Virgin. It degrades the atonement by making its benefits a matter of barter; it leads to idolatry and image-worship; it snatches from the believer the great gift bought with the blood of Christ, by thrusting in a priest between him and his heavenly Father. It has kept the people from the Word of God and compelled them to accept forced and unscholarly interpretations of it. It has lowered the tone of morality. It has quenced [sic] free thought, stifled free speech, and threatens to throttle free government. It has limited the advancement of every country on which its hand has been laid. If the religion of Rome becomes ours, then a civilization like that of Italy will be ours too. [Loomis, 1887: 87–88]

Adherence by immigrants to Catholicism was thus thought to be the chief encumbrance to their achievement of an American character. "They come to us, these people, with their splendid possibilities of character," Dr. Howard B. Grose, a Baptist home missions official, said of the new immigrants. "But," he added, "they come from countries which know nothing of our ideals or our institutions." His solution was to evangelize the immigrants, and thereby to Americanize them. "The Americanization of the alien is essential for the preservation of American ideals and institutions," Grose (quoted in Sanford, 1909: 98) insisted.

So, Catholicism's speedy removal from the city and replacement with a proper evangelicalism of any sort became a top priority of much urban

church work. A new Protestant, by the fact of his or her religion alone, drew closer to becoming fully American. "To make newcomers both Christians and good citizens," historian of American religion Robert T. Handy (1971: 75) notes, "seemed to be but the two sides of the same coin to the evangelical mind of the time." As one analyst of the Protestant home missions movement (Abel, 1933: 3–4) recounted:

This belief had its source in the social philosophy of American Protestant-ism, according to which there exists a vital and determining link between the spirit of evangelical Protestantism and the ideals of American institu-tions and ways of living. According to this view the best American citizen is the one who is most thoroughly imbued with the ideas of Protestant Christianity and who, through his membership in a Protestant church, stays under the influence of "the most constructive" element in the community. The most effective way, then, to make good Americans of the foreign-born and their descendants is to draw them into the membership of Protestant churches.

The Protestant urban missionary effort had, besides its explicit aim of Americanizing the immigrant, a latent function as well. This function, "hardly less important" than fostering assimilation of the alien, was, to put it simply, "to maintain the dominant position of the Protestant church in American civilization" (Abel, 1933: 6; cf. Handy, 1971: 73–79). "The real issue, as far as the Protestant churches are concerned," charged Theo-dore Abel (1933: 8) in his study of Protestant evangelization among the immigrants, "is not so much the alleged inadequacy of the Catholic church as the concern for their own position in American life, which is thought to be threatened by the influx of large masses of Catholics."

An historian of cooperative Protestantism in the second half of the nineteenth century echoes this point of view, while paying due respect to the social changes which were the antecedents of evangelical reaction:

Immigration swelled the population and contributed a dangerous hetero-geneity to culture and religion . . . Population shifted to the cities and overflowed the western frontier, thereby changing the context and locus of power for American culture. The geometric growth of Roman Catho-lics and the expansion of Mormonism into states neighboring Utah threat-ened the political fabric of the Republic. (Evangelicals assumed both religions so controlled their members that they voted according to Church dictates, thereby threatening that independence of mind requi-site to democracy . . . ) To cap it all, a high level of illiteracy and intemper-ance provided the means for socialism and secularism to attack the moral

base of America at the very time when a "tendency to class distinctions within and without the Church" (evangelical denominations now appealed primarily to the middle class) hindered the one agency capable of defending the nation. These developments were evil because they threatened the reality upon which American evangelical identity rested. Introduction of conflicting moralities, cultural attachments and religious allegiances augured ill for the evangelical Religion of the Republic and its national mission. How could evangelical America transmit its high culture, morality, and proper religious perspective to the world if America ceased to be evangelical? The dangers appeared to be real. The American mission was at stake. [Jordan, 1982: 154–155; cf. Jordan, 1973: 318]

The threat represented by the continued presence in American society of enormous numbers of foreign Catholics could be handled by the constituent denominations of the Protestant majority only if they were to agree to join forces and work together. Indeed, the evangelical churches themselves were aware of this necessity. "Unless there is a coming together of the evangelical forces in this land of ours, we seem to be engaged in a losing fight," a group of prominent Protestant churchmen admitted in a plea for interdenominational cooperation in domestic missionary activity issued in 1908. "The manner of co-operation is secondary. The necessity of it is explicit, imperative, insistent" (Hill, 1909: 216).

Among the "ten imperative reasons" the churchmen offered for co-operation was the shocked realization that "the Roman Catholic Church is rushing ahead by leaps and bounds" (Hill, 1909: 222, 223). The Federal Council of the Churches of Christ in America, at whose founding meeting in that year this alarm was voiced, had composed a "Committee on Home Missions" to consider possible avenues of action. The fledgling committee warned in an ominously worded paper that "the foreign populations have swarmed to the great centers until the very existence of Protestantism in some of the cities is being endangered." Church workers already in the field, the committee recognized, "are engaged in a heroic fight, but," they feared, these denominational missionaries "are slowly backing away." The panel therefore concluded gravely that "co-operative action is the only hope" for urban Protestantism (Hill, 1909: 223).

Others attending the Federal Council's first meeting pledged to aid cooperative endeavors by bringing together members of diverse Protestant bodies in common labors. The Reverend W. I. Haven, Secretary of the American Bible Society, alerted the church delegates gathered in Philadelphia to the services that his group was prepared to supply to any evangelistic project, conducted under any appropriate auspices.

Now we stand ready to put in your hands at the merest cost of production, and oftentimes at much less than that, for your missionary work, the gospels and the New Testament in over sixty-five languages, and we stand ready to give you whole Bibles in many of these languages; and if there is anything we can do to help you to go to these people with this simple message of the New Testament, we are with you, whatever may be your church, whatever may be your denomination, to be your fellow-laborer. [quoted in Sanford, 1909: 99]

Cooperation meant for Protestants not just a valuable merging of effort, but a streamlining of the missionary task itself, for, as the Council's Committee on the Church and the Immigrant Problem explained:

It is true of the vast majority of immigrants, as it is true of men and women in heathen countries, that differences in form of government and points of theology, which seem very important to us here are exceedingly unimportant to them. The necessity of defining and exalting evangelical truth is so much greater than the need of emphasizing denominational differences, that federated effort becomes more reasonable and possible in home missions and foreign missions than in our regular church work. Immigrants are only confused by our many names and our many differences. [Davis, 1909: 258]

What is noteworthy about Protestant efforts to deal with growing numbers of Catholics at the turn of the century is not that they occurred, but that in occurring they apparently obliterated the practical importance of many long-standing denominational divisions. Immigrants were to be recast into Americans; implied in this transformation was their adoption of some brand of evangelical Protestantism – it mattered not which, as all were better than their lazy and superstitious Catholicism. Attempts to proselytize immigrants along strictly denominational lines, in any event, would not succeed. Such campaigns would not be sufficient to the task, they furthermore would waste resources, and, in all likelihood, they would not be understood by the very persons to whom their narrow messages were directed. In the end, the Bible would be made available to all immigrants on the same terms that governed its circulation among evangelicals, as a code of common belief. The weapon of persuasion afforded by Scripture was to be denied to none who did not themselves deny its truth.

Thus did the urban mission challenge unify a disparate Protestant family by the first years of the twentieth century. A diversifying religious environment spelled conflict with non-Protestants, and especially with Catholics, and furnished the "active motive sufficient to overcome de-

nominational self-consciousness and inertia" which Niebuhr (1954: 270) had decided would be required to stir the Protestant churches later to move toward union.

Although the examples in this section have been limited to subcultural contact via missionary work in American cities, religious conflict can be seen to have generated as readily Protestant solidarity in other areas of urban life, most notably in politics and social reform. On a whole range of issues, from agitation for temperance to legislation on schooling (Tyack, 1974) to the regulation of the Sabbath, religious affiliation was a principal line of cleavage (cf. Jensen, 1971), a line on one side of which urban Protestants largely congregated.

Whether the process of dedifferentiation described here was sym-metrical — that is, whether the many differences within American Catholi-cism at this time were bridged when it battled the Protestant majority — is not as clear. On the one hand, many conservative prelates in the late nineteenth-century Church were highly suspicious of contact with the prevailing national culture, which was permeated by a generalized Protes-tantism, for they feared its potential effects on the faithful. They therefore opposed attempts by liberal Catholic bishops (cf. Cross, 1958) to elude or defuse nativism by "Americanizing" the immigrants. Instead, the conserva-tives encouraged the persistence of Catholic ethnic diversity as a means of resisting the inroads of native American culture, with its Protestant influ-ences. They took as a motto the admonition (quoted in Linkh, 1975: 4) that "he who loses his language also loses his faith." Internal diversity, then, while it may have been a handicap to a majority seeking to maintain its superior position, was recognized by some to be a useful kind of refuge for a minority group fighting assimilation.

On the other hand, historical accounts of particular incidents of Protestant-Catholic conflict in the nineteenth century suggest that ethnic divisions within Catholicism were overlooked when the fortunes of the whole group were challenged. Indeed, as one historian of the immigrant Church, Jay P. Dolan (1975: 161) points out, "as the church took on an intensified degree of ethnic diversity, it needed to develop a measure of unity and control lest it split apart into independent national churches." One source of unity which obligingly grew in proportion to the ethnic diversity of American Catholicism was Protestant nativism. When the operation of parochial schools in New York City was threatened by the refusal of the city government to approve public aid, "divisions among Catholics," according to Dolan (1975: 164), "were glossed over" as Bishop John Hughes "molded his flock into a united opposition party."

The data collected for this study do not permit a test of whether Catholics drew together in the face of nativist Protestants. However, the statistics do allow the opposite reaction to be measured. In the following

two sections, turn-of-the-century church membership data are scrutinized for signs of Protestant consolidation in response to religious conflict. Clearly, leaders of American Protestantism at this time saw the need and set in motion the mechanisms for interdenominational cooperation (not to mention, well in the future, church union). Whether these efforts had any effect, however, on the structure of Protestant church membership in the most populous American cities—that is, on the unity of American Protestantism as a cultural movement—is another matter. There is no evidence to indicate that decisions of individuals during this period to switch affiliations converged on one or any group of denominations. Nevertheless, the very fact of conflict may have so altered the urban religious environment that Protestantism as a cultural entity was rendered more unified by the first years of this century than it was in the final decade of the last. The analyses summarized next test this possibility.

## Urban Subcultural Conflict and Protestant Diversity

Table 8.1 describes ordinary least squares (OLS) regression analyses of diversity among Protestants in 1906. By controlling scores for 1890 on that same diversity index, the models in this table are constructed so as to analyze *changes* in Protestant diversity between 1890 and 1906 (Land and Felson, 1976: 580–585). The independent variables of interest in these analyses are three related measures of alien presence in the urban cultural environment in 1890. They are: the segment of a city's population that was descended from foreign stock, the number of its inhabitants born abroad, and its Catholic Church membership. Since total population in 1890 supplements 1890 diversity as a control in every equation, the form of the three predictors used here means that they are not scaled directly to city size. Instead, the population or membership counts in these equations are equivalent to measures of proportions of total population (cf. Bollen and Ward, 1979: 437, 441–443). The three predictors are inserted in the model one at a time, and the results from these regressions are displayed in Equations 8.1a through 8.1c.

Because of obvious empirical similarities among the principal independent variables, the coefficients in Table 8.1 are quite stable across the three equations, and the estimates of alien presence are identical in sign and in achieved level of statistical significance. No matter how it is measured, the proportion of a city's population that is *not* derived from a traditional, native Protestant background is negatively related to changes in Protestant diversity over the ensuing sixteen-year period.[2] In every case, moreover, the *t*-statistic associated with the particular coefficient for foreign or Catholic population is statistically significant. These findings suggest that cities in which, by 1890, foreigners or Catholics (or, as

Table 8.1. *Results of ordinary least squares (OLS) analyses of the effects of alien cultural presence in American cities in 1890 on changes in Protestant denominational diversity, 1890–1906 (unstandardized regression coefficients)*

| Equation number | Dependent variable | Control variables | | | Measures of alien presence, 1890 (in millions) | | | $R^2$ | N |
|---|---|---|---|---|---|---|---|---|---|
| | | Constant | Diversity among Protestants, 1890 | Total population (in millions), 1890 | Foreign stock population | Foreign born population | Catholic Church membership | | |
| 8.1a | Diversity among Protestants, 1906 | +.357 | +.586 | +.190 | −.249[a] | — | — | .60 | 122 |
| 8.1b | Diversity among Protestants, 1906 | +.359 | +.585 | +.135 | — | −.352[b] | — | .60 | 122 |
| 8.1c | Diversity among Protestants, 1906 | +.357 | +.589 | +.118 | — | — | −.472[c] | .59 | 122 |

[a] $t = 2.546; p < .02.$   [b] $t = 2.348; p < .02.$   [c] $t = 2.329; p < .02.$

is likely, people who were both) were strongly represented, underwent soon thereafter a process whereby heterogeneity among Protestants was eventually reduced. Protestantism, in other words, was consolidated at the structural level when, and in the same places that, non-"American" elements were in the ascendant.

One way to interpret this change is to conceive of patterns in church membership as an interorganizational response to religious competition, and the threats it poses to group solidarity. These threats are transmitted by the intergroup contact that greater diversity across all groups facilitates. Lower Protestant diversity, seen in this light, provides quantitative support for an assertion which Fischer (1975b: 1327) had earlier conceded lacked "solid evidence," the assertion "that confrontation with 'odd' strangers in the subculturally heterogeneous city does lead to recoil and the embracing of own-group values."

But, these results suggest, subcultural conflict can do more: in this historical instance, conflict apparently determined which values were to be regarded as defining the "own-group," and it thereby redrew the very boundaries which distinguished the competing parties. Although the nineteenth century witnessed "a great increase in the number of separate denominations," Douglass (1934: 40) insisted that these new organizations had "a diminishing significance attaching to their differences, so that it became possible for integrating forces to affect the total situation as they could not at any earlier date." Denominational differences within Protestantism once were more generally regarded as genuine and important (for example, in the period before the Civil War), but it appears that with the arrival in cities during the late nineteenth century of large numbers of Catholics and Jews—persons bearing radically different religious assumptions and habits—the ranks of Protestant denominations closed, lending substance in social life for the first time to the designation of "Protestant."

Continuing conflict among Christian groups, according to Mead (1954c: 316), "meant that ever changing patterns of antagonism and competition were developed, and, by the same token, ever changing patterns of alignments and cooperation." The analyses discussed in the next section seek to trace aspects of one particularly historic religious alignment which, it is argued, happened at the turn of the century.

## Subcultural Conflict and Denominational Realignment

If the interpretation of diminished Protestant diversity offered above is correct, further evidence for it as a consequence of subcultural conflict ought to lie in the relationships over time between the two religious diversity indexes themselves. In the situation where the distribution of

Protestants, Catholics, Jews, and others in a city's pool of church members was relatively uniform, the disincentive to internal differentiation within Protestantism must have been pronounced: every evangelical body needed to be counted together, as one, in order for Protestants to outnumber affiliates of the "unevangelical" churches. If profiles of religious membership were formed at the turn of the century in accordance with such limiting conditions in the cultural environment, one would expect Protestants, in the initial presence of high Protestant-Catholic-Jewish-Other diversity, to have coalesced, and thus to exhibit lower diversity at the later time point.

In contrast, where Protestant-Catholic-Jewish-Other diversity in 1890 was comparatively low, either Catholics so predominated that no plausible coalition could have achieved a majority for Protestants, or none was necessary, as a Protestant majority was the cause of the low level of overall diversity in the first place. Under either circumstance, Protestantism would have met no external barrier to differentiation, and diversity might well have increased with time, as Protestantism's constituent populations became more varied.[3]

To summarize, if subcultural conflict was the basis for net historical differences in Protestant diversity, there should exist a negative relationship between Protestant-Catholic-Jewish-Other diversity in 1890 and additions to diversity among Protestants by 1906. Substantively, Protestant diversity should have decreased between 1890 and 1906 in cities where, other things being equal, overall religious diversity in 1890 was high, and the competition for cultural influence in which the major religious faiths participated was most intense. Conversely, Protestant diversity should have increased where overall diversity at first was low, and the relations among different Protestant denominations therefore were forged in the comfortable context of a larger numerical superiority or, alternatively, in the safety of the neglect accorded a Protestantism in declension by the religion of the new majority.

Table 8.2 addresses these hypotheses. To begin, Equation 8.2a demonstrates the existence of a strong and positive cross-sectional relationship between Protestant-Catholic-Jewish-Other diversity and diversity among Protestants in 1890. It seems that, in 1890, diversity across the major faiths and diversity within Protestantism flourished in the same places. This held true in 1906 as well: Equation 8.2b reports a less prominent but still positive relationship between the two diversity measures at the later time.

These results alone are insufficient, however, to invalidate the hypotheses elaborated above, which anticipated a negative relation to pertain between the two types of diversity. It is possible, after all, for Protestant diversity and its more general counterpart to be positively related at both

Table 8.2. *Results of ordinary least squares (OLS) analyses of the effects of Protestant-Catholic-Jewish-Other diversity on Protestant denominational diversity in 1890 and 1906 (unstandardized regression coefficients)*

| Equation number | Dependent variable | Constant | Diversity among Protestants, 1890 | Protestant-Catholic-Jewish-Other diversity, 1890 | Protestant-Catholic-Jewish-Other diversity, 1906 | $R^2$ | $N$ |
|---|---|---|---|---|---|---|---|
| 8.2a | Diversity among Protestants, 1890 | +.694 | — | +.269[a] | — | .13 | 122 |
| 8.2b | Diversity among Protestants, 1906 | +.815 | — | — | +.062[b] | .01 | 119 |
| 8.2c | Diversity among Protestants, 1906 | +.787 | — | +.117[c] | — | .04 | 122 |
| 8.2d | Diversity among Protestants, 1906 | +.362 | +.611 | −.047[d] | — | .58 | 122 |
| 8.2e | Diversity among Protestants, 1906 | +.357 | +.613 | −.070[e] | +.037[f] | .58 | 119 |

[a] $t = 4.252; p < .001.$   [b] $t = 1.305; .10 < p < .20.$   [c] $t = 2.277; p < .05.$   [d] $t = 1.281; p = .20.$   [e] $t = 1.428; .10 < p < .20.$
[f] $t = 0.880; .30 < p < .40.$

time points, and also to vary inversely across the historical period the two points bound. Although neither of the first two equations extends the analysis over time, there is reason to suspect that such an extension would yield different results. The powerful cross-sectional relationship connecting the diversity measures for 1890 is reduced by 1906, implying that the cities with high scores on both indexes in 1890 are not, as a group, the same ones with mutually high scores in 1906.

Equation 8.2c, which introduces as a predictor of Protestant diversity a lagged version of diversity across the major faiths, presents something of a surprise. The 1890 values of Protestant-Catholic-Jewish-Other diversity are positively and statistically significantly associated with diversity among Protestants in 1906. The coefficient in this equation marked "c" indicates that Protestant diversity in 1906 was high in the same cities which supported diversity in the wider religious environment in 1890. Yet, this is basically a static relationship, albeit one which joins variables from two points in time. Equations 8.2d and 8.2e improve on 8.2c, for this final pair of models incorporates diversity among Protestants in 1890 as a control, and thereby renders the dependent variable, for practical purposes, a measure of change.

Cross-sectionally and over a lag interval, a positive relationship holds between the two diversity measures. However, it may be concluded from Equation 8.2d that Protestant-Catholic-Jewish-Other diversity in 1890 is actually a negative predictor of the change in Protestant diversity which had accumulated over sixteen years. The outcome of this more refined specification of the model, further, is in agreement with the hypothesis.

The inclusion, in Equation 8.2e, of a term for Protestant-Catholic-Jewish-Other diversity in 1906 represents the principal independent variable as the dependent variable already is formulated, as a change measure. In this equation, the coefficient for the indicator of diversity across the major faiths in 1906 is positive, but it is not statistically significant. Thus, whatever the dynamic that induced Protestant consolidation between 1890 and 1906, it probably did not operate in direct proportion to contemporaneous changes in the wider religious environment. Either Protestant-Catholic-Jewish-Other diversity in 1890 spawned a single shift in the distribution of Protestant church membership, or the effects of its later development are located in a period beyond that which is treated by these data.

These results suggest, then, that an adjustment of religious group boundaries accompanied urban subcultural conflict at the turn of the century. They imply additionally that this adjustment was not an increment in an ongoing process, but was more likely an historical shift of singular causes, requiring approximately a generation before it became evident.

## Discussion

The consolidation of Protestant membership by 1906 in cities where foreigners and Catholics were prevalent in 1890 need not have occurred by an accumulation of separate, individual decisions. On the contrary, there is no historical evidence from religious statistics to suggest that denominational switching within Protestantism was more common during the turn-of-the-century era than at any other time. Indeed, it would be difficult to determine anything about the religious affiliations of particular sets of individuals from the Census data compiled for this study, because aggregate data on the same cities from successive decades refer, in all likelihood, to substantially different groups of people (Clubb et al., 1981: 107–116).

The people were different by virtue of similar processes operating in two concentric areas. First, the pool of church members in any city was more a stream than a pool, in that believers were forever trickling off and being replenished. Religious organizations at any one time involved just a segment of a city's adults, and the segment changed in both its external dimensions and internal composition when the newly committed joined and the disaffected dropped away. The larger population changed as well: immigration, it was noted in Chapters 1 and 4, was rapidly swelling the populations of many American cities at the turn of the century, constantly depositing new actors – church members and potential members – into the urban religious environment. Furthermore, numerous persons who were not necessarily new to America were nevertheless not very settled (Chudacoff, 1972; Thernstrom, 1968; Thernstrom and Knights, 1970). They moved from city to city and contributed, by their departures and arrivals, to the frequent renewal of urban religious environments.

What developed out of subcultural conflict at the turn of the century, then, was almost certainly not a directed wave of conversions, but more probably, a "shaking out," on the structural level, of the varieties of Protestantism represented in different American cities. Changes in the composition of religious membership in many cities in this period were wrought not by individuals, moving laterally across denominational boundaries, but by organizations, rising or falling as they gained members from among the new urban populations or lost them to other churches, to lack of interest, or to unbelief. If this view is correct, the factors which selected the religious survivors in most cities had less to do with personal choices than with the size, power, and preparedness for competition of Protestant church organizations.

Religious bodies such as the Salvation Army and Christian Science were tailored to modern life chances and life-styles, and thus they enjoyed a

comparative advantage in appeals to city dwellers. Yet others no doubt prospered simply by being the largest church in the local environment, and as such, the one with the widest net (knit of personal ties and hoisted by organizational resources) to cast for recruits. Conversely, smaller churches, particularly those not born in sectarian fervor, by this logic were ill-suited to the struggles taking place around them.

A coincidence of these processes—growth in a few already large congregations and the extinction of many smaller ones—would have been adequate to produce a marked decrease in Protestant diversity in many cities over time. This is not to say, however, that this change could not also have been a response to wider religious and cultural conditions. It is only to observe that this change took place on the structural level, and not as the result either of the intentions of Protestant church members or of a conscious policy of Protestant collaboration.

Nevertheless, the finding is all the more intriguing because of where it is positioned. It demonstrates anew how ideological trends may be clues to the existence of correlative changes on the structural level; and, while structures do not always explain ideas—and need not—that the two classes of social phenomena vary together is not unimportant. In this case, the ideology of Protestant cooperation and the statistical fact of Protestant consolidation were probably both responses to larger demographic conditions. Population growth and heterogeneity in the late nineteenth century no doubt intensified cultural conflict, which in turn made for a turbulent religious environment. By the start of the twentieth century, Catholicism rose from the confusion to be a new force in American society, leaving room, resources, and role, then, for only a lean and organized Protestant opposition.

The broadest sociological suggestion of this line of reasoning is that the religious "frame of reference" shifts in a religiously more heterogeneous environment. From a nation of evangelical denominations and foreign churches, the United States developed its triple structure of religious affiliation: Protestant, Catholic, and Jewish (Herberg, 1955). Such a shift was thought not to have occurred in America until roughly after the Second World War, with the "denomination-blurring homogenization of the suburban church" (Lambert, 1960: 154) and the secularization which presumably accompanied suburban living (cf. Lambert, 1960; Marty, 1959; Winter, 1961). Yet this chapter has uncovered evidence for the historian Oscar Handlin's (1954: 222) opinion that "a fundamental tripartite division . . . had begun to take form earlier in the century." How changes caused by turn-of-the-century religious diversity prefabricated the current structure of American denominationalism is a question which is pursued in the final chapter.

# "Matters Merely Indifferent"

## Religious Diversity and American Denominationalism

The organizational reaction to "unevangelical" elements in the urban population set the historical stage, just after the turn of the century, for the inauguration of an era of cooperation among Protestants (cf. Davis, 1973: 192) which was unprecedented in its attempts to integrate church work in areas as varied as religious education, foreign missions, domestic evangelization, and social action. "The first decade of the century," commented Protestant researcher H. Paul Douglass (1934: 43), "is marked as an epoch of cooperation and federation."

Chief among the signs of increasing cooperation was the founding, in 1908, of the Federal Council of the Churches of Christ in America. The Federal Council, the forerunner of the present-day National Council of Churches, joined thirty-three Protestant denominations in common spiritual and social causes (Hutchison, 1941; Sanford, 1916). Still other initiatives toward cooperation were undertaken even earlier. The standardization of Protestant Sunday School curricula was begun in 1900 with the guidance of the Editorial Association. The Laymen's Missionary Movement, organized in 1906, represented interdenominational collaboration in the administration of missions. And in 1908, the same year that the Federal Council was founded, domestic evangelism was coordinated for the first time on a large scale by the Home Missions Council and the Council of Women for Home Missions (Douglass, 1934: 43).

Widespread cooperation on social issues, much of it conducted under the auspices of the Federal Council, served as a prelude to a more sweeping movement for Protestant church union which gained momentum in the second and third decades of this century. It additionally cleared the way for several notable "short-cuts" around Protestant sectarianism, including campaigns "from the ground up" for local church comity, and the contemporaneous rise of community and federated churches as organizational forms in American religion (Douglass, 1934: 44, 48–49).

## Religious Diversity and American Denominationalism

The religious diversity of the late nineteenth century played an important role in establishing America's current system of religious denominationalism, a system in which interdenominational cooperation by Protestants has been only one feature. Other aspects include an attitude of toleration toward diverse beliefs, under the conviction that "there is an indefinite plurality of morally acceptable denominations" (Parsons, 1963: 62–63, 66; quotation at 66).

In addition, the denominational era has witnessed a gravitation of religious ideology in America toward a vague uniformity (Herberg, 1955; Hudson, 1961; Lambert, 1960), to the point where religious choice is compared to consumer decision-making (Berger, 1963; Berger and Luckmann, 1966), and the specifics of one's faith (though not its ethical foundation) are consigned to the company of, to harken one last time to the words of the Puritan Nathaniel Ward (1969: 10), "matters merely indifferent." As Talcott Parsons (1963: 64–65) described the significance, or lack of significance, of specific allegiances under denominationalism, "if some should shift to another denomination, it is not to be taken too tragically, since the new affiliation will in most cases be included in the deeper moral community."

A "deeper moral community," the existence of which Parsons (1963: 62) relied upon as his explanation for why religious diversity did not plunge America into a perpetual "state of latent religious war," took form in the twentieth century precisely because the communities of belief which had in the past been kept intact by individual religious bodies by then had become increasingly untenable. This erosion of the potential for commitment, Chapter 7 makes clear, followed from the fact of religious pluralism and stemmed, more specifically, from the difficulty of sustaining permanent and exclusive boundaries in a diversified religious environment. The difficulty is especially pronounced if, as Chapter 8 indicates was true at the turn of the century, religion already serves as an axis of political and social conflict, for then religious definitions may be loosened to facilitate coalition building.

Religious diversity at the turn of the century, and the conflict it generated, managed to remove certain old distinctions among religious groups and to accentuate new, broader ones. The evidence for this conclusion appears in a number of the chapters of this study. The addition, by 1890, of foreign and nonwhite persons to the native white populations of rapidly growing American cities, Chapter 4 revealed, did more to diversify urban religious environments over the ensuing sixteen years than did simply increasing demographic scale, without regard for the composition of the cities' populations. Yet the conflict of the new city-dwellers with

the existing urban culture and its evangelical Protestant establishment produced, the analyses in Chapter 8 suggest, a consolidation of Protestant church membership across the turn of the century. At the same time that Protestantism underwent consolidation, it experienced, according to Chapter 7, an increase in its standing relative to the size of its constituency. These findings collectively imply an emphasis, dictated by social change, on the wider religious group boundaries setting off Protestants, Catholics, Jews, and others. They furthermore certify the preliminary success of the adjustments the new emphasis brought. In broader terms, the findings point to a reorganization of American denominationalism into a system of three major faiths, at least one of which (Protestantism) now functions, as a practical matter, as a cartel of different church bodies that are descended from like traditions (Berger, 1963).

Diversity, then, though a distinguishing mark of American religion, has over the past century effected its own limitation. Such an eventual limit was foreseen by some. William Adams Brown, a Presbyterian systematic theologian, wrote as early as 1922 that "the picture of American Christianity as a strife of warring sects is a serious misrepresentation. The chief danger of denominationalism is not that it leads us to attack our fellow-Christians, but that it makes us content to ignore them" (Brown, 1922: 73). What Brown did not say, but what this study contends beyond his remarks, is that Protestant diversity could be ignored safely only after the appearance in cities by the late nineteenth century of masses whose religious loyalties and habits were literally foreign. One hundred years after the formal separation of church and state in the United States, Catholics, Jews, and others diversified urban religion over again, but with respect to an almost entirely new set of categories (Handy, 1966b, 1971). The most noticeable results of this second diversification of American religion were conflict between Catholics and Protestants and organizational change of a lasting sort within Protestantism itself.

Stanley Lieberson (1980: 380) has posited a similar historical development in the field of race relations in the United States since the late nineteenth century.[1] "Group boundaries shift and float in multiethnic or multiracial settings more than some recognize," he states. "Antagonisms and dispositions change in accordance with the group context." In particular, the ambitions for personal achievement of white immigrants to America in the late nineteenth and early twentieth centuries were assisted, Lieberson explains, by the arrival in northern cities of southern blacks.

In an environment newly diversified from the standpoint of race, the foreign-born no longer occupied the lowest rank in an imaginary queue symbolizing the relative desirability of different social groups in the eyes of employers, schools, political parties, and other institutional actors

whose choices powerfully determined the life chances of group members. Because the European immigrants were at least the same race as white Americans, "negative dispositions toward them would be muffled and modified." In this manner, Lieberson (1980: 380–381) concludes, "ethnic ties and allegiances float and shift in accordance with the threats and alternatives that exist. The presence of blacks made it harder to discriminate against the new Europeans because the alternative was viewed even less favorably."

In a slightly different vein, Olivier Zunz (1982), in his extensive study of social change in Detroit between 1880 and 1920, demonstrates how a "restructuring of social relations took place" there as different immigrant groups were incorporated into the industrial life of the city. After the inclusion of these groups, class distinctions, claims Zunz (1982: 403), replaced ethnic ones as the central components of Detroit's social organization. Industrial production assumed every worker under "a new, single opportunity structure," a structure, Zunz (1982: 401) asserts, that integrated urban life in a way that a vanishing "traditional ethnic matrix" did not. If this account is accurate, Zunz's work provides another example of how a heterogeneous group context made it possible for subsequent events to designate, in this case, "by default" (Zunz, 1982: 402), a new set of socially salient individual characteristics which then was used to structure intergroup relations.

One structural parallel of shifting racial preferences or ethnic allegiances in this period involved religion. A legacy of Protestant sectarianism in major cities was rendered intolerable at the turn of the century by the religious rivalries posed by Catholics, Jews, and others, and by the new diversity their joint presence signaled. Whatever the differences among evangelicals, they were considered minor compared to the deep cultural divisions separating Protestantism from Catholicism and Judaism. Protestants discovered previously unrecognized affinities and endowed their collaborative work with a special urgency just as Catholicism and Judaism, both seemingly more unitary, rose to present serious competition to the Protestant vision of the American nation as a "righteous empire" (Marty, 1970).

## Conclusion

This study establishes the need for revision in standard historical approaches to the development of denominationalism in American society. It goes still further in suggesting a general intergroup dynamic which has operated, previous research hints, in other social spheres where diversity of some type prevailed. Most of all, however, its results and the manner in which they are qualified highlight the weaknesses of global theories of

social change uninformed by history and insensitive to aspects of context. Instead, they demonstrate the truth of Wade Clark Roof's (1985: 79) insistence that "religious trends cannot be understood fully by theories of secularization which link religious decline to relatively continuous processes such as industrial expansion, urbanization, or the diffusion of scientific knowledge." Roof believes positively that social studies of religion need "explanatory paradigms that allow for the shifts and irregularities that actually occur over the historical course" (Roof, 1985: 79).

The statistical analyses reported in Chapter 5 uncover little that is consistent in the relationship between industrialization and religious diversity, and still less that may be interpreted readily with the perspectives supplied by the sweeping theories which have been proposed for their presumed connection. While it is possible that the two phenomena are wholly unrelated, it may be inferred from the failure in Chapter 5 to estimate consistent regression models for different types of diversity at different times that, at the very least, the nature of diversity's historical association with industrialization might have been locationally or temporally specific. Religious diversity possibly was more related to certain kinds of industrial activity than simply to aggregate changes in industrial scale.

Chapters 6 and 7 alone appear to sustain general conclusions. In these two chapters, there are traces of relationships, admittedly sometimes modest ones, between cultural conditions and religious variables. In Chapter 6, illiteracy is shown for the most part to have depressed levels of religious diversity over time. Chapter 7 shows diversity in turn to be a cause of the secularization which commentators had long ago begun to associate with urban places.

These results are especially interesting in light of the research on determinants of religious diversity reported in Chapters 4 and 5. Chapter 5 uncovered few reliable examples of relations between diversity and the scale and development of manufacturing activity in American cities. The findings of Chapter 4, while somewhat more substantial, were limited to statistical traces of population movements; structural factors like population size and growth, in themselves, proved to be unrelated to diversity. Chapters 6 and 7, however, demonstrate the sensitive link between measures of religious diversity and cultural conditions. This is in spite of the fact that diversity appeared *not* to respond to changes in basic institutions like the economy, and to basic processes like urbanization, which are thought by some sociologists to constitute the social structural underpinnings of the organization of modern religion.

In Chapter 7, diversity is negatively related (with one notable exception) to increases in levels of church membership across the turn of the century. It is this exception, however, which returns the study to a mode of

analysis which combines concern for the implications of theory with historical specificity. The single exception to diversity's pattern of negative effects on church membership levels in Chapter 7 occurs with respect to Protestants, implying an important deviation from the expectation, established by sociological theory, of a weakening of all religious groups in a pluralistic environment. Chapter 7 offers an interpretation of this anomaly which not only ratifies historical and organizational analyses of Protestantism, but introduces the social-historical analyses in Chapter 8.

Protestantism, this interpretation argues, may actually attract more members to its ranks under conditions of diversity because of its peculiar organization, which dates from the turn of the century. Internally, American Protestantism is still nominally differentiated, but externally, its many bodies approach the national culture as a unified force. It can make specialized appeals for commitment, yet act in a coordinated fashion in political and social conflict. Now that overt conflict between Catholics and Protestants in the United States has been muted (Noll, 1987), the organization of the Protestant denominations is perhaps the most lasting effect of turn-of-the-century religious diversity.

In a more passive way, this effect has made possible varied resorts to the values of a generalized Protestant ethos as a legitimation for social movements throughout the twentieth century. Whether by the renamed Moral Majority or the National Council of Churches, Protestants have continually been implored to unite, to realize both the trivial nature of their differences and the importance of the work at hand. Indeed, the difference between the new Christian right and mainline Protestant cooperative bodies such as the NCC better defines the current split in American Protestantism than does any set of more minute doctrines.[2] That what differences that exist among Protestants are located in the conditions for and goals of their cooperation, and not in the very idea of joint action, is a product of the turn of the century. As such, it is a consequence which has transcended its historical causes and which promises to be one factor from the past which will figure prominently in the future of American religion.

# Cities in the Study

Listed alphabetically below are the 122 cities which serve as the units of analysis in the empirical portions of this study. They are the universe of cities in the United States with 25,000 or more inhabitants in 1890. The group originally numbered 124, but two places returned separately in the 1890 Census—Brooklyn and Long Island City, New York—were consolidated, under the Greater New York Charter of 1898, into boroughs of the City of New York. Formerly autonomous Brooklyn became one borough, whereas Long Island City was combined with several other municipalities to form the Borough of Queens. Statistics for Brooklyn and Long Island City in 1890 have been added to those of New York City in that year to simulate a geographical unit comparable to the New York of 1906.

Other cities as well grew by consolidation during this period, but the annexed areas were too small to have been returned as distinct urban places in the 1890 enumeration of religious organizations. Thus, data with which to make desired adjustments to religious measures are not available from published Census sources.

Data on changes in land area between 1890 and 1910 could be located (in McKenzie, 1933: 336–339) for 73 of the largest cities in the sample. Twenty cities experienced no growth in area during this period. Of the 53 cities that did add territory, the median increment was 6.4 square miles. These figures appear to validate Victor Jones's (1953: 551) observation that there occurred "few significant annexations after 1890" and before the immediate post-Second World War years. Both suggest in addition that artificial increases in church membership between 1890 and 1906 due to annexation are probably not great.

Akron, Ohio
Albany, New York
Allegheny, Pennsylvania
Allentown, Pennsylvania
Altoona, Pennsylvania
Atlanta, Georgia
Auburn, New York
Augusta, Georgia

Baltimore, Maryland
Bay City, Michigan
Binghamton, New York
Birmingham, Alabama
Boston, Massachusetts
Bridgeport, Connecticut
Brockton, Massachusetts
Buffalo, New York
Cambridge, Massachusetts
Camden, New Jersey
Canton, Ohio
Charleston, South Carolina
Chattanooga, Tennessee
Chelsea, Massachusetts
Chicago, Illinois
Cincinnati, Ohio
Cleveland, Ohio
Columbus, Ohio
Covington, Kentucky
Dallas, Texas
Davenport, Iowa
Dayton, Ohio
Denver, Colorado
Des Moines, Iowa
Detroit, Michigan
Dubuque, Iowa
Duluth, Minnesota
Elizabeth, New Jersey
Elmira, New York
Erie, Pennsylvania
Evansville, Indiana
Fall River, Massachusetts
Fort Wayne, Indiana
Galveston, Texas
Grand Rapids, Michigan
Harrisburg, Pennsylvania
Hartford, Connecticut
Haverhill, Massachusetts
Hoboken, New Jersey
Holyoke, Massachusetts
Houston, Texas
Indianapolis, Indiana
Jersey City, New Jersey
Kansas City, Kansas
Kansas City, Missouri
LaCrosse, Wisconsin

Lancaster, Pennsylvania
Lawrence, Massachusetts
Lincoln, Nebraska
Little Rock, Arkansas
Los Angeles, California
Louisville, Kentucky
Lowell, Massachusetts
Lynn, Massachusetts
Manchester, New Hampshire
Memphis, Tennessee
Milwaukee, Wisconsin
Minneapolis, Minnesota
Mobile, Alabama
Nashville, Tennessee
Newark, New Jersey
New Bedford, Massachusetts
New Haven, Connecticut
New Orleans, Louisiana
New York, New York
Norfolk, Virginia
Oakland, California
Omaha, Nebraska
Paterson, New Jersey
Pawtucket, Rhode Island
Peoria, Illinois
Philadelphia, Pennsylvania
Pittsburgh, Pennsylvania
Portland, Maine
Portland, Oregon
Providence, Rhode Island
Quincy, Illinois
Reading, Pennsylvania
Richmond, Virginia
Rochester, New York
Sacramento, California
Saginaw, Michigan
St. Joseph, Missouri
St. Louis, Missouri
St. Paul, Minnesota
Salem, Massachusetts
Salt Lake City, Utah
San Antonio, Texas
San Francisco, California
Savannah, Georgia
Scranton, Pennsylvania
Seattle, Washington

Sioux City, Iowa
Somerville, Massachusetts
Springfield, Massachusetts
Springfield, Ohio
Syracuse, New York
Tacoma, Washington
Taunton, Massachusetts
Terre Haute, Indiana
Toledo, Ohio
Topeka, Kansas
Trenton, New Jersey
Troy, New York
Utica, New York
Washington, D.C.
Waterbury, Connecticut
Wheeling, West Virginia
Wilkes-Barre, Pennsylvania
Williamsport, Pennsylvania
Wilmington, Delaware
Worcester, Massachusetts
Yonkers, New York
Youngstown, Ohio

# Church Membership and Population in 122 Cities, 1890 and 1906

Church membership and population totals at 1890 and 1906 for the 122 cities in the analysis are provided below.

Ratios of membership to population are included as well. These ratios may be regarded as negative indicators of secularization. A preferable denominator for the ratios would have been the adult and adolescent population of each city, because the church membership figures exclude baptized infants and small children. Indeed, estimates relying on restricted population totals appear throughout the literature. For instance, Michael Argyle (1958: 28) has reported that, nationwide in 1906, church membership was a trait of 55 percent of persons then at least thirteen years of age. However, city population data by age for 1906 were not readily available, so, at both points, for consistency, total population is recorded.

Auburn, Elmira, and Rochester, New York are missing data on Roman Catholic Church membership in 1906. Hence, total church membership and the church membership ratio for 1906 could not be calculated for them. In addition, the Census did not report 1906 population estimates for either Los Angeles or San Francisco, again making the church membership ratio for those cities in that year impossible to calculate.

| City | Total church membership, 1890 | Total population, 1890 | Ratio, 1890 | Total church membership, 1906 | Total population, 1906 | Ratio, 1906 |
|------|------|------|------|------|------|------|
| Akron | 10,404 | 27,601 | .377 | 18,370 | 50,738 | .362 |
| Albany | 44,597 | 94,923 | .470 | 59,612 | 98,537 | .605 |
| Allegheny | 32,666 | 105,287 | .310 | 61,456 | 145,240 | .423 |
| Allentown | 9,658 | 25,228 | .383 | 19,985 | 41,595 | .480 |
| Altoona | 11,227 | 30,337 | .370 | 26,715 | 47,910 | .558 |
| Atlanta | 27,237 | 65,533 | .416 | 59,479 | 104,984 | .567 |
| Auburn | 10,620 | 25,858 | .411 | — | 32,963 | — |

| City | Total church membership, 1890 | Total population, 1890 | Ratio, 1890 | Total church membership, 1906 | Total population, 1906 | Ratio, 1906 |
|---|---|---|---|---|---|---|
| Augusta | 16,936 | 33,300 | .509 | 22,890 | 43,125 | .531 |
| Baltimore | 175,995 | 434,439 | .405 | 224,968 | 553,669 | .406 |
| Bay City | 13,282 | 27,839 | .477 | 24,725 | 40,587 | .609 |
| Binghamton | 13,099 | 35,005 | .374 | 19,758 | 43,785 | .451 |
| Birmingham | 12,214 | 26,178 | .467 | 26,383 | 45,869 | .575 |
| Boston | 244,048 | 448,477 | .544 | 376,728 | 602,278 | .626 |
| Bridgeport | 19,983 | 48,866 | .409 | 50,936 | 84,274 | .604 |
| Brockton | 9,598 | 27,294 | .352 | 20,516 | 49,340 | .416 |
| Buffalo | 115,160 | 255,664 | .450 | 195,302 | 381,819 | .512 |
| Cambridge | 29,094 | 70,028 | .415 | 45,896 | 98,544 | .466 |
| Camden | 16,709 | 58,313 | .287 | 29,223 | 84,849 | .344 |
| Canton | 9,631 | 26,189 | .368 | 12,894 | 38,440 | .335 |
| Charleston | 24,117 | 54,955 | .439 | 27,942 | 56,317 | .496 |
| Chattanooga | 9,830 | 29,100 | .338 | 17,469 | 34,297 | .509 |
| Chelsea | 9,664 | 27,909 | .346 | 11,589 | 37,932 | .306 |
| Chicago | 388,145 | 1,099,850 | .353 | 833,441 | 2,049,185 | .407 |
| Cincinnati | 115,777 | 296,908 | .390 | 159,663 | 345,230 | .462 |
| Cleveland | 94,385 | 261,353 | .361 | 146,338 | 460,327 | .318 |
| Columbus | 28,992 | 88,150 | .329 | 63,261 | 145,414 | .435 |
| Covington | 15,575 | 37,371 | .417 | 31,435 | 46,436 | .677 |
| Dallas | 11,711 | 38,067 | .308 | 32,471 | 52,793 | .615 |
| Davenport | 7,491 | 26,872 | .279 | 11,839 | 40,706 | .291 |
| Dayton | 27,090 | 61,220 | .443 | 53,359 | 100,799 | .529 |
| Denver | 33,613 | 106,713 | .315 | 58,699 | 151,920 | .386 |
| Des Moines | 16,142 | 50,093 | .322 | 26,905 | 78,323 | .344 |
| Detroit | 83,397 | 205,876 | .405 | 194,160 | 353,535 | .549 |
| Dubuque | 14,003 | 30,311 | .462 | 22,575 | 43,070 | .524 |
| Duluth | 7,206 | 33,115 | .218 | 22,312 | 67,337 | .331 |
| Elizabeth | 16,569 | 37,764 | .439 | 28,616 | 62,185 | .460 |
| Elmira | 12,935 | 30,893 | .419 | — | 35,734 | — |
| Erie | 18,320 | 40,634 | .451 | 34,540 | 59,993 | .576 |
| Evansville | 13,832 | 50,756 | .273 | 31,634 | 63,957 | .495 |
| Fall River | 39,138 | 74,398 | .526 | 71,877 | 105,942 | .678 |
| Fort Wayne | 18,344 | 35,393 | .518 | 22,304 | 50,947 | .438 |
| Galveston | 13,748 | 29,084 | .473 | 21,157 | 34,355 | .616 |
| Grand Rapids | 21,367 | 60,278 | .354 | 43,306 | 99,794 | .434 |
| Harrisburg | 12,229 | 39,385 | .310 | 22,909 | 55,735 | .411 |
| Hartford | 23,127 | 53,230 | .434 | 43,717 | 95,822 | .456 |
| Haverhill | 12,539 | 27,412 | .457 | 17,357 | 37,961 | .457 |
| Hoboken | 14,777 | 43,648 | .339 | 22,529 | 66,689 | .338 |
| Holyoke | 18,828 | 35,637 | .528 | 34,530 | 50,778 | .680 |
| Houston | 8,712 | 27,557 | .316 | 29,983 | 58,132 | .516 |
| Indianapolis | 32,156 | 105,436 | .305 | 84,815 | 219,154 | .387 |
| Jersey City | 63,865 | 163,003 | .392 | 104,637 | 237,952 | .440 |
| Kans. City, Kans. | 6,667 | 38,316 | .174 | 22,079 | 77,912 | .283 |

| City | Total church membership, 1890 | Total population, 1890 | Ratio, 1890 | Total church membership, 1906 | Total population, 1906 | Ratio, 1906 |
|---|---|---|---|---|---|---|
| Kans. City, Mo. | 31,600 | 132,716 | .238 | 61,503 | 182,376 | .337 |
| LaCrosse | 9,480 | 25,090 | .378 | 19,938 | 29,115 | .685 |
| Lancaster | 12,119 | 32,011 | .379 | 18,336 | 47,129 | .389 |
| Lawrence | 26,583 | 44,654 | .595 | 48,363 | 71,548 | .676 |
| Lincoln | 8,653 | 55,154 | .157 | 19,114 | 48,232 | .396 |
| Little Rock | 8,298 | 25,874 | .321 | 17,969 | 39,959 | .450 |
| Los Angeles | 18,229 | 50,395 | .362 | 81,771 | — | — |
| Louisville | 73,355 | 161,129 | .455 | 147,330 | 226,129 | .652 |
| Lowell | 38,214 | 77,696 | .492 | 66,766 | 95,173 | .702 |
| Lynn | 17,383 | 55,727 | .312 | 31,571 | 78,748 | .401 |
| Manchester | 18,601 | 44,126 | .422 | 45,282 | 64,703 | .700 |
| Memphis | 17,333 | 64,495 | .269 | 37,477 | 125,018 | .300 |
| Milwaukee | 68,249 | 204,468 | .334 | 155,206 | 317,903 | .488 |
| Minneapolis | 65,184 | 164,738 | .396 | 96,819 | 273,825 | .354 |
| Mobile | 21,729 | 31,076 | .699 | 33,652 | 42,903 | .784 |
| Nashville | 30,195 | 76,168 | .396 | 44,198 | 84,703 | .522 |
| Newark | 69,988 | 181,830 | .385 | 115,307 | 289,634 | .398 |
| New Bedford | 18,894 | 40,733 | .464 | 43,936 | 76,746 | .572 |
| New Haven | 32,684 | 81,298 | .402 | 67,650 | 121,227 | .558 |
| New Orleans | 95,716 | 242,039 | .395 | 186,497 | 314,146 | .594 |
| New York | 875,823 | 2,352,150 | .372 | 1,838,482 | 4,113,043 | .447 |
| Norfolk | 13,611 | 34,871 | .390 | 28,533 | 66,931 | .426 |
| Oakland | 18,490 | 48,682 | .380 | 41,750 | 73,812 | .566 |
| Omaha | 18,658 | 140,452 | .133 | 33,900 | 124,167 | .273 |
| Paterson | 28,612 | 78,347 | .365 | 45,967 | 112,801 | .408 |
| Pawtucket | 13,984 | 27,633 | .506 | 22,327 | 44,211 | .505 |
| Peoria | 11,874 | 41,024 | .289 | 28,779 | 66,365 | .434 |
| Philadelphia | 335,189 | 1,046,964 | .320 | 558,866 | 1,441,735 | .388 |
| Pittsburgh | 105,757 | 238,617 | .443 | 205,847 | 375,082 | .549 |
| Portland, Me. | 13,958 | 36,425 | .383 | 20,263 | 55,167 | .367 |
| Porland, Ore. | 16,750 | 46,385 | .361 | 40,282 | 109,884 | .367 |
| Providence | 66,715 | 132,146 | .505 | 131,214 | 203,243 | .646 |
| Quincy | 15,995 | 31,494 | .508 | 31,496 | 39,108 | .805 |
| Reading | 22,402 | 58,661 | .382 | 38,976 | 91,141 | .428 |
| Richmond | 38,114 | 81,388 | .468 | 54,506 | 87,246 | .625 |
| Rochester | 59,037 | 133,896 | .441 | — | 185,703 | — |
| Sacramento | 9,059 | 26,386 | .343 | 12,070 | 31,022 | .389 |
| Saginaw | 16,012 | 46,322 | .346 | 20,698 | 48,742 | .425 |
| St. Joseph | 14,588 | 52,324 | .279 | 25,280 | 118,004 | .214 |
| St. Louis | 131,186 | 451,779 | .290 | 302,531 | 649,320 | .466 |
| St. Paul | 71,113 | 133,156 | .534 | 103,639 | 203,815 | .508 |
| Salem | 16,348 | 30,801 | .531 | 22,163 | 37,961 | .584 |
| Salt Lake City | 17,502 | 44,843 | .390 | 34,452 | 61,202 | .563 |
| San Antonio | 11,102 | 37,673 | .295 | 31,141 | 62,711 | .497 |
| San Francisco | 92,872 | 298,997 | .311 | 142,919 | — | — |

| City | Total church membership, 1890 | Total population, 1890 | Ratio, 1890 | Total church membership, 1906 | Total population, 1906 | Ratio, 1906 |
|---|---|---|---|---|---|---|
| Savannah | 18,905 | 43,189 | .438 | 36,713 | 68,596 | .535 |
| Scranton | 30,122 | 75,215 | .400 | 70,776 | 118,692 | .596 |
| Seattle | 6,839 | 42,837 | .160 | 49,479 | 104,169 | .475 |
| Sioux City | 8,207 | 37,806 | .217 | 12,117 | 42,520 | .285 |
| Somerville | 13,032 | 40,152 | .325 | 25,683 | 70,798 | .363 |
| Springfield, Mass. | 18,207 | 44,179 | .412 | 39,941 | 70,798 | .564 |
| Springfield, Ohio | 14,271 | 31,895 | .447 | 16,908 | 42,069 | .402 |
| Syracuse | 31,615 | 88,143 | .359 | 66,697 | 118,880 | .561 |
| Tacoma | 9,052 | 36,006 | .251 | 14,151 | 55,392 | .255 |
| Taunton | 10,551 | 25,448 | .415 | 17,903 | 30,953 | .578 |
| Terre Haute | 8,889 | 30,217 | .294 | 16,335 | 52,805 | .309 |
| Toledo | 32,378 | 81,434 | .398 | 44,082 | 159,980 | .276 |
| Topeka | 11,554 | 31,007 | .373 | 15,716 | 41,886 | .375 |
| Trenton | 23,473 | 57,458 | .409 | 41,310 | 86,355 | .478 |
| Troy | 40,945 | 60,956 | .672 | 46,924 | 76,513 | .613 |
| Utica | 18,631 | 44,007 | .423 | 45,846 | 65,099 | .704 |
| Washington | 94,572 | 230,392 | .410 | 136,759 | 307,716 | .444 |
| Waterbury | 16,041 | 28,646 | .560 | 35,260 | 61,903 | .570 |
| Wheeling | 14,293 | 34,522 | .414 | 22,017 | 41,494 | .531 |
| Wilkes-Barre | 15,738 | 37,718 | .417 | 35,780 | 60,121 | .595 |
| Williamsport | 11,484 | 27,132 | .423 | 17,189 | 29,735 | .578 |
| Wilmington | 21,293 | 61,431 | .347 | 38,095 | 85,140 | .447 |
| Worcester | 32,629 | 84,655 | .385 | 69,588 | 130,078 | .535 |
| Yonkers | 14,083 | 32,033 | .440 | 48,211 | 64,110 | .752 |
| Youngstown | 11,527 | 33,220 | .347 | 17,740 | 52,710 | .337 |

# Categorization of Religious Bodies, 1890 and 1906

Below are arrayed the denominational categories used in constructing the two indexes of religious diversity employed in this study's empirical analyses of church membership in 1890 and 1906. With rare exceptions, the original categorizations of the Census statisticians have been preserved, and the original labels for their categories retained. When classifications were rearranged, the primary motivation was to ensure the comparability of religious designations over time. Decisions on which groups to shift were thus guided principally by historical considerations, such as the existence of a common parent body or the shared ethnicity of combined memberships.

Because some data, particularly the data for 1890, were not minutely disaggregated, several obvious errors (for example, the inclusion in 1890 of members of the Reformed Catholic Church with Latin rite and Orthodox faithful) could not be corrected. For this same reason, members of some smaller Protestant bodies (e.g., Moravians) are counted in 1890 as "Other" rather than as "Protestant." The gross numbers involved in these arithmetic misallocations, however, are small; they should not sway any results.

The Protestant-Catholic-Jewish-Other diversity index relies, as its name implies, on just four broad categories of religious affiliation. They are noted in CAPITAL letters at the left margin, and all groups named to the right and below are subsumed under those labels. The divisions of importance when diversity among Protestants is calculated are indicated by *italics*. Seventy-one distinct Protestant bodies are represented in the sample of cities in 1890. For the diversity index, they were collapsed into 21 categories, representing larger denominational "families." The 127 Protestant bodies reporting in 1906 were similarly fit into 26 general classifications. Preliminary calculations of diversity measures using completely disaggregated membership data yielded results only slightly different from those based on these broader groupings.

## Statistics of Churches, 1890

PROTESTANT

*Adventist bodies*
Advent Christians
Churches of God in Christ Jesus
Evangelical Adventists
Life and Advent Union
Seventh-Day Adventists

*Regular Baptist bodies*
Colored Baptists
Northern Baptists
Southern Baptists

*Other Baptist bodies*
Freewill Baptists
Primitive Baptists
Seventh-Day Baptists

*Congregationalists*

*Disciples of Christ*

*Episcopal bodies*
Protestant Episcopal Church
Reformed Episcopal Church

*Evangelical Association*

*Friends bodies*
Friends (Hicksite)
Friends (Orthodox)
Friends (Primitive)
Friends (Wilburite)

*German Evangelical bodies*
German Evangelical Protestants
German Evangelical Synod

*Lutheran bodies*
Buffalo Synod
Danish Church Association
Danish Church in America
General Council
General Synod
German Augsburg Synod
Hauges Synod
Icelandic Synod
Immanuel Synod
Independent Congregations
Joint Synod of Ohio
Michigan Synod
Norwegian Church in America

Synodical Conference
United Norwegian Church of America
United Synod in the South

Principal Methodist bodies
*Methodist Episcopal Church*
*Methodist Episcopal Church, South*

*Black Methodist bodies*
African Methodist Episcopal Church
African Methodist Episcopal Zion Church
African Union Methodist Protestant Church
Colored Methodist Episcopal Church
Evangelist Missionary Church
Union American Methodist Episcopal Church
Zion Union Apostolic Church

*Other Methodist bodies*
Free Methodist Church
Independent Methodist Church
Methodist Protestant Church
Primitive Methodist Church
Wesleyan Methodist Connection

Principal Presbyterian bodies
*Presbyterian Church in the United States of America* (Northern Presbyterians)
*Presbyterian Church in the United States* (Southern Presbyterians)

*Other Presbyterian bodies*
Associate Church of North America
Associate Reformed Synod of the South
Cumberland Presbyterian Church
Cumberland Presbyterian Church (Colored)
Reformed Presbyterian Church (Covenanted)
Reformed Presbyterian Church in North America (General Synod)
Reformed Presbyterian Church in the United States and Canada
Reformed Presbyterian Church in the United States (Synod)
United Presbyterian Church
Welsh Calvinistic Methodist Church

*Reformed bodies*
Christian Reformed Church
Reformed Church in America
Reformed Church in the United States

*Unitarians*

*United Brethren bodies*
United Brethren in Christ
United Brethren in Christ (Old Constitution)

*Universalists*

CATHOLIC
>  Armenian Church
>  Greek Catholic (Uniates)
>  Greek Orthodox Church
>  Reformed Catholic Church
>  Roman Catholic Church
>  Russian Orthodox Church


JEWISH
>  Jewish Congregations (Orthodox)
>  Jewish Congregations (Reformed)


OTHER
>  Apostolic Mennonites
>  Brethren in Christ
>  Catholic Apostolic Church
>  Chinese Temples
>  Christadelphians
>  Christians (Christian Connection)
>  Christian Church, South
>  Christian Scientists
>  Christian Union
>  Church of God (Winebrennerian)
>  Church of Jesus Christ of Latter-day Saints
>  Church of the New Jerusalem
>  Church Triumphant (Koreshan Ecclesia)
>  Church Triumphant (Schweinfurth)
>  Dunkards, or German Baptists (Conservative)
>  Dunkards, or German Baptists (Progressive)
>  Friends of the Temple
>  General Conference Mennonites
>  Independent Congregations
>  Mennonites
>  Moravians
>  Plymouth Brethren (I and II)
>  Reorganized Church of Jesus Christ of Latter Day Saints
>  River Brethren
>  Salvation Army
>  Schwenkfeldians
>  Social Brethren
>  Society for Ethical Culture
>  Spiritualists
>  Theosophical Society
>  United Zion's Children

## Census of Religious Bodies, 1906

PROTESTANT

*Adventist bodies*
Advent Christian Church
Churches of God (Adventist), Unattached Congregations
Churches of God in Christ Jesus
Evangelical Adventists
Life and Advent Union
Seventh-Day Adventist Denomination

Principal Baptist bodies
*National Baptist Convention (Colored)*
*Northern Baptist Convention*
*Southern Baptist Convention*

*Other Baptist bodies*
Colored Primitive Baptists in America
Free Baptists
Freewill Baptists
General Baptists
Primitive Baptists
Seventh-Day Baptists
Two-Seed-in-the-Spirit Predestinarian Baptists

*Church of Christ, Scientist*

*Congregationalists*

*Disciples, or Christians, and related bodies*
Christians (Christian Connection)
Churches of Christ
Disciples of Christ

*Episcopal bodies*
Protestant Episcopal Church
Reformed Episcopal Church

*Evangelical bodies*
Evangelical Association
United Evangelical Church

*Friends bodies*
Friends (Primitive)
Orthodox Conservative Friends (Wilburite)
Religious Society of Friends (Hicksite)
Society of Friends (Orthodox)

*German Evangelical bodies*
German Evangelical Protestant Ministers' Association
German Evangelical Protestant Ministers' Conference
German Evangelical Synod of North America

*Lutheran bodies*
Apostolic Lutheran Church (Finnish)

Church of the Lutheran Brethren of America (Norwegian)
Danish Evangelical Lutheran Church in America
Evangelical Lutheran Church in America (Eielsen's Synod)
Evangelical Lutheran Jehovah Conference
Evangelical Lutheran Joint Synod of Ohio and Other States
Evangelical Lutheran Synodical Conference of America
Evangelical Lutheran Synod of Iowa and Other States
Evangelical Lutheran Synod of Michigan and Other States
Finnish Evangelical Lutheran Church of America (Suomi Synod)
Finnish Evangelical Lutheran National Church
General Council of the Evangelical Lutheran Church in North America
General Synod of the Evangelical Lutheran Church in the United States of
    America
Hauge's Norwegian Evangelical Lutheran Synod
Immanuel Synod of the Evangelical Lutheran Church of North America
Lutheran Synod of Buffalo
Norwegian Lutheran Free Church
Slovak Evangelical Lutheran Synod of America
Swedish Evangelical Free Mission
Swedish Evangelical Mission Covenant of America
Synod for the Norwegian Evangelical Lutheran Church in America
United Danish Evangelical Lutheran Church in America
United Norwegian Lutheran Church in America
United Synod of the Evangelical Lutheran Church in the South

Principal Methodist bodies
  *Methodist Episcopal Church*
  *Methodist Episcopal Church, South*

*Black Methodist bodies*
  African Methodist Episcopal Church
  African Methodist Episcopal Zion Church
  African Union Methodist Protestant Church
  Colored Methodist Episcopal Church
  Congregational Methodist Church
  Reformed Methodist Union Episcopal Church (Colored)
  Union American Methodist Episcopal Church (Colored)

*Other Methodist bodies*
  Free Methodist Church of North America
  Methodist Protestant Church
  Primitive Methodist Church in the United States of America
  Wesleyan Methodist Connection of America

Principal Presbyterian bodies
  *Presbyterian Church in the United States of America* (Northern Presbyte-
    rians)
  *Presbyterian Church in the United States* (Southern Presbyterians)

*Other Presbyterian bodies*
  Associate Reformed Synod of the South

Colored Cumberland Presbyterian Church
Cumberland Presbyterian Church
General Synod of the Reformed Presbyterian Church in North America
Reformed Presbyterian Church in the United States and Canada
Synod of the Reformed Presbyterian Church of North America
United Presbyterian Church of North America
Welsh Calvinistic Methodist Church

*Reformed bodies*
Christian Reformed Church
Hungarian Reformed Church
Reformed Church in America
Reformed Church in the United States

*Salvationist bodies*
American Salvation Army
Salvation Army

*Unitarians*

*United Brethren bodies*
Church of the United Brethren in Christ
Church of the United Brethren in Christ (Old Constitution)

*Universalists*

*Other Protestant bodies*
Apostolic Christian Church
The Brethren Church (Progressive Dunkers)
Brethren in Christ
Catholic Apostolic Church
Central Illinois Conference of Mennonites
Christadelphians
Christian Catholic Church in Zion
Christian Israelite Church
Christian Union
Church of Christ in God
Church of Daniel's Band
Church of God and Saints of Christ (Colored)
Church of the Living God (Apostolic Church)
Church of the Living God (Christian Workers for Friendship)
General Conference of Mennonites of North America
General Eldership of the Churches of God in North America
German Baptist Brethren Church (Conservative)
Heavenly Recruit Church
Hephzibah Faith Missionary Association
Independent Churches
International Apostolic Holiness Union
Mennonite Brethren in Christ
Mennonite Church
Metropolitan Church Association

Missionary Church Association
Moravian Church (Unitas Fratum)
New Apostolic Church
Nonsectarian Churches of Bible Faith
Old Order German Baptist Brethren
Peniel Missions
Pentecostal Church of the Nazarene
Pentecostal Union Church
Pentecost Bands of the World
Plymouth Brethren (I, II, III, and IV)
Reformed Catholic Church
Schwenkfelders
Volunteers of America
Yorker (Old Order) Brethren

CATHOLIC
Armenian Church
Greek Orthodox Church
Polish National Church of America
Roman Catholic Church
Russian Orthodox Church
Servian Orthodox Church
Syrian Orthodox Church

JEWISH
Jewish congregations

OTHER
Bahai Faith
Buddhists (Japanese Temples)
Church of Jesus Christ of Latter-day Saints
General Church of the New Jerusalem
General Convention of the New Jerusalem in the United States
Reorganized Church of Jesus Christ of Latter Day Saints
Society for Ethical Culture
Spiritualists
Temple Society in the United States (Friends of the Temple)
Theosophical Society (American Section)
Theosophical Society in America
Theosophical Society (New York)
Vedanta Society

# Composition of Church Membership in 122 Cities, 1890 and 1906

The proportions of total church membership in each city in 1890 and 1906 affiliated with America's two largest religious subcommunities, Protestantism and Catholicism, are presented below. For the most part, these statistics describe well the overall religious divisions in each city, as nowhere—except Salt Lake City—do the combined figures for Jews and members of other religious bodies in either year exceed 10 percent of total church membership. In Salt Lake City, Latter-day Saints (Mormons), of course, account for 82 percent of church membership in 1890 and 70 percent in 1906.

Blanks appear in the table because Auburn, Elmira, and Rochester, New York all are missing data on Roman Catholic Church membership in 1906, thus rendering impossible the calculation of relative proportions of church membership in that year for any of these cities' religious groups.

| City | Proportion Protestant, 1890 | Proportion Protestant, 1906 | Proportion Catholic, 1890 | Proportion Catholic, 1906 |
|------|------|------|------|------|
| Akron | .666 | .785 | .319 | .203 |
| Albany | .361 | .334 | .609 | .654 |
| Allegheny | .586 | .472 | .413 | .525 |
| Allentown | .825 | .826 | .166 | .171 |
| Altoona | .731 | .598 | .247 | .399 |
| Atlanta | .908 | .902 | .075 | .094 |
| Auburn | .540 | — | .457 | — |
| Augusta | .816 | .830 | .161 | .167 |
| Baltimore | .532 | .538 | .438 | .452 |
| Bay City | .293 | .313 | .658 | .673 |
| Binghamton | .566 | .600 | .421 | .398 |
| Birmingham | .707 | .718 | .205 | .268 |
| Boston | .216 | .296 | .759 | .696 |
| Bridgeport | .401 | .259 | .579 | .736 |

172

| City | Proportion Protestant, 1890 | Proportion Protestant, 1906 | Proportion Catholic, 1890 | Proportion Catholic, 1906 |
|---|---|---|---|---|
| Brockton | .362 | .325 | .625 | .661 |
| Buffalo | .348 | .328 | .634 | .667 |
| Cambridge | .285 | .269 | .689 | .729 |
| Camden | .688 | .585 | .310 | .414 |
| Canton | .529 | .882 | .450 | .118 |
| Charleston | .797 | .717 | .156 | .277 |
| Chattanooga | .787 | .893 | .173 | .100 |
| Chelsea | .375 | .298 | .621 | .648 |
| Chicago | .286 | .285 | .676 | .703 |
| Cincinnati | .335 | .323 | .625 | .666 |
| Cleveland | .406 | .521 | .555 | .459 |
| Columbus | .564 | .532 | .416 | .451 |
| Covington | .351 | .279 | .649 | .721 |
| Dallas | .702 | .706 | .280 | .286 |
| Davenport | .461 | .471 | .522 | .503 |
| Dayton | .579 | .525 | .391 | .470 |
| Denver | .421 | .522 | .537 | .455 |
| Des Moines | .681 | .837 | .271 | .145 |
| Detroit | .408 | .330 | .549 | .662 |
| Dubuque | .254 | .240 | .746 | .759 |
| Duluth | .624 | .441 | .371 | .549 |
| Elizabeth | .443 | .394 | .537 | .605 |
| Elmira | .437 | — | .533 | — |
| Erie | .330 | .354 | .657 | .644 |
| Evansville | .550 | .432 | .408 | .558 |
| Fall River | .144 | .120 | .832 | .876 |
| Fort Wayne | .602 | .758 | .378 | .236 |
| Galveston | .353 | .260 | .596 | .727 |
| Grand Rapids | .608 | .550 | .347 | .446 |
| Harrisburg | .778 | .871 | .143 | .116 |
| Hartford | .440 | .345 | .530 | .628 |
| Haverhill | .345 | .327 | .598 | .660 |
| Hoboken | .276 | .266 | .713 | .723 |
| Holyoke | .166 | .136 | .834 | .859 |
| Houston | .607 | .529 | .385 | .458 |
| Indianapolis | .671 | .621 | .261 | .373 |
| Jersey City | .269 | .254 | .717 | .742 |
| Kansas City, Kans. | .578 | .538 | .379 | .442 |
| Kansas City, Mo. | .584 | .662 | .377 | .320 |
| LaCrosse | .451 | .367 | .541 | .628 |
| Lancaster | .646 | .756 | .264 | .236 |
| Lawrence | .187 | .139 | .809 | .856 |
| Lincoln | .679 | .666 | .297 | .311 |
| Little Rock | .831 | .693 | .121 | .293 |
| Los Angeles | .606 | .510 | .338 | .461 |

| City | Proportion Protestant, 1890 | Proportion Protestant, 1906 | Proportion Catholic, 1890 | Proportion Catholic, 1906 |
|---|---|---|---|---|
| Louisville | .527 | .412 | .460 | .579 |
| Lowell | .250 | .182 | .745 | .814 |
| Lynn | .416 | .291 | .539 | .699 |
| Manchester | .237 | .163 | .731 | .832 |
| Memphis | .579 | .844 | .369 | .145 |
| Milwaukee | .466 | .339 | .514 | .655 |
| Minneapolis | .399 | .504 | .581 | .483 |
| Mobile | .734 | .578 | .249 | .414 |
| Nashville | .792 | .858 | .199 | .136 |
| Newark | .402 | .357 | .562 | .633 |
| New Bedford | .250 | .163 | .688 | .832 |
| New Haven | .472 | .320 | .500 | .675 |
| New Orleans | .268 | .198 | .702 | .797 |
| New York | .266 | .203 | .680 | .779 |
| Norfolk | .881 | .844 | .103 | .148 |
| Oakland | .472 | .351 | .433 | .631 |
| Omaha | .506 | .490 | .411 | .488 |
| Paterson | .398 | .377 | .586 | .609 |
| Pawtucket | .223 | .251 | .776 | .747 |
| Peoria | .521 | .384 | .430 | .610 |
| Philadelphia | .481 | .456 | .489 | .524 |
| Pittsburgh | .427 | .380 | .538 | .608 |
| Portland, Me. | .493 | .488 | .480 | .510 |
| Portland, Ore. | .358 | .530 | .546 | .449 |
| Providence | .301 | .211 | .660 | .781 |
| Quincy | .457 | .352 | .524 | .648 |
| Reading | .655 | .737 | .335 | .258 |
| Richmond | .892 | .834 | .094 | .158 |
| Rochester | .441 | — | .537 | — |
| Sacramento | .287 | .342 | .662 | .588 |
| Saginaw | .468 | .498 | .528 | .499 |
| St. Joseph | .535 | .564 | .404 | .398 |
| St. Louis | .387 | .295 | .579 | .696 |
| St. Paul | .263 | .284 | .720 | .706 |
| Salem | .225 | .207 | .755 | .791 |
| Salt Lake City | .091 | .134 | .077 | .163 |
| San Antonio | .410 | .321 | .566 | .655 |
| San Francisco | .183 | .152 | .761 | .833 |
| Savannah | .781 | .793 | .190 | .200 |
| Scranton | .327 | .309 | .632 | .682 |
| Seattle | .719 | .471 | .249 | .504 |
| Sioux City | .524 | .643 | .463 | .344 |
| Somerville | .417 | .318 | .583 | .674 |
| Springfield, Mass. | .469 | .314 | .523 | .678 |
| Springfield, Ohio | .655 | .716 | .315 | .281 |
| Syracuse | .476 | .347 | .472 | .643 |

| City | Proportion Protestant, 1890 | Proportion Protestant, 1906 | Proportion Catholic, 1890 | Proportion Catholic, 1906 |
|---|---|---|---|---|
| Tacoma | .443 | .686 | .552 | .301 |
| Taunton | .318 | .217 | .678 | .783 |
| Terre Haute | .583 | .677 | .409 | .302 |
| Toledo | .406 | .700 | .554 | .281 |
| Topeka | .756 | .830 | .186 | .162 |
| Trenton | .434 | .418 | .556 | .573 |
| Troy | .273 | .324 | .708 | .670 |
| Utica | .506 | .293 | .462 | .704 |
| Washington | .594 | .669 | .386 | .324 |
| Waterbury | .255 | .215 | .736 | .781 |
| Wheeling | .540 | .516 | .439 | .464 |
| Wilkes-Barre | .417 | .374 | .548 | .619 |
| Williamsport | .744 | .776 | .253 | .220 |
| Wilmington | .580 | .455 | .404 | .539 |
| Worcester | .370 | .286 | .617 | .704 |
| Yonkers | .329 | .204 | .664 | .794 |
| Youngstown | .527 | .814 | .458 | .173 |

# A Typology of Urban Religious Change, 1890–1906

Below, 118 cities in the sample are classified on the basis of changes which occurred between 1890 and 1906 in the sizes of the Protestant and Catholic fractions of their reported total church membership (see Appendix D).

Four cities had to be excluded from this typology: Auburn, Elmira, and Rochester, New York lack data on Roman Catholic Church membership in 1906; Latter-day Saints (Mormons) predominated in Salt Lake City at both time points, so that city could not be classified.

**Cities with Protestant Majorities, 1890 and 1906** *(N = 43)*

CHANGES, 1890–1906

*Protestants gain, Catholics lose*
Akron
Binghamton
Canton
Chattanooga
Des Moines
Fort Wayne
Harrisburg
Kansas City, Mo.
Lancaster
Memphis
Nashville
Reading
St. Joseph
Sioux City
Springfield, Ohio
Terre Haute
Topeka
Washington
Williamsport
Youngstown

176

*Both groups gain*
  Allentown
  Augusta
  Baltimore
  Birmingham
  Dallas
  Savannah

*Protestants lose, Catholics gain*
  Altoona
  Atlanta
  Camden
  Charleston
  Columbus
  Dayton
  Grand Rapids
  Houston
  Indianapolis
  Kansas City, Kans.
  Lincoln
  Little Rock
  Los Angeles
  Mobile
  Norfolk
  Richmond
  Wheeling

## Cities in Religious Transition *(N = 20)*

CHANGES, 1890–1906

  *Protestant majority to no majority*
    Omaha

  *Protestant majority to Catholic majority*
    Allegheny
    Duluth
    Evansville
    Louisville
    Peoria
    Seattle
    Utica
    Wilmington

  *No majority to Catholic majority*
    Oakland
    Philadelphia
    Portland, Me.
    Syracuse

*Catholic majority to Protestant majority*
Cleveland
Denver
Minneapolis
Portland, Ore.
Tacoma
Toledo

*Catholic majority to no majority*
Saginaw

## Cities with Catholic Majorities, 1890 and 1906 *(N = 55)*

CHANGES, 1890–1906

*Catholics lose, Protestants gain*
Boston
Davenport
Erie
Pawtucket
Sacramento
St. Paul
Troy

*Both groups gain*
Bay City

*Catholics gain, Protestants lose*
Albany
Bridgeport
Brockton
Buffalo
Cambridge
Chelsea
Chicago
Cincinnati
Covington
Detroit
Dubuque
Elizabeth
Fall River
Galveston
Hartford
Haverhill
Hoboken
Holyoke
Jersey City
LaCrosse
Lawrence
Lowell

Lynn
Manchester
Milwaukee
Newark
New Bedford
New Haven
New Orleans
New York
Paterson
Pittsburgh
Providence
Quincy
St. Louis
Salem
San Antonio
San Francisco
Scranton
Somerville
Springfield, Mass.
Taunton
Trenton
Waterbury
Wilkes-Barre
Worcester
Yonkers

# Religious Diversity Scores for 122 Cities, 1890 and 1906

Scores on the two indexes of religious diversity which serve as key variables in the empirical analyses of the cities in this study are listed below. The technique for computing these scores is illustrated in detail by Lieberson (1969; cf. Agresti and Agresti, 1977; Gibbs and Poston, 1975; Teachman, 1980). A short summary of the process will suffice here.

A city's score on either index is calculated by squaring, successively, the relative proportions of church membership reported for each relevant religious group, summing these quantities across all such groups represented in the city, and subtracting this total from one. The calculation is complicated in one minor way: the total number of members of "Other" religious bodies is first divided arbitrarily into three segments, of one-half, one-third, and one-sixth of the total, respectively, before squaring and deduction from one. This procedure, recommended by Lieberson (1969: 861), is designed to adjust the index to reflect the heterogeneous composition of the residual category and, accordingly, to prevent its size from affecting the diversity score in as direct a manner as do the sizes of the other, more descriptive, classifications. One exception to this practice was allowed: because Latter-day Saints (Mormons) were in the majority at both time points in their home base, Salt Lake City, their membership was extracted from the residual category and treated as a fourth religious subcommunity in the calculation of that city's overall level of religious diversity.

Diversity scores in theory may range from zero to one, but in actual practice, the upper bound merely approaches unity, as the number of categories into which the population has been divided increases. It is possible to standardize the diversity scores to eliminate the truncation of range that is an artifact of the number of subclasses in the population. This adjustment is accomplished by dividing the raw diversity scores by $1 - (1/N)$, where $N$ is the number of categories across which the population may be distributed; a diversity score is thus represented as a proportion of its theoretical maximum (Land, 1970: 275–276). However, for purposes of description and most kinds of comparison, the unstandardized scores are superior; hence, no standardization has been attempted here.

Because the number of categories employed in calculating the index of diver-

sity among Protestants is greater than the number upon which the overall diversity index is based, the Protestant diversity scores, inspection of the table below will reveal, are uniformly higher. This comparison may be grasped nonmathematically by recalling that the diversity indexes are interpreted substantively as the probability that any two church members in a city, chosen at random, will have different religious affiliations. Obviously, the greater the number of religious distinctions recognized in any population, the more likely it will be to fail to match pairs of persons simply by chance.

Auburn, Elmira, and Rochester, New York are missing data required for the calculation of the 1906 Protestant-Catholic-Jewish-Other diversity index.

| City | Protestant-Catholic-Jewish-Other diversity, 1890 | Protestant-Catholic-Jewish-Other diversity, 1906 | Diversity among Protestants, 1890 | Diversity among Protestants, 1906 |
|---|---|---|---|---|
| Akron | .455 | .342 | .861 | .880 |
| Albany | .499 | .461 | .854 | .850 |
| Allegheny | .486 | .502 | .864 | .864 |
| Allentown | .292 | .289 | .729 | .716 |
| Altoona | .405 | .483 | .801 | .841 |
| Atlanta | .169 | .178 | .755 | .843 |
| Auburn | .500 | — | .785 | .782 |
| Augusta | .308 | .283 | .723 | .773 |
| Baltimore | .524 | .506 | .860 | .891 |
| Bay City | .479 | .448 | .804 | .832 |
| Binghamton | .502 | .482 | .790 | .805 |
| Birmingham | .450 | .413 | .825 | .860 |
| Boston | .377 | .428 | .842 | .809 |
| Bridgeport | .504 | .392 | .824 | .852 |
| Brockton | .478 | .457 | .736 | .819 |
| Buffalo | .477 | .447 | .822 | .858 |
| Cambridge | .443 | .395 | .780 | .844 |
| Camden | .431 | .487 | .776 | .760 |
| Canton | .518 | .208 | .839 | .863 |
| Charleston | .339 | .409 | .822 | .851 |
| Chattanooga | .350 | .193 | .854 | .878 |
| Chelsea | .474 | .490 | .763 | .831 |
| Chicago | .461 | .425 | .837 | .865 |
| Cincinnati | .496 | .452 | .824 | .875 |
| Cleveland | .526 | .518 | .892 | .901 |
| Columbus | .509 | .513 | .837 | .857 |
| Covington | .456 | .402 | .851 | .881 |
| Dallas | .429 | .420 | .854 | .878 |
| Davenport | .515 | .525 | .865 | .862 |
| Dayton | .511 | .503 | .874 | .893 |
| Denver | .534 | .520 | .875 | .880 |

| City | Protestant-Catholic-Jewish-Other diversity, 1890 | Protestant-Catholic-Jewish-Other diversity, 1906 | Diversity among Protestants, 1890 | Diversity among Protestants, 1906 |
|---|---|---|---|---|
| Des Moines | .462 | .278 | .863 | .877 |
| Detroit | .531 | .453 | .848 | .842 |
| Dubuque | .379 | .366 | .813 | .817 |
| Duluth | .473 | .504 | .858 | .822 |
| Elizabeth | .515 | .479 | .747 | .797 |
| Elmira | .524 | — | .839 | .833 |
| Erie | .460 | .460 | .846 | .831 |
| Evansville | .529 | .501 | .874 | .875 |
| Fall River | .287 | .219 | .808 | .831 |
| Fort Wayne | .494 | .370 | .693 | .725 |
| Galveston | .517 | .404 | .861 | .867 |
| Grand Rapids | .509 | .499 | .848 | .854 |
| Harrisburg | .372 | .227 | .813 | .831 |
| Hartford | .525 | .486 | .759 | .806 |
| Haverhill | .522 | .457 | .827 | .830 |
| Hoboken | .416 | .407 | .772 | .787 |
| Holyoke | .277 | .244 | .801 | .795 |
| Houston | .484 | .510 | .838 | .860 |
| Indianapolis | .479 | .475 | .857 | .886 |
| Jersey City | .414 | .384 | .848 | .854 |
| Kansas City, Kans. | .521 | .516 | .798 | .883 |
| Kansas City, Mo. | .516 | .459 | .872 | .896 |
| LaCrosse | .503 | .471 | .742 | .689 |
| Lancaster | .511 | .373 | .740 | .820 |
| Lawrence | .311 | .248 | .839 | .857 |
| Lincoln | .450 | .459 | .861 | .863 |
| Little Rock | .292 | .434 | .850 | .883 |
| Los Angeles | .518 | .528 | .856 | .892 |
| Louisville | .511 | .496 | .827 | .889 |
| Lowell | .383 | .304 | .835 | .848 |
| Lynn | .536 | .427 | .802 | .848 |
| Manchester | .409 | .281 | .841 | .852 |
| Memphis | .526 | .267 | .856 | .840 |
| Milwaukee | .519 | .456 | .623 | .607 |
| Minneapolis | .503 | .512 | .857 | .846 |
| Mobile | .399 | .495 | .623 | .797 |
| Nashville | .334 | .246 | .820 | .875 |
| Newark | .522 | .471 | .833 | .859 |
| New Bedford | .463 | .282 | .854 | .870 |
| New Haven | .526 | .441 | .757 | .796 |
| New Orleans | .435 | .326 | .877 | .856 |
| New York | .465 | .352 | .852 | .861 |
| Norfolk | .213 | .266 | .765 | .829 |

| City | Protestant-Catholic-Jewish-Other diversity, 1890 | Protestant-Catholic-Jewish-Other diversity, 1906 | Diversity among Protestants, 1890 | Diversity among Protestants, 1906 |
|------|------|------|------|------|
| Oakland | .587 | .478 | .868 | .882 |
| Omaha | .571 | .521 | .863 | .877 |
| Paterson | .498 | .486 | .818 | .843 |
| Pawtucket | .348 | .380 | .800 | .802 |
| Peoria | .543 | .480 | .842 | .862 |
| Philadelphia | .529 | .517 | .845 | .857 |
| Pittsburgh | .528 | .486 | .862 | .882 |
| Porland, Me. | .526 | .502 | .808 | .853 |
| Portland, Ore. | .569 | .518 | .886 | .891 |
| Providence | .473 | .346 | .843 | .850 |
| Quincy | .516 | .457 | .798 | .856 |
| Reading | .459 | .391 | .770 | .762 |
| Richmond | .196 | .279 | .484 | .786 |
| Rochester | .517 | — | .862 | .854 |
| Sacramento | .478 | .535 | .891 | .871 |
| Saginaw | .502 | .503 | .787 | .790 |
| St. Joseph | .549 | .524 | .877 | .906 |
| St. Louis | .515 | .429 | .863 | .900 |
| St. Paul | .412 | .421 | .827 | .813 |
| Salem | .379 | .331 | .823 | .842 |
| Salt Lake City | .320 | .469 | .805 | .868 |
| San Antonio | .511 | .468 | .866 | .889 |
| San Francisco | .386 | .284 | .876 | .900 |
| Savannah | .353 | .330 | .647 | .699 |
| Scranton | .492 | .439 | .823 | .850 |
| Seattle | .422 | .524 | .856 | .868 |
| Sioux City | .511 | .468 | .846 | .830 |
| Somerville | .486 | .445 | .794 | .792 |
| Springfield, Mass. | .506 | .442 | .754 | .782 |
| Springfield, Ohio | .471 | .409 | .862 | .867 |
| Syracuse | .548 | .465 | .875 | .868 |
| Tacoma | .499 | .438 | .861 | .854 |
| Taunton | .440 | .340 | .805 | .809 |
| Terre Haute | .494 | .450 | .865 | .868 |
| Toledo | .527 | .431 | .792 | .829 |
| Topeka | .393 | .285 | .867 | .889 |
| Trenton | .503 | .497 | .796 | .835 |
| Troy | .424 | .446 | .812 | .821 |
| Utica | .530 | .419 | .834 | .860 |
| Washington | .498 | .448 | .787 | .852 |
| Waterbury | .394 | .343 | .771 | .811 |
| Wheeling | .515 | .519 | .809 | .839 |
| Wilkes-Barre | .525 | .477 | .853 | .851 |

| City | Protestant-Catholic-Jewish-Other diversity, 1890 | Protestant-Catholic-Jewish-Other diversity, 1906 | Diversity among Protestants, 1890 | Diversity among Protestants, 1906 |
|---|---|---|---|---|
| Williamsport | .383 | .350 | .849 | .859 |
| Wilmington | .500 | .503 | .739 | .799 |
| Worcester | .483 | .423 | .789 | .818 |
| Yonkers | .451 | .329 | .809 | .808 |
| Youngstown | .512 | .307 | .876 | .882 |

# A Note on Weighted Least Squares (WLS) Regression Analysis

There is reason to suspect that with historical Census data, such as those employed in this study, error would not be a constant element of each observation, but rather would increase in proportion to the size of the total count. For example, counts of church membership in larger cities probably contain more spurious entries than statistics of religious affiliation for smaller places. Any ordinary least squares (OLS) model, then, will lose its predictive power as observations on the dependent variable increase in size.

As a consequence, variance around the fit to these data of an OLS model will be correlated with predictors in the model that are also functions of scale. This problem is especially acute in equations where, to avoid resort to ratio measures, population is entered as an explicit control for the effects of scale on other variables (Bollen and Ward, 1979: 437, 441–443; Kasarda and Nolan, 1979: 222–223, 225n; Pendleton et al., 1979: 470). Residual variance around predictions of the dependent variable will increase as the size of observations increases. The presence of this relation, however, violates one of the fundamental assumptions under which any OLS regression analysis is conducted, namely that individual disturbance terms are, as a group, homoscedastic (i.e., they exhibit a constant variance across the range of values of the dependent variable).

In short, larger values are troublesome under such conditions in that they yield greater residuals from regression; they are, by implication, empirically less trustworthy and practically less useful in estimating true regression slopes than are the smaller observations. Weighted least squares (WLS) analysis (Berry and Feldman, 1985: 77–88; Bollen and Ward, 1979: 444–446; Fligstein, 1981: 120, 210–212; Kasarda and Nolan, 1979: 223, 225n; Rao and Miller, 1971: 77–80; Wonnacott and Wonnacott, 1970: 132–135) remedies this imbalance in a straightforward manner. The solution is sought in the proportional reduction of suspect data points (and hence a reduction in their influence on the regression calculations) in accordance with some size factor. The reduction is accomplished, in research applications, by transformation of the regression equation into a statistically more sound algebraic equivalent. In the WLS analyses in this study, each term in the

185

equation is divided by a population variable also appearing in the model. Data are thus "weighted" by the reciprocal of the population of the city from which they were drawn, and the common contribution of scale is removed. This procedure has the additional advantages of alleviating skewness and lowering multicollinearity among the explanatory variables.

The reexpressed quantities are then analyzed, using OLS, for their effects on the dependent variable, which has likewise been transformed. The value of the intercept in the resulting estimated equation is interpreted as the coefficient for population, while the slope associated with population's reciprocal is actually the intercept.

Besides this minor transposition, one further complication is introduced in deriving WLS estimates from OLS on transformed data: conventional goodness-of-fit statistics for OLS equations provided by statistical packages are inappropriate to the WLS case (Buse, 1973; Hibbs, 1974: 269n, 288n, 302n). Furthermore, there is no widely accepted analogue in WLS to the familiar OLS coefficient of determination $(R^2)$. $R^2$ estimated for a weighted equation using the OLS formula will retain its customary meaning only if the intercepts in the original and in the transformed equations are identical (Buse, 1973: 108); this is seldom the case. For this reason, coefficients of determination have been omitted from the statistics reported for all WLS regression equations in the tables of this study.

# Notes

Chapter I. "As Slavery Never Did"

1. Wendell Phillips (1811–1884) was a native of Boston, and was educated at the Harvard Law School. He devoted the entirety of his adult life to social activism, including a long period in the leadership of the movement to abolish slavery. A noted orator, Phillips appealed as well for prohibition, women's suffrage, and the right of labor to organize. In 1870, Phillips ran as the Prohibitionist candidate for Governor of Massachusetts; in 1879, he delivered the eulogy at the funeral of his friend and fellow abolitionist, William Lloyd Garrison. For a full biography of Phillips, see Bartlett (1961).

2. Weber (1967: 20–40) provides a detailed statistical description of the process of urbanization in the United States over the nineteenth century, with much commentary helpful to understanding this change.

3. Immigration to the United States reached its historical height in the following year, 1907, when 1,285,349 new arrivals landed.

4. The data points are marked by letters indicating the immigrant group whose numbers they gauge ("N" for northwestern Europeans, "C" for central Europeans, "E" for eastern Europeans, and "S" for southern Europeans). The points are connected by line segments (for northwestern Europeans), dots (for central Europeans), crosses (for eastern Europeans), or short dashes (for southern Europeans).

5. For an assessment of this work's strengths and weaknesses, as well as of its significance after one hundred years, see Gaustad (1986).

6. Smith's (1960) three other significant decades are the 1790s (the prelude to the Second Great Awakening), the 1850s (the peak of antebellum revival activity), and the 1950s (the period of the so-called "religious revival"). A slightly different periodization of American religious history, featuring *four* "awakenings" (1730–1760, 1800–1830, 1890–1920, and 1960–1990) is outlined by William G. McLoughlin (1978).

7. H. Paul Douglass (1934: 25, 40) and Robert T. Handy (1953: 20n) are also among those analysts of church history who have proposed 1890 as one possible point of transition in any narrative about Christianity in America. Most

recently, Phillip E. Hammond (1983: 282) has presented the argument for the importance of this period in its simplest terms: "between 1880 and 1920," he asserts, "something really new occurred in American Protestantism" (cf. Hammond, 1985: 55–56). The writings of others, however, emphasize historical continuity, and accordingly, slight the disruption of religion in the nineteenth century caused by urbanization. "Many interpreters of the so-called 'social gospel' have assumed that prior to 1907 or 1890 the hope of a kingdom on earth was practically nonexistent, while Christians directed all their expectations to the heavenly city," H. Richard Niebuhr (1956: 151) charged. "Not only Edwards and Hopkins, but many of their followers in the succeeding decades appear as witnesses to dispute the correctness of this conception." Also discerning precedents for turn-of-the-century religious developments is Smith. "It is true," he admits, "that at the end of the century liberal theology and social Christianity replenished the dying stream of interdenominational harmony. But its headwaters were the springs of brotherly zeal which broke forth in the generation of Robert Baird and A. B. Earle" (Smith, 1957: 85; see also 148–149).

8.   Cities of this size are the smallest geographical subdivisions for which the Census reported religious data. Actually, there existed 124 cities with populations of 25,000 or more in 1890. Because two of these cities – Brooklyn and Long Island City, New York – were consolidated, under the Greater New York Charter of 1898, into boroughs of the City of New York, their 1890 data were merged with those of New York City to ensure the comparability of units over time. This adjustment leaves a group of 122 cases for analysis. A complete list of the cities in the analysis, along with further information about them as a group, is furnished in Appendix A.

9.   Information on a city's year of incorporation is taken from Bureau of the Census (1917). Because the distributions of these two variables are skewed, their arithmetic means are exaggerated indicators of the age and size of the cities selected for analysis. The mean year of legal incorporation of the cities is 1840, their mean 1890 population approximately 115,000.

10.   The other cities of more than one million people in 1900 were Chicago (1,698,575) and Philadelphia (1,293,697).

11.   The five states are Massachusetts, New Jersey, New York, Ohio, and Pennsylvania.

12.   Appendix B contains a list of Census population and church membership totals for 1890 and 1906 for the cities in the analysis. These data are used to compute church membership ratios for each of the cities at both times; these statistics are reported as well in Appendix B.

13.   The two cities which lost total population in the years between 1890 and 1906 were Lincoln and Omaha, Nebraska. Lincoln had a population of 55,154 in 1890, but the Census Bureau estimated that only 48,232 people lived there in 1906, a net loss of 6,922 persons. Omaha had 140,452 inhabitants in 1890, but its population dropped 16,285 – to 124,167 – by 1906 (Carroll, 1894: 91 and Bureau of the Census, 1910: 380–381).

14.   The nine cities in the group which more than doubled in size between 1890 and 1906 were: Duluth, Minnesota; Houston, Texas; Indianapolis, Indiana; Kansas

City, Kansas; Portland, Oregon; St. Joseph, Missouri; Seattle, Washington; Waterbury, Connecticut; and Yonkers, New York.

**15.** Change of equal severity (if on an absolutely smaller scale) occurred in this interval within American Judaism. One estimate holds that the Jewish population of the United States tripled in the years between 1880 and 1900 (Handy, 1971: 74). Unfortunately, the Census data on Jewish religious membership for 1890 and 1906 are not fully comparable (for reasons that are elaborated in Chapter 2), so quantitative summaries of religious change must here be sacrificed. The scope of qualitative change in American Judaism during this time was nevertheless great. This historical period witnessed substantial shifts, both in the composition of the Jewish community and in the direction of its religious behavior. Assimilationist pressures in the latter half of the 1800s had yielded the Reform "tradition," a vital adaptation of ancient beliefs to a new culture. However, prospects for the dominance of this accommodative interpretation of Judaism early in the second century of American nationhood, or for the rapid secularization of the Jewish faith by theological compromise, were buried for a time by the eastern European component of the "new immigration" (Glazer, 1957: 43–78).

Chapter II. "Numbering Israel"

**1.** Throughout this discussion, general phrases such as "religious statistics" and "data on religion" are meant to indicate, more narrowly, census-style counts of persons identified as members of one or another religious group. Surveys of religious belief, experience, and activity—later research brought on by social scientists—are subject to a somewhat different class of criticisms, and are therefore not addressed at any length here.

**2.** The Lord ordered a separate census of this group, embracing all males aged one month and older, some time later (Numbers 3 and 4).

**3.** Religious scruples about the possible repercussions of census taking were common in eighteenth-century England and France, too. See Wolfe (1932: 358, 367–369) for some descriptions. The prohibition persists to this day among some groups. See Harris (1985: 255) for one explanation.

**4.** Returns from this Census are reported by state in Kennedy (1853: 29–45).

**5.** Tables comparing Census church statistics for 1850, 1860, and 1870 by state and by denomination, and a detailed breakdown of the 1870 totals for each state by denomination are contained in Walker (1872: 514–527).

**6.** The schedule itself is reprinted in Wright, with Hunt (1900: 786–794).

**7.** Oddly, statistics on *membership* were not collected for churches in any United States Census until 1880. Previous canvasses relied solely upon estimates of a church's seating accommodations to suggest its congregation's size (cf. Goodman, 1977; Pritchard, 1984: 245, 264n). Roger Kent Finke (1984: 203–219) and Finke and Rodney Stark (1986) have developed regression-based methods for transforming counts of seats into church membership estimates, thus completing the Census time series for the latter half of the nineteenth century.

**8.** This characterization of Seaton was offered by Henry Randall Waite, head of "Statistics of Churches, Schools, and Libraries" for the 1880 Census, whose corre-

spondence with the Reverend William Hull on the lack of a report on churches was quoted in Hull (1889).

9. The other, in Walker's opinion, was the failure of the Census to complete its inquiry on private schools.

10. Colonel Robert Ingersoll (1833–1899), the nineteenth century's most prominent symbol of free-thinking agnosticism, was a lawyer and son of a Congregational minister. From 1856 until his death, he toured the country, speaking against supernaturalism and what he challenged as religious superstition.

11. Henry King Carroll (1848–1931), a Methodist leader, was also a journalist, and religious and political editor of *The Independent,* a Protestant weekly newspaper (see, e.g., Carroll, 1891a, 1891b, 1891c, 1891d). In the second half of his long career, Carroll became an Associate Secretary of the Federal Council of Churches and wrote on the life of Francis Asbury, one of American Methodism's first bishops (Carroll, 1923).

12. The text of this law (32 Stat. L., 51) is reprinted in W. S. Holt (1929: 172–175).

13. Rodney Stark and his colleagues (Stark et al., 1981: 138) suggest that sharp declines in the reported numbers of Southern Baptists and Southern Baptist churches between 1926 and 1936 are probably attributable to "the massive uprooting of rural America, especially in the Dust Bowl region" at the onset of the Depression. "These missing Baptists," they assert, "were simply gone from the farms and small towns where they had been in 1926 and had not yet showed up on the rolls of Baptist churches elsewhere." This explanation possesses a moderate degree of plausibility (cf. Brunner and Lorge, 1937: 299–328; Handy, 1960; Kincheloe, 1937; Landis, 1935), and an element of historiographical drama to boot (cf. Carter, 1954: 222; Garrison, 1933: 261–265), but Stark and his colleagues seem not to be aware of the contemporary controversies surrounding the Census of Religious Bodies. A more mundane reason for the apparent losses among Southern Baptists resides in the documented unwillingness of their ministers to cooperate with the 1936 Census (Murphy, 1941: 18n, 20n, 51). Stark et al. in this instance disregard their own admonition that "we must keep a close eye on the history of specific groups if we are to interpret their membership statistics correctly" (Stark et al., 1981: 139). The Southern Baptists, in their 1937 *Handbook* (cited in Murphy, 1941: 18n), claimed 24,671 churches in 1936. This number implies a slight *gain* over the decade, and not the *decrease* of almost 41 percent found in the Census. This is one of the admittedly rare cases in which denominational statistics appear to be more worthy of trust than those generated by the Census.

14. A contemporary account of the Third Reich's strategies to co-opt, and failing that, to persecute German Christians is given by Bendiscioli (1939).

15. N. J. Demerath, III (1968: 369) guesses that the legislators' neglect of the Census of Religious Bodies occurred "perhaps because of the war." The Second World War had ended a year and a half before the Census schedules were mailed, however; the meaning of this speculation is therefore unclear.

16. More concerted, but likewise unsuccessful, have been campaigns by social scientists and their professional organizations (such as the Population Association

of America) to add a question on religious affiliation to the schedule for the decennial Census of Population (cf. Good, 1959; Petersen, 1962).

**17.**   Original returns of the Census's data on religion are unfortunately not for the most part available today to historical researchers. Some schedules of religious statistics from the decennial censuses of 1850 through 1880 are currently held by the National Archives, whereas others are in the possession of universities, state libraries, or historical societies. Only a portion has been microfilmed. The returns for the 1890 count of church membership burned in a fire in 1921 that destroyed most of the materials from the Eleventh Census. Furthermore, the questionnaires from the 1906, 1916, and 1936 Censuses of Religious Bodies were "disposed of by authorization of Congress" (Davidson and Ashby, 1964: 108). The only manuscripts to have been retained were from the 1926 canvass (National Archives, 1950: 50). They reside in the General Branch of the National Archives, but the 92 feet of records they comprise have not been microfilmed. (Special thanks are due Jerry Hess of the National Archives and Records Service, who supplied the above information.)

**18.**   This process was not duplicated for Eastern Orthodox churches in 1906, although they too regarded all baptized persons as members. "The number of adult males without families is so large," in these groups, the Bureau of the Census (1909: 13) explained, "that the figures may be taken as fairly comparable with those of other bodies." In addition, "no deduction has been made" from membership in the Polish National Church, "because of the small number involved."

**19.**   One source (Brown, 1922: 69) recommended multiplying these counts by *four* in order to arrive at a projection for the size of the entire Jewish population.

**20.**   For earlier and even more extreme estimates of membership concentration, derived from data on church seating capacities in the Censuses of 1850 and 1860, consult Pritchard (1984: 248–250).

**21.**   Moberg credits neither Smith nor Good for this opinion, although Smith's demography text is cited elsewhere in the chapter from which this quotation is drawn (Moberg, 1962: 37, 48). Rather, an official Commerce Department document, *Appraisal of Census Programs* (United States Department of Commerce, 1954), is identified as the source for the condemnation. The reference is erroneous, however. The report does not find any fault with Census religious statistics; it evades the topic of their value altogether. "Since the Committee has made no investigation of this area," the section on "Religious Bodies" (United States Department of Commerce, 1954: 55) reads, "it does not feel qualified to offer recommendations." The data are finally vindicated by Moberg, albeit in small print, in the annotated references at the end of the chapter. There, he instructs readers that the Censuses of Religious Bodies "contain a wealth of statistical and other information about American denominations useful for many purposes in sociological and historical studies" (Moberg, 1962: 48–49). Nevertheless, the negative assessment of Census religious data has survived. The stigma was broadcast to Europe by Joseph S. Roucek, whose article – in English – in the Italian journal *Sociologia Religiosa* (Roucek, 1964) reiterated the Smith-Good-Moberg criticism.

**22.**   Note, in addition, the regular use of Census of Religious Bodies data as an

authoritative standard for comparison in the many volumes on the adaptation of the local church produced under the auspices of the Institute of Social and Religious Research. The results of the Institute's studies are summarized in Douglass and Brunner (1935). The Census data have also been used extensively in social science textbooks (e.g., Kolb and Brunner, 1935; Moberg, 1962; Smith, 1947, 1948).

**23.** Church membership totals for Unitarians, Universalists, and Christian Scientists displayed an exceptional pattern. These more secularized groups exhibited a greater degree of apparent affinity for urban modernity, and their numbers in the population correlated strongly in a positive direction with a city's quality of life (Thorndike, 1939: 97).

**24.** Fry (1930b: 12) reported a similar negative correlation between statewide church membership and suicide rates, using data from the 1926 Census of Religious Bodies.

**25.** Cf. Bainbridge and Stark (1981); Stark et al. (1983); and Wasserman (1978). They do not cite Porterfield's research.

**26.** With respect neither to elementary schools nor to hospitals, however, did Catholic Church involvement seem to be spurred by a religious environment in which specific groups traditionally perceived to be hostile to Catholicism (such as Baptists) predominated. In fact, Westhues (1971a: 466–467) found the opposite to be true: a hostile environment discouraged Catholic social service. This mode of analysis was later extended by Westhues (1976) to a study of Catholic school enrollments in Canadian provinces.

**27.** They have replicated these results in a parallel study of religion in Canada (Bainbridge and Stark, 1982). For a critique of the application of the Stark and Bainbridge cult formation model to Canada, see Bibby and Weaver (1985). A more general critique, the first one to be published, is by Wallis and Bruce (1984; cf. Wallis and Bruce, 1986: 47–80). See also Wallis (1984: 59–64, 92–102, 1985: 140–145). A description by the original authors of work to date on–and a defense of–their controversial project to develop a new sociological theory of religious behavior is contained in Bainbridge and Stark (1984); see also Stark and Bainbridge (1985, 1987).

Chapter III. "An Infinite Variety of Religions"

**1.** For a readable summary of these historical influences, see Miller (1976).

**2.** The text of the brief statute is reprinted in Commager, ed. (1963: 125–126). All quotations are taken from this source.

**3.** For reviews of how denominational diversity has been treated in historical scholarship on American religion, see Ahlstrom (1975a, 1975b), Ernst (1982), Hutchison (1974), and Moore (1986: 3–21).

**4.** This measure is essentially the same as one which is employed frequently by sociologists as an indicator of the degree of the division of labor in a society (Clemente, 1972; Gibbs and Martin, 1962; Gibbs and Poston, 1975; Labovitz and Gibbs, 1964; Land, 1970: 275–276; Rushing and Davies, 1970; Smith and Snow, 1976; Swanson, 1973; Willis, 1982), and by economists as an indicator of the

concentration of producers in a market (cf. Hall and Tideman, 1967). For concise reviews of much of this material, see Carter and Keon (1986), Patil and Taillie (1982), and White (1986). Several alternative indexes were investigated, including Henri Theil's (1972) information theory-based, logarithmic measure of "entropy" in a frequency distribution (cf. Allison, 1978; Teachman, 1980), and a "coefficient of variation" elaborated by Paul D. Allison (1978, 1980). Lieberson's measure was adopted primarily for its ease of computation and the intuitively appealing substantive interpretation its scores allow (Goodman and Kruskal, 1959: 155; Teachman, 1980: 343–344; see also Lieberson, 1978, 1981).

5.   Groups considered in this latter measure number 21 for 1890 and 26 for 1906. Construction of the Protestant diversity index required collapsing data reported for a great number of individual bodies into final composite categories, representing larger denominational "families." For the 1890 version of the Protestant index, 71 distinct designations were aggregated into 21 broad categories of affiliation. The 127 Protestant bodies reporting in 1906 were similarly assumed into 26 such groupings. The categorization of religious bodies followed in this study is reproduced and explained in detail in Appendix C. Because the merged groups were all very small, diversity scores calculated with the aggregated data do not depart widely from scores derived from data which were not aggregated.

6.   Interestingly, the other Far Western cities in the sample, with the exception of San Francisco (which had a large Catholic immigrant population), also ranked near the top of the diversity hierarchy. For more information, and to make further comparisons, consult Appendix F.

Chapter IV. "A Motley of Peoples and Cultures"

1.   This conclusion persists today as one of the broadest axioms of the "human ecology" school of urban theory (see, e.g., Blau, 1977: 162–163; Clemente and Sturgis, 1972: 176–177; Schnore, 1958). For example, Amos H. Hawley (1950: 122), the theorist who codified many of the earliest insights in sociological human ecology, asserts directly that "every increment in size increases the extent to which specialization may be developed."

2.   Fischer (1976: 25–39) labels these, respectively, the "determinist" and the "compositional" approaches to urbanism.

3.   An exception is Borhek and Curtis's (1975: 137–181) effort at analyzing, from the standpoint of a sociology of knowledge, the underpinnings of belief in urban society, and how urbanization transforms belief. Their book is a valuable introduction to the questions examined in this chapter, and in Chapters 6 and 7 of this study.

4.   Counting numbers of religious groups instead of measuring the distribution of church membership in a city reflects a superficial conception of religious diversity – that is, diversity as a variety of religious organizational labels and not as a heterogeneity among participants in the regularized patterns of behavior which constitute the entire social institution. A group-based measure does not penetrate the core of the religious institution; rather, it represents it by the external dimensions of its formal structure. Such representations are not always valid, however.

To illustrate, the vast majority of religious groups have small memberships. The Census, literally going one better the Bible's promise that "whenever two or more of you are gathered . . . ," actually credited as churches some organizations with as few as one member in a city (exactly the membership, for example, of the Church of God and Saints of Christ in Syracuse, New York in 1906). Thus, in a count of groups, many bodies only nominally represented in certain cities are imparted a significance far out of proportion to their numbers. Their presence in a city signifies little about how organized religious life and correlative social action was carried on there differently across wide segments of its people. The number of religious bodies in a city serves better as a quantitative indicator of sectarian religious innovation, and it is all the more important as such because of the often irregular and fleeting character of sects. Viewed in this way, a positive relationship between numbers of religious bodies and urbanization should not be offered as evidence of a broad process of differentiation, for it might as easily be an artifact of the style of religious adaptation of rural migrants to the urban moral order (Holt, 1940; cf. Dynes, 1956; Nelsen and Whitt, 1972; Singleton, 1975).

5. Although Singleton (1979: 225–227) employed a formula for computing religious diversity identical to the one used here, this study, with data from 1890 and 1906, failed to replicate *any* of his statistical estimates of religious diversity, for Los Angeles or for other cities he mentions by name (e.g., Singleton, 1979: xvi). The differences in results are too great to be accounted for by rounding error or by Singleton's practice of interpolating 1906 data back to 1900. Indeed, for his index scores to be valid, there would have to have been a distribution of religious membership across church categories in Los Angeles which was more radically uneven than that of any major American city at the turn of the century. What is more, no means of aggregating denominational groupings (and thus artificially generating religious homogeneity) that was attempted yielded numbers as low. In personal communications, Singleton (1982a, 1982b) explained that his data on church membership, while drawn at the start from the same Census enumerations as are cited herein, were eventually adjusted by him to bring them into conformity with additional information he culled from parish membership records, denominational archives, and other sources. A note to this effect in one of his book's appendixes was omitted by his publisher, he said.

6. Probabilities (*p*-values) for *t* (two-tailed test) for correlation or regression coefficients are listed in the tables, or in the footnotes to the tables. Although achieved levels of significance are reported for most statistical tests computed in this study, the .05 standard is employed throughout in the interpretation of results.

7. A precautionary inspection of scatterplots of the relationships between city size and both types of diversity revealed no noticeable evidence of curvilinearity.

8. Recall from the first chapter that the units of analysis in this study are cities with populations in 1890 of at least 25,000. This restriction was necessary because neither the 1890 decennial Census nor the 1906 Census of Religious Bodies published distributions of church membership by denomination for less populous jurisdictions, although such data were gathered and were compiled in the computation of state and national totals. One can only speculate about how

the limitation of the focus of this study to larger places has affected its analyses of religious diversity. It probably has excluded some of the most religiously homogeneous American settlements, because historical studies of such communities have emphasized their small size. On the other hand, it is hard to imagine an effect of population size – if one exists at all – which is so constricted as to have the range of variation in religious affiliations it can produce confined to a level below 25,000. The possibility of a threshold of maximum diversity due to scale somewhere *above* the lower population boundary of 25,000 is investigated statistically later in this section.

9.  Multiple methods, beyond those recounted above, were employed to test the hypothesis that city size was related to religious heterogeneity. One strategy was to enter the 1890 population total as the sole population indicator, under the assumption that the cultural effect of any given city size lagged behind the date at which it was reached. In another analysis, the population and diversity measures for 1890 and 1906 were transformed into difference scores, and a "regression of first differences" (Wonnacott and Wonnacott, 1970: 140) was computed. However, the use of difference scores has been criticized in the methodological literature (see, e.g., Blau and Duncan, with Tyree, 1967: 152–161, 194–199; Bohrnstedt, 1969: 128; Fuguitt and Lieberson, 1974; Kessler, 1977). Weighted least squares (WLS; see Appendix G) was invoked in a third analysis to alleviate skewness and multicollinearity among the population variables and to correct for heteroscedasticity (Wonnacott and Wonnacott, 1970: 132–135; cf. Berry and Feldman, 1985: 77–88; Bollen and Ward, 1979: 444–446; Fligstein, 1981: 120, 210–212; Kasarda and Nolan, 1979: 223, 225n; Rao and Miller, 1971: 77–80). To weight the data, each term in the equation was divided by population in 1906. Finally, to put to rest concern that the lagged diversity scores interfered with the estimation of the standard errors for the remaining coefficients, regression analyses on "residualized difference scores" (Bohrnstedt, 1969: 118–120; Pendleton, Warren, and Chang, 1979: 461–462; Schuessler, 1974: 395) were performed. Specifically, these analyses of residuals were designed to explain variance in the 1906 diversity variables with the influence of their 1890 versions already removed. In every instance with these alternatives, the different data analysis tack yielded essentially the same findings. For that reason, Table 4.3 presents the OLS results, which are simpler in their derivation and more familiar than the statistics generated by other methods.

10.  Niebuhr's book, originally published in 1929, was written from the standpoint of a theologian, one concerned about compromise of the Christian message by churches that were too closely bound to the social statuses and earthly aspirations of their members. As such, the analysis he pursued is highly critical of denominationalism. In addition, however, it displays a broad sense of history, coupled with a strong grasp of the dynamics of formal organizations. For this reason, *The Social Sources* is instructive even today to students of American religion, and it has rightfully earned their regard as a "classic" (cf. Eister, 1973).

11.  Data with which to calculate these proportions for 1890 are taken from tables of the Census Office (1892). The statistical method employed in this chapter's quantitative analyses of data on nativity and race is known as weighted

least squares (WLS). Because the WLS procedure represents a deliberate, if uncomplicated, variation on standard ("ordinary") least squares techniques, a brief introduction to the method, its logic, and its benefits and limitations, is provided in Appendix G. The terms in every equation estimated in Tables 4.4 through 4.11 were weighted beforehand by total population in 1890.

**12.**   The 1890 Census designation for this category was "Colored," a term embracing Asians and "civilized" American Indians as well as blacks.

**13.**   The numbers of blacks in the populations of major northern cities increased markedly after 1890, although migration to the North was not to reach its historic proportions until the time of the First World War. In Chicago, New York, and Pittsburgh, for example, the black population more than doubled between 1890 and 1900, and in many places it came to exceed that of nearly any new white immigrant group at the turn of the century (Lieberson, 1980: 284, 286–287).

**14.**   The cities regarded as "southern" for the purposes of this study are those that are located within the Census Bureau's current-day South Atlantic, East South Central, and West South Central regions. Specifically, the 22 cities so classified include: Atlanta and Augusta, Georgia; Baltimore, Maryland; Birmingham, Alabama; Charleston, South Carolina; Chattanooga, Tennessee; Covington, Kentucky; Dallas, Galveston, and Houston, Texas; Little Rock, Arkansas; Louisville, Kentucky; Memphis, Tennessee; Mobile, Alabama; Nashville, Tennessee; New Orleans, Louisiana; Norfolk and Richmond, Virginia; San Antonio, Texas; Savannah, Georgia; Washington, D.C.; and Wheeling, West Virginia.

**15.**   This last finding is one of the more intriguing to have been generated here, but because its interpretation carries implications for the history of interreligious relations in America, discussion of it in this chapter would be misplaced. Chapter 8 undertakes an entire set of analyses based on exactly this theme.

Chapter V. "A New Society"

**1.**   George M. Marsden (1980: 204), in a new interpretation of fundamentalism, accords the movement—as a religious ideology—a greater degree of complexity and autonomy than have other authors. He nevertheless explains the sources of the peculiar intensity and timing of fundamentalist sentiment by reference to a kind of "culture shock" which beset Victorian Protestants. These conservative Christians "had retained the dominant beliefs of the culture in which they were raised," and "now found themselves living," in the first decades of the twentieth century, "in a society where these same beliefs were widely considered outdated, or even bizarre." Fundamentalism insulated such "immigrants" to modernity from a widening diversity of worldviews, and so functioned, Marsden claims, as "their own equivalent of the urban ghetto."

**2.**   Some critics apparently had charged that the 1890 manufacturing data were, in fact, *too* complete, and were thus ill-suited to comparison with similar statistics from previous censuses. This complaint, ironically, compelled one former official of the Census (Stuart, 1898), in defending the data, not only to acknowledge, but to stress their limitations.

3. All dollar values were coded just as they were recorded in each Census. Adjustments in value on the basis of price changes between 1890 and 1905, which would have rendered the figures in constant dollars, were not attempted. The difference, anyway, between the 1890 and 1905 versions of the Wholesale Price Index for manufactured commodities is small (86.6 in 1890 vs. 88.5 in 1905, with 100 set at 1913's level), implying approximate equality in prices for manufactured products at these two time points (Bureau of the Census, 1975: 203). The Wholesale Price Index for all commodities, calibrated in 1967 dollars, rose from 28.9 to 31.0 in this decade and one-half, whereas the Bureau of Labor Statistics' Consumer Price Index for all items was unchanged (at 27, where 1967 = 100) across this period (Bureau of the Census, 1975: 199, 211).

4. "Value added" is defined for the purposes of this study as the value of manufactured product in excess of the cost of materials. This indicator is, at best, a crude measure of the value added concept. Because the costs of labor (wages) and miscellaneous expenses (e.g., rentals) are not deducted from the value of a city's total industrial product, value added in manufacturing is overstated for all cities, and even more crucially, within cities, for industries where goods were produced by labor-intensive processes and with relatively inexpensive materials (as, for example, in dressmaking).

5. This variable is simply the number of categories in the Census's standard code of industries in which one or more firms appeared in 1890. It therefore measures something of the breadth of any city's manufacturing activity.

6. Under ordinary circumstances, the simultaneous inclusion in a regression analysis of multiple variables with overlapping empirical referents would invite the statistical problem of multicollinearity. However, because weighted least squares (WLS) transformations substantially reduce intercorrelation among the independent variables, each of the measures of manufacturing may be used in the presence of the others and still not risk inflation of the estimates of their standard errors.

7. Total population in 1890 is adopted as the weighting factor for all terms in the equations in Table 5.1.

8. The multiple regression analyses conducted for Chapters 4, 5, and 6 make successive use of different sets of regressors on the same dependent variable (religious diversity). If any presumably influential independent factor is omitted from an equation, that equation is automatically misspecified, and the coefficients estimated are therefore not to be trusted. Yet, the suspicion here of specification error without an estimation of its empirical effects or the designation of an alternative model is not a major criticism. The charge sounds more damning than it truly is, first because "specification errors may engender biases that are real but nonetheless quantitatively trivial" (Duncan, 1975: 110); and second, because "it is easy to suggest the name of a variable that has been overlooked, though not always so easy to justify a 'true' model that includes it" (Duncan, 1975: 111). For both these reasons, there is good cause to regard the simplified models employed in Chapters 4 through 6 as adequate. In this chapter, the repeated use of the lagged dependent variable as a predictor in effect controls for all conditions in the status quo ante with causal impact on religious diversity. Furthermore, since the analyses in Chap-

ter 6 incorporate group-specific literacy statistics, it would make little sense to carry over into those equations the additional population composition variables that had been proven significant in the analyses contained in Chapter 4. Thus, any misspecification of models committed by not transporting statistically significant variables from chapter to chapter probably generates only negligibly small amounts of bias. The reserved posture toward model-building reflected in these data analyses serves to ratify Otis Dudley Duncan's sentiment that "it is not enough for a skeptical critic to say, 'The model is improperly specified, hence the estimates of structural coefficients are biased.' He must, on the contrary – or *you* must, taking the role of critic – propose a new, 'true' model that shows just wherein the initial model errs, and then compare the two to infer as much as possible about the consequences of the specification error" (Duncan, 1975: 107–108). In accordance with Duncan's advice, the eight multiple regression equations which together comprise the complete analyses of industrialization and religious diversity in this chapter were reestimated. For each equation, the model specified in the tables was augmented by terms for two variables – counts of each city's foreign-born and nonwhite populations in 1890 – whose salience was demonstrated by results discussed in Chapter 4. On the whole, statistics in the new equations suggest interpretations identical to the ones offered in the text of Chapter 5. Furthermore, a notable stability is evident in the magnitudes of even the coefficients for the less influential terms. More specifically, results in five of the eight equations were fully replicated; three others exhibited minor variations, but none undermined the validity of the explications provided in this text. Of the 92 new unstandardized coefficients which were produced in this check, 76 had companions in the old equations to which they could be compared. Of these, just seven coefficients (none of them statistically significant in the first instance) changed signs. Fully eight of the ten coefficients that achieved significance at the .05 level the first time duplicated that performance in a new equation carrying the additional pair of control variables. A ninth coefficient slipped to approximately the .09 level of significance, while the last fell to .16. Conversely, three coefficients of marginal salience in the original calculations rose to statistical significance in their respecified models. Framed equation by equation, however, the conclusions one might draw about the effects of manufacturing activity on religious diversity are substantially the same as before the respecifications.

9.    In Table 5.2, the weighting term for WLS is total population in 1906.

10.    Total population in 1906 again is the common divisor of the terms in these two equations.

11.    Recent survey research (Greeley and Jacobsen, 1978) has shown that differences among ethnic groups in characteristic occupational choices were still evident through the 1970s.

Chapter VI. "No Fast Friend to Policy or Religion"

1.    Persons ten years of age or older who were unable to *write* in *any* language were, for the purposes of the Census, considered illiterate. Some persons could read but not write; almost all persons who could not read also were unable to

write. At best, then, the inability to write functions as an approximate indicator of illiteracy. This definition, further, substantially underestimates the linguistic difficulties of foreigners, many of whom could write in their native language, but not in English. The numbers of illiterate persons in principal American cities in 1890 were reported by the Census Office (1897). These figures were additionally disaggregated by nativity and race, and the detailed counts were coded for this study. Base data on the age distributions of urban populations in 1890, which are necessary in order to calculate accurate estimates of literacy among adults and adolescents, were compiled also from tabulations of the Census Office (1897).

2.   Ethnicity probably played a role in the differences among cities with respect to the literacy of their foreign populations, but data on illiteracy by ethnic group for cities in 1890 were not published by the Census Office. Thus the means to resolve this question quantitatively are not currently available.

3.   However, for a frontal attack on Stone's assertions about religion and literacy, based on a close consideration of sources and documents from the German Reformation, see Strauss (1984).

4.   However, compare the predictions of these theories to the findings of longitudinal, cross-national empirical research on political development (e.g., Flora, 1973).

5.   Illiteracy is the conceptual obverse of literacy, or, more concretely, its empirical lack. The Census Office reported its literacy data in this negative form, which is why an indicator of illiteracy, rather than literacy, is the key independent variable in this analysis. Since one is simply the absence of the other, this choice should make no substantive difference in the findings.

6.   In Table 6.1, the terms in each equation were first weighted by total population, ten years of age and older, in 1890. The analyses in Table 6.2 employed this same quantity, broken down by race, while those conducted for Table 6.3 relied solely on 1890 white population, ten and over, as a weighting factor.


Chapter VII. "God's Bible at the Devil's Girdle"


1.   By 1920, more than 51 percent of Americans lived in a town or city with a population of at least 2,500 persons.

2.   This conception of urbanization has survived to this day, if the characterization of it as a "menace" to historical religion has not retained its negative implications. For instance, the theologian and social critic Harvey Cox, in his popular discussion of *The Secular City* (first published in 1965) repeats the old theme in a new, more positive light. The high mobility Cox describes as a part of urban life "does play havoc with traditional religion. It separates people from the holy places. It mixes them with neighbors whose gods have different names and who worship them in different ways" (Cox, 1966: 47). Yet he goes on to praise the role of urbanization in contributing to the creation of a new religious order. Urbanization, Cox explains, precisely because it *is* destructive of old orthodoxies, serves as a kind of urban renewal program for the City on the Hill, clearing the spiritual landscape of the structures of petrified practice, and leaving the site

barren but nonetheless ready for the arrival of the future "religionless Christianity" of the radical theologians.

3.  For an appreciation of Nathaniel Ward as a prescient thinker on the relationship between religious liberty and the shape of religious institutions, see Miller (1935).

4.  For critical reviews of the secularization literature, see Coleman (1978), Dobbelaere (1981, 1984), Glasner (1977), Lyon (1981, 1985, 1987), Robertson (1971), and Shiner (1967a, 1967b).

5.  Recall the discussion of this phenomenon in Chapter 3.

6.  A possible exception to this pattern was life in early Pennsylvania, one of the so-called "middle colonies," whose "diversity promoted a rule of religious pluralism in the republic that has persisted to this day" (Zuckerman, 1982: 13). How meaningful this pluralism was, though, is difficult to estimate from the historical record. Laura L. Becker (1982: 198), for example, found that just before the Revolution the town of Reading "was clearly characterized by religious diversity." What this fact implies for patterns of contact among members of different religious groups, Becker concedes, is not so clear. "Physical proximity," she notes (Becker, 1982: 196), "does not guarantee meaningful interaction between individuals." Yet "the citizens of Reading were quite broad minded in their attitudes toward other faiths" (Becker, 1982: 204). Religious intermarriage was not infrequent, loans of money routinely were made across religious boundaries, and townspeople often chose as witnesses to their legal declarations and as executors of their estates persons of different religious backgrounds. Church members in Reading additionally shared facilities and even clergy. Likewise, Stephanie Grauman Wolf (1976: 7) opens her study of Germantown, an "urban village" outside Philadelphia, with the observation that "the very heterogeneity and unplanned development of the area speak directly to the later growth of the country at large." In eighteenth-century Germantown, "the variety of ethnic backgrounds . . . was surpassed, almost at once, by the diversity of religious belief and practice" (Wolf, 1976: 129). The significance of this diversity is indicated as well by Wolf (1976: 242): "The dilemma of maintaining religious conviction where each church has an equal share of 'the truth' and of maintaining power where each religion must compete in the open market for public support was seriously raised, perhaps for the first time, in colonial America." Historians have documented similar patterns of religious diversity in another of the "middle colonies" – New York. New York "represented, in germinal form, the very nation that had come into existence by the late nineteenth century" (Klein, 1972: 138). See also Bonomi (1971: 25, 1986); Klein (1974: esp. 97–109, 183–204); Pointer (1982: esp. 101–146); and Smith (1969; cf. Smith, 1973: esp. 179–246). Although evidence of diversity in this one part of the country predates widespread urbanization there, diversity's effects were nevertheless very much the same. The evident "outward indifference" of many colonists to religion "is closely related," according to Martin E. Lodge (1971: 212), "to the denominational heterogeneity of the Middle Colonies. The multiplicity of religions, more than any other single factor, appears to have provided the layman with the incentive to question his inherited faith. Opportunities for doubting one's beliefs were more limited in Europe and in

New England, where a dominant church either suppressed its rivals or relegated them to a distinctly inferior position. But in the Middle Colonies, dozens of denominations competed on a more or less equal footing and the babble of creeds inevitably obscured the old certainties."

7.   For current-day survey evidence supporting the idea that religious heterogeneity promotes interreligious contacts, see Blum (1985).

8.   The results in Table 7.1 are ordered vertically; all equations therefore should be read *down* the columns of the table. Total population in 1906 was used as the weighting factor in Equation 7.1a. In Equations 7.1b and 7.1c, the population "at risk" to Protestantism was the divisor.

9.   Only Jewish heads of families were reported in the membership data of the 1906 Census of Religious Bodies. More complete membership counts did appear in the 1890 Census report, however (Engelman, 1947: 147).

10.   Herberg's conclusion is drawn in part from Ruby Jo Reeves Kennedy's (1944) discovery of a "triple melting-pot" in patterns of ethnic and religious intermarriage in New Haven, Connecticut between 1870 and 1940. Italian and Irish Catholics, for example, were found to marry outside their ethnic boundaries with greater frequency over time, but marriages across religious communities were seldom in evidence. See also Kennedy (1952), for an update of this research, and Peach (1980), for a careful and critical reexamination.

Chapter VIII. "If the Religion of Rome Becomes Ours"

1.   Protestant and Catholic percentages of total church membership in 1890 and 1906, for each city in the analysis, are listed in Appendix D. In the section after it, Appendix E, 118 of the cities are organized, for ease in description, into a typology based on their relative proportions of Protestants and Catholics and on changes in these proportions over time. Forty-three cities in the study maintained Protestant majorities between 1890 and 1906; in 55, Catholics predominated in both years; and in 20, the religious situation was more fluid, with neither group holding sway at both times. Jews, although also growing in number in the concluding decades of the nineteenth century, were still not enough of a presence in most cities to compete seriously for cultural dominance.

2.   The results in Equations 8.1a and 8.1b are similar in substance to those reported in Equations 4.10a and 4.10b, which were computed for Chapter 4. Discussion of this pattern of findings, however, has been deferred until now.

3.   For an analysis with a similar approach, see Alger (1974). Her biographical data illustrate how, among leading members of religious bodies in the American colonies, support for independence varied according to their group's social standing and the heterogeneity of the region. Leaders in high-status groups that were unchallenged for cultural dominance were more likely to be supportive of independence, as were representatives of low-status groups. Competing privileged groups in a diverse religious environment, on the other hand, could risk no division and win no improvements by backing the Revolution. They tended toward loyalism as a defense of their social position.

Chapter IX. "Matters Merely Indifferent"

1.   For a critical discussion of Lieberson's book, see Sullivan (1982).
2.   Historian Mark A. Noll (1987) documents a shift in the axes of Protestant vs. Catholic conflict along these same lines, and offers some reflections on possible future directions.

# REFERENCES

Abel, Theodore. 1933. *Protestant Home Missions to Catholic Immigrants.* New York: Institute of Social and Religious Research.

Abell, Aaron Ignatius. 1943. *The Urban Impact on American Protestantism, 1865–1900.* Cambridge, Mass.: Harvard University Press.

Abrahamson, Mark. 1974. "The Social Dimensions of Urbanism." *Social Forces* 52 (March): 376–383.

Agresti, Alan, and Barbara F. Agresti. 1977. "Statistical Analysis of Qualitative Variation." Pp. 204–237 in *Sociological Methodology, 1978,* edited by Karl F. Schuessler. San Francisco: Jossey-Bass.

Ahlstrom, Sydney E. 1975a. *A Religious History of the American People: Volume 1.* New York: Doubleday.

1975b. *A Religious History of the American People: Volume 2.* New York: Doubleday.

1978. *"E Pluribus Unum:* Religious Pluralism and the American Ideal." *Soundings* 61 (Fall): 328–338.

Albanese, Catherine L. 1981. *America: Religions and Religion.* Belmont, Calif.: Wadsworth.

Alger, Janet Merrill. 1974. "The Impact of Ethnicity and Religion on Social Development in Revolutionary America." Pp. 327–339 in *Ethnicity and Nation-Building: Comparative, International, and Historical Perspectives,* edited by Wendell Bell and Walter E. Freeman. Beverly Hills, Calif.: Sage.

Allison, Paul D. 1978. "Measures of Inequality." *American Sociological Review* 43 (December): 865–880.

1980. "Inequality and Scientific Productivity." *Social Studies of Science* 10 (May): 163–179.

American Economic Association. 1899. *The Federal Census: Critical Essays by Members of the American Economic Association; Collected and Edited by a Special Committee.* New York: Macmillan.

Angell, Robert Cooley. 1951. *The Moral Integration of American Cities.* Chicago: University of Chicago Press.

Angoff, Charles, and H. L. Mencken. 1931. "The Worst American State: Part III." *The American Mercury* 24 (November): 355–371.

Argyle, Michael. 1958. *Religious Behavior.* New York: Free Press.

Azzi, Corry, and Ronald Ehrenberg. 1975. "Household Allocation of Time and Church Attendance." *Journal of Political Economy* 83 (February): 27–53.

Bainbridge, William Sims, and Laurie Russell Hatch. 1982. "Women's Access to Elite Careers: In Search of a Religion Effect." *Journal for the Scientific Study of Religion* 21 (September): 242–254.

Bainbridge, William Sims, and Rodney Stark. 1981. "Suicide, Homicide, and Religion: Durkheim Reassessed." *The Annual Review of the Social Sciences of Religion* 5: 33–56.

        1982. "Church and Cult in Canada." *Canadian Journal of Sociology* 7 (Fall): 351–366.

        1984. "Formal Explanation of Religion: A Progress Report." *Sociological Analysis* 45 (Summer): 145–158.

Bartlett, Irving H. 1961. *Wendell Phillips: Brahmin Radical.* Boston: Beacon.

Bass, Archer B. 1929. *Protestantism in the United States.* New York: Crowell.

Becker, Laura L. 1982. "Diversity and Its Significance in an Eighteenth-Century Pennsylvania Town." Pp. 196–221 in *Friends and Neighbors: Group Life in America's First Plural Society,* edited by Michael Zuckerman. Philadelphia: Temple University Press.

Beecher, Lyman. 1864. "Downfall of the Standing Order." Pp. 342–349 in *Autobiography, Correspondence, Etc., of Lyman Beecher, D.D.: Volume I,* edited by Charles Beecher. New York: Harper Bros.

Bender, Thomas. 1982. *Community and Social Change in America.* Baltimore: Johns Hopkins University Press.

Bendiscioli, Mario. 1939. *Nazism versus Christianity,* translated by Gerald Griffin. London: Skeffington.

Berger, Peter L. 1963. "A Market Model for the Analysis of Ecumenicity." *Social Research* 30 (Spring): 77–93.

        1967. *The Sacred Canopy: Elements of a Sociological Theory of Religion.* New York: Doubleday.

        1969. *A Rumor of Angels: Modern Society and the Rediscovery of the Supernatural.* New York: Doubleday.

Berger, Peter L., Brigitte Berger, and Hansfried Kellner. 1974. *The Homeless Mind: Modernization and Consciousness.* New York: Random House.

Berger, Peter L., and Thomas Luckmann. 1966. "Secularization and Plural-

ism." *International Yearbook for the Sociology of Religion* 2: 73–86.

Bernard, Richard M., and Bradley R. Rice. 1975. "Political Environment and the Adoption of Progressive Municipal Reform." *Journal of Urban History* 1 (February): 149–174.

Berry, William D., and Stanley Feldman. 1985. *Multiple Regression in Practice.* Beverly Hills, Calif.: Sage.

Bibby, Reginald W., and Harold R. Weaver. 1985. "Cult Consumption in Canada: A Further Critique of Stark and Bainbridge." *Sociological Analysis* 46 (Winter): 445–460.

Blau, Peter M. 1977. *Inequality and Heterogeneity: A Primitive Theory of Social Structure.* New York: Free Press.

　1981. "Introduction: Diverse Views of Social Structure and Their Common Denominator." Pp. 1–23 in *Continuities in Structural Inquiry,* edited by Peter M. Blau and Robert K. Merton. Beverly Hills, Calif.: Sage.

Blau, Peter M., and Otis Dudley Duncan, with Andrea Tyree. 1967. *The American Occupational Structure.* New York: Wiley.

Blum, Terry C. 1985. "Structural Constraints on Interpersonal Relations: A Test of Blau's Macrosociological Theory." *American Journal of Sociology* 91 (November): 511–521.

Bohrnstedt, George W. 1969. "Observations on the Measurement of Change." Pp. 113–133 in *Sociological Methodology, 1969,* edited by Edgar F. Borgatta. San Francisco: Jossey-Bass.

Bollen, Kenneth A., and Sally Ward. 1979. "Ratio Variables in Aggregate Data Analysis: Their Uses, Problems, and Alternatives." *Sociological Methods and Research* 7 (May): 431–450.

Bonomi, Patricia U. 1971. *A Factious People: Politics and Society in Colonial New York.* New York: Columbia University Press.

　1986. *Under the Cope of Heaven: Religion, Society, and Politics in Colonial America.* New York: Oxford University Press.

Bonomi, Patricia U., and Peter R. Eisenstadt. 1982. "Church Adherence in the Eighteenth-Century British American Colonies." *The William and Mary Quarterly* 39 (April): 245–286.

Borhek, James T., and Richard F. Curtis. 1975. *A Sociology of Belief.* New York: Wiley.

Brauer, Jerald C. 1966. "Religious Freedom as a Human Right." Pp. 45–64 in *Religious Liberty: An End and a Beginning; the Declaration on Religious Freedom: An Ecumenical Discussion,* edited by John Courtney Murray, S.J. New York: Macmillan.

Brown, William Adams. 1922. *The Church in America: A Study of the Present Condition and Future Prospects of American Protestantism.* New York: Macmillan.

Brunner, Edmund deS., and Irving Lorge. 1937. *Rural Trends in Depression Years: A Survey of Village-Centered Agricultural Communities, 1930–1936.* New York: Columbia University Press.

Bureau of the Census. 1907. *Manufactures: 1905; Part II: States and Territories.* Washington, D.C.: Government Printing Office.

1909. *Bulletin 103; Religious Bodies: 1906.* Washington, D.C.: Government Printing Office.

1910. *Special Reports; Religious Bodies: 1906; Part I: Summary and General Tables.* Washington, D.C.: Government Printing Office.

1915. *The Story of the Census: 1790–1915.* Washington, D.C.: Bureau of the Census.

1917. *General Statistics of Cities: 1916; Including Statistics of Parks, Playgrounds, Museums and Art Galleries, Zoological Collections, Music and Entertainments, Swimming Pools and Bathing Beaches, and Other Features of the Recreational Service.* Washington, D.C.: Government Printing Office.

1930. *Religious Bodies: 1926; Volume I: Summary and Detailed Tables.* Washington, D.C.: Government Printing Office.

1975. *Historical Statistics of the United States: Colonial Times to 1970, Part I.* Washington, D.C.: Bureau of the Census.

Burr, Nelson R., with James Ward Smith and A. Leland Jamison. 1961. *A Critical Bibliography of Religion in America.* Princeton, N.J.: Princeton University Press.

Buse, A. 1973. "Goodness of Fit in Generalized Least Squares Estimation." *The American Statistician* 27 (June): 106–108.

Canevin, J. F. Regis. 1917. "Loss and Gain in the Catholic Church in the United States (1800–1916)." *The Catholic Historical Review* 2 (January): 377–385.

Carroll, Henry K. 1891a. "The Census of Religious Bodies: Statistics of Fourteen Denominations." *The Independent* 43 (January 22): 120–121.

1891b. "Census Statistics of Churches." *The Independent* 43 (June 4): 840A–840B.

1891c. "The Census of Catholics." *The Independent* 43 (July 30): 1137–1139.

1891d. "Fourth Census Bulletin of Churches." *The Independent* 43 (December 17): 1877–1880.

1894. *Report on Statistics of Churches in the United States at the Eleventh Census: 1890.* Washington, D.C.: Government Printing Office.

1912. *The Religious Forces of the United States: Enumerated, Classified, and Described; Returns for 1900 and 1910 Compared with the Government Census of 1890; Condition and Characteristics of*

*Christianity in the United States: Revised and Brought Down to 1910.* New York: Scribner.

1923. *Francis Asbury in the Making of American Methodism.* New York: Methodist Book Concern.

Carter, Nancy M., and Thomas L. Keon. 1986. "Research Note: The Rise and Fall of the Division of Labour, the Past 25 Years." *Organization Studies* 7: 57–74.

Carter, Paul A. 1954. *The Decline and Revival of the Social Gospel: Social and Political Liberalism in American Protestant Churches, 1920–1940.* Ithaca, N.Y.: Cornell University Press.

Cassedy, James H. 1984. *American Medicine and Statistical Thinking, 1800–1860.* Cambridge, Mass.: Harvard University Press.

Census Office. 1892. *Compendium of the Eleventh Census: 1890; Part I. –Population.* Washington, D.C.: Government Printing Office.

1894. *Compendium of the Eleventh Census: 1890; Part II: Vital and Social Statistics; Educational and Church Statistics; Wealth, Debt, and Taxation; Mineral Industries; Insurance; Foreign Born Population; Manufactures.* Washington, D.C.: Government Printing Office.

1897. *Report on Population of the United States at the Eleventh Census: 1890; Part II.* Washington, D.C.: Government Printing Office.

Chapin, F. Stuart. 1914. "Immigration as a Source of Urban Increase." *Quarterly Publications of the American Statistical Association* 14 (September): 223–227.

Chudacoff, Howard P. 1972. *Mobile Americans: Residential and Social Mobility in Omaha, 1880–1920.* New York: Oxford University Press.

Clark, Earle. 1915. "Contributions to Urban Growth." *Quarterly Publications of the American Statistical Association* 14 (September): 654–671.

Clemente, Frank. 1972. "The Measurement Problem in the Analysis of an Ecological Concept: The Division of Labor." *Pacific Sociological Review* 15 (January): 30–40.

Clemente, Frank, and Richard B. Sturgis. 1972. "The Division of Labor in America: An Ecological Analysis." *Social Forces* 51 (December): 176–182.

Clubb, Jerome M., Erik W. Austin, and Michael W. Traugott. 1981. "Demographic and Compositional Change." Pp. 105–135 in *Analyzing Electoral History: A Guide to the Study of American Voter Behavior,* edited by Jerome M. Clubb, William H. Flanigan, and Nancy H. Zingale. Beverly Hills, Calif.: Sage.

Coe, George A., with J. L. Gillen, Cecil C. North, Edwin C. Walker, T. J. Riley, and J. E. Cutler. 1910. "Notes on the Recent Census of Religious Bodies." *American Journal of Sociology* 15 (May): 806–816.

Cohen, Patricia Cline. 1982. *A Calculating People: The Spread of Numeracy in Early America.* Chicago: University of Chicago Press.

Coleman, John A. 1978. "The Situation for Modern Faith." *Theological Studies* 39 (December): 601–632.

Commager, Henry Steele. 1950. *The American Mind: An Interpretation of American Thought and Character Since the 1880s.* New Haven, Conn.: Yale University Press.

    1977. *The Empire of Reason: How Europe Imagined and America Realized the Enlightenment.* New York: Doubleday.

    ed. 1963. *Documents of American History; Volume I: To 1898; Seventh Edition.* East Norwalk, Conn.: Appleton-Century-Crofts.

Commager, Henry Steele, and Richard Brandon Morris. 1959. "Editors' Introduction." Pp. ix-xii in Harold U. Faulkner, *Politics, Reform, and Expansion: 1890–1900.* New York: Harper Bros.

Cox, Harvey. 1966. *The Secular City: Secularization and Urbanization in Theological Perspective.* New York: Macmillan.

Cressy, David. 1980. *Literacy and the Social Order: Reading and Writing in Tudor and Stuart England.* Cambridge University Press.

Cross, Robert D. 1958. *The Emergence of Liberal Catholicism in America.* Cambridge, Mass.: Harvard University Press.

    1967. "Introduction." Pp. xi-xlii in *The Church and the City: 1865–1910,* edited by Robert D. Cross. Indianapolis, Ind.: Bobbs-Merrill.

Cumbler, John T. 1979. *Working-Class Community in Industrial America: Work, Leisure, and Struggle in Two Industrial Cities, 1880–1930.* Westport, Conn.: Greenwood.

Currie, Robert, Alan Gilbert, and Lee Horsley. 1977. *Churches and Churchgoers: Patterns of Church Growth in the British Isles Since 1700.* New York: Oxford University Press.

Davidson, Katherine H., and Charlotte M. Ashby. 1964. *Preliminary Inventory of the Records of the Bureau of the Census (Record Group 29).* Washington, D.C.: The National Archives.

Davis, Lawrence B. 1973. *Immigrants, Baptists, and the Protestant Mind in America.* Urbana: University of Illinois Press.

Davis, Ozora S. 1909. "The Church and the Immigrant." Pp. 254–262 in *Federal Council of the Churches of Christ in America: Report of the First Meeting of the Federal Council, Philadelphia, 1908,* edited by Elias B. Sanford. New York: Revell.

Demerath, N. J., III. 1968. "Trends and Anti-trends in Religious Change." Pp. 349–445 in *Indicators of Social Change: Concepts and Measurements,* edited by Eleanor Bernert Sheldon and Wilbert E. Moore. New York: Russell Sage Foundation.

Dentler, Robert A., and Kai T. Erikson. 1959. "The Functions of Deviance in Groups." *Social Problems* 7 (Fall): 98–107.

Deutsch, Albert. 1944. "The First U.S. Census of the Insane (1840) and Its Use as Pro-slavery Propaganda." *Bulletin of the History of Medicine* 15 (May): 469–482.

Diamond, Sigmund. 1963. "Introduction." Pp. 3–22 in *The Nation Transformed: The Creation of an Industrial Society,* edited by Sigmund Diamond. New York: Braziller.

Dobbelaere, Karel. 1981. "Secularization: A Multidimensional Concept." *Current Sociology / La Sociologie contemporaine* 29 (Summer): 3–213.

———. 1984. "Secularization Theories and Sociological Paradigms: Convergences and Divergences." *Social Compass* 31: 199–219.

Dolan, Jay P. 1975. *The Immigrant Church: New York's Irish and German Catholics, 1815–1865.* Baltimore: Johns Hopkins University Press.

Dollar, Charles M., and Richard J. Jensen. 1971. *Historian's Guide to Statistics: Quantitative Analysis and Historical Research.* New York: Holt, Rinehart & Winston.

Douglass, H. Paul. 1934. *Church Unity Movements in the United States.* New York: Institute of Social and Religious Research.

———. 1938. "Religion: The Protestant Faiths." Pp. 505–527 in *America Now: An Inquiry into Civilization in the United States,* edited by Harold E. Stearns. New York: Literary Guild.

Douglass, H. Paul, and Edmund deS. Brunner. 1935. *The Protestant Church as a Social Institution.* New York: Russell & Russell.

Duncan, Otis Dudley. 1975. *Introduction to Structural Equation Models.* New York: Academic Press.

Durkheim, Emile. 1933. *The Division of Labor in Society,* translated by George Simpson. New York: Free Press.

———. 1969. "Individualism and the Intellectuals," translated by S. Lukes and J. Lukes. *Political Studies* 17 (March): 19–30.

———. 1982. *The Rules of the Sociological Method,* edited by Steven Lukes and translated by W. D. Halls. New York: Free Press.

Dynes, Russell R. 1956. "Rurality, Migration, and Sectarianism." *Rural Sociology* 21 (March): 25–28.

Eckler, A. Ross. 1972. *The Bureau of the Census.* New York: Praeger.

Eister, Allan W. 1973. "H. Richard Niebuhr and the Paradox of Religious Organization: A Radical Critique." Pp. 355–408 in *Beyond the Classics?: Essays in the Scientific Study of Religion,* edited by Charles Y. Glock and Phillip E. Hammond. New York: Harper & Row.

Engelman, Uriah Zvi. 1935. "The Jewish Synagogue in the United States." *American Journal of Sociology* 41 (July): 44–51.

———. 1947. "Jewish Statistics in the U.S. Census of Religious Bodies (1850–1936)." *Jewish Social Studies* 9 (April): 127–174.

Erikson, Kai T. 1966. *Wayward Puritans: A Study in the Sociology of Deviance.* New York: Wiley.

Ernst, Eldon G. 1982. "Beyond the Protestant Era in American Religious Historiography." Pp. 123–145 in *In the Great Tradition: In Honor of Winthrop S. Hudson, Essays on Pluralism, Voluntarism, and Revivalism,* edited by Joseph D. Ban and Paul R. Dekar. Valley Forge, Penna.: Judson Press.

Faulkner, Harold Underwood. 1931. *The Quest for Social Justice: 1898–1914.* New York: Macmillan.

    1959. *Politics, Reform, and Expansion: 1890–1900.* New York: Harper Bros.

Finke, Roger Kent. 1984. The Churching of America: 1850–1980. Unpublished Ph.D. Dissertation. Department of Sociology, University of Washington.

Finke, Roger, and Rodney Stark. 1986. "Turning Pews into People: Estimating 19th Century Church Membership." *Journal for the Scientific Study of Religion* 25 (June): 180–192.

Fischer, Claude S. 1972. " 'Urbanism as a Way of Life': A Review and an Agenda." *Sociological Methods and Research* 1 (November): 187–242.

    1975a. "The Effect of Urban Life on Traditional Values." *Social Forces* 53 (March): 420–432.

    1975b. "Toward a Subcultural Theory of Urbanism." *American Journal of Sociology* 80 (May): 1319–1341.

    1976. *The Urban Experience.* San Diego, Calif.: Harcourt Brace Jovanovich.

Fishlow, Albert. 1966. "The American Common School Revival: Fact or Fancy?" Pp. 40–67 in *Industrialization in Two Systems: Essays in Honor of Alexander Gerschenkron,* edited by Henry Rosovsky. New York: Wiley.

Fligstein, Neil. 1981. *Going North: Migration of Blacks and Whites from the South, 1900–1950.* New York: Academic Press.

Flora, Peter. 1973. "Historical Processes of Social Mobilization: Urbanization and Literacy, 1850–1965." Pp. 213–258 in *Building States and Nations: Models and Data Resources, Volume I,* edited by S. N. Eisenstadt and Stein Rokkan. Beverly Hills, Calif.: Sage.

Frank, Douglas W. 1986. *Less Than Conquerors: How Evangelicals Entered the Twentieth Century.* Grand Rapids, Mich.: Eerdmans.

Frazier, E. Franklin. 1964. *The Negro Church in America.* Liverpool University Press.

Fry, C. Luther. 1930a. "Organized Religion." *American Journal of Sociology* 35 (May): 1042–1051.

1930b. *The U.S. Looks at Its Churches.* New York: Institute of Social and Religious Research.

Fry, C. Luther, and Mary Frost Jessup. 1933. "Changes in Religious Organizations." Pp. 1009–1060 in *Recent Social Trends in the United States: Report of the President's Research Committee on Social Trends, Volume II.* New York: McGraw-Hill.

Fuguitt, Glenn V., and Stanley Lieberson. 1974. "Correlation of Ratios or Difference Scores Having Common Terms." Pp. 128–144 in *Sociological Methodology, 1973–1974,* edited by Herbert L. Costner. San Francisco: Jossey-Bass.

Furet, Francois, and Jacques Ozouf. 1981. "Three Centuries of Cultural Cross-Fertilization: France." Pp. 214–231 in *Literacy and Social Development in the West: A Reader,* edited by Harvey J. Graff. Cambridge University Press.

Garrison, Winfred Ernest. 1933. *The March of Faith: The Story of Religion in America Since 1865.* New York: Harper Bros.

Gaustad, Edwin Scott. 1976. *Historical Atlas of Religion in America: Revised Edition.* New York: Harper & Row.

1985. "Regionalism in American Religion." Pp. 155–172 in *Religion in the South,* edited by Charles Reagan Wilson. Jackson: University Press of Mississippi.

1986. *"Our Country:* One Century Later." Pp. 85–101 in *Liberal Protestantism: Realities and Possibilities,* edited by Robert S. Michaelson and Wade Clark Roof. New York: Pilgrim Press.

Gibbs, Jack P., and Walter T. Martin. 1962. "Urbanization, Technology, and the Division of Labor: International Patterns." *American Sociological Review* 27 (October): 667–677.

Gibbs, Jack P., and Dudley L. Poston, Jr. 1975. "The Division of Labor: Conceptualization and Related Measures." *Social Forces* 53 (March): 468–476.

Giddings, Franklin H. 1910. "The Social Marking System." *American Journal of Sociology* 15 (May): 721–740.

Gilbert, Alan D. 1980. *The Making of Post-Christian Britain: A History of the Secularization of Modern Society.* New York: Longman.

Gillette, John M. 1911. "The Drift to the City in Relation to the Rural Problem." *American Journal of Sociology* 16 (March): 645–667.

Gillette, John M., and George R. Davies. 1915. "Measure of Rural Migration and Other Factors of Urban Increase in the United States." *Quarterly Publications of the American Statistical Association* 14 (September): 642–653.

Glaab, Charles N., and A. Theodore Brown. 1967. *A History of Urban America.* New York: Macmillan.

Glasner, Peter E. 1977. *The Sociology of Secularisation: A Critique of a Concept.* New York: Routledge & Kegan Paul.

Glazer, Nathan. 1957. *American Judaism.* Chicago: University of Chicago Press.

Glock, Charles Y. 1959. "The Religious Revival in America?" Pp. 25–42 in *Religion and the Face of America,* edited by Jane C. Zahn. Berkeley, Calif.: University Extension, University of California.

Good, Dorothy. 1959. "Questions on Religion in the United States Census." *Population Index* 25 (January): 3–16.

Goodman, Leo A., and William H. Kruskal. 1959. "Measures of Association for Cross Classifications. II: Further Discussion and References." *Journal of the American Statistical Association* 54 (March): 123–163.

Goodman, Paul. 1977. "A Guide to American Church Membership Data Before the Civil War." *Historical Methods Newsletter* 10 (Fall): 183–190.

Goody, Jack, and Ian Watt. 1963. "The Consequences of Literacy." *Comparative Studies in Society and History* 5 (April): 304–345.

Graff, Harvey J. 1979. *The Literacy Myth: Literacy and Social Structure in the Nineteenth-Century City.* New York: Academic Press.

Gray, Virginia. 1970. "Anti-evolution Sentiment and Behavior: The Case of Arkansas." *Journal of American History* 57 (September): 352–366.

Greeley, Andrew M. 1972. *Unsecular Man: The Persistence of Religion.* New York: Schocken.

Greeley, Andrew M., and Christian Wells Jacobsen. 1978. "Editorial Research Note." *Ethnicity* 5 (March): 1–13.

Greenberg, Joseph H. 1956. "The Measurement of Linguistic Diversity." *Language* 32 (January-March): 109–115.

Greenberg, Stephanie W. 1981. "Industrial Location and Ethnic Residential Patterns in an Industrializing City: Philadelphia, 1880." Pp. 204–232 in *Philadelphia: Work, Space, Family, and Group Experience in the Nineteenth Century; Essays Toward an Interdisciplinary History of the City,* edited by Theodore Hershberg. New York: Oxford University Press.

Grob, Gerald N. 1971. "Introduction." Pp. 1–73 in *Insanity and Idiocy in Massachusetts: Report of the Commission on Lunacy, 1855,* by Edward Jarvis, with a critical introduction by Gerald N. Grob. Cambridge, Mass.: Harvard University Press.

Hall, Marshall, and Nicolaus Tideman. 1967. "Measures of Concentration." *Journal of the American Statistical Association* 62 (March): 162–168.

Hall, Thomas Cuming. 1930. *The Religious Background of American Culture.* Boston: Little, Brown.

Hammond, Phillip E. 1983. "In Search of a Protestant Twentieth Century: American Religion and Power Since 1900." *Review of Religious Research* 24 (June): 281–294.

1985. "The Curious Path of Conservative Protestantism." *The Annals of the American Academy of Political and Social Science* 480 (July): 53–62.

1986. "Religion in the Modern World." Pp. 143–158 in *Making Sense of Modern Times: Peter L. Berger and the Vision of Interpretive Sociology,* edited by James Davison Hunter and Stephen C. Ainlay. New York: Routledge & Kegan Paul.

Handlin, Oscar. 1951. *The Uprooted: The Epic Story of the Great Migrations that Made the American People.* Boston: Little, Brown.

1954. *The American People in the Twentieth Century.* Cambridge, Mass.: Harvard University Press.

Handy, Robert T. 1953. "The Protestant Quest for a Christian America." *Church History* 22 (March): 8–20.

1960. "The American Religious Depression, 1925–1935." *Church History* 29 (March): 3–16.

1966a. "Introduction." Pp. 3–16 in *The Social Gospel in America, 1870–1920: Gladden, Ely, Rauschenbusch,* edited by Robert T. Handy. New York: Oxford University Press.

1966b. "The Voluntary Principle in Religion and Religious Freedom in America." Pp. 129–139 in *Voluntary Associations: A Study of Groups in Free Societies; Essays in Honor of James Luther Adams,* edited by D. B. Robertson. Richmond, Va.: John Knox Press.

1971. *A Christian America: Protestant Hopes and Historical Realities.* New York: Oxford University Press.

Harrell, David Edwin, Jr. 1985. "Religious Pluralism: Catholics, Jews, and Sectarians." Pp. 59–82 in *Religion in the South,* edited by Charles Reagan Wilson. Jackson: University Press of Mississippi.

Harris, Lis. 1985. *Holy Days: The World of a Hasidic Family.* New York: Macmillan.

Harrison, Michael I., and Bernard Lazerwitz. 1982. "Do Denominations Matter?" *American Journal of Sociology* 88 (September): 356–377.

Hart, Hornell. 1942. "Religion." *American Journal of Sociology* 47 (May): 888–897.

Hawley, Amos H. 1950. *Human Ecology: A Theory of Community Structure.* New York: Ronald Press.

Hays, Samuel P. 1957. *The Response to Industrialism: 1885–1914.* Chicago: University of Chicago Press.

1960. "History as Human Behavior." *Iowa Journal of History* 58 (July): 193–206.

Hechter, Michael. 1975. *Internal Colonialism: The Celtic Fringe in Brit-*

*ish National Development, 1536–1966.* Berkeley and Los Angeles: University of California Press.

Herberg, Will. 1955. *Protestant-Catholic-Jew: An Essay in American Religious Sociology.* New York: Doubleday.

Hershberg, Theodore, Michael Katz, Stuart Blumin, Laurence Glasco, and Clyde Griffen. 1974. "Occupation and Ethnicity in Five Nineteenth-Century Cities: A Collaborative Inquiry." *Historical Methods Newsletter* 7 (June): 174–216.

Hibbs, Douglas A., Jr. 1974. "Problems of Statistical Estimation and Causal Inference in Time-Series Regression Models." Pp. 252–308 in *Sociological Methodology, 1973–1974,* edited by Herbert L. Costner. San Francisco: Jossey-Bass.

Higham, John. 1955. *Strangers in the Land: Patterns of American Nativism, 1860–1925.* New Brunswick, N.J.: Rutgers University Press.

Hill, Edgar P. 1909. "Co-operation in Home Missions." Pp. 216–225 in *Federal Council of the Churches of Christ in America: Report of the First Meeting of the Federal Council, Philadelphia, 1908,* edited by Elias B. Sanford. New York: Revell.

Hirsch, Susan E. 1978. *Roots of the American Working Class: The Industrialization of Crafts in Newark, 1800–1860.* Philadelphia: University of Pennsylvania Press.

Holt, Arthur E. 1929. "Religion." *American Journal of Sociology* 34 (May): 1116–1128.

Holt, John B. 1940. "Holiness Religion: Cultural Shock and Social Reorganization." *American Sociological Review* 5 (October): 740–747.

Holt, W. Stull. 1929. *The Bureau of the Census: Its History, Activities, and Organization.* Washington, D.C.: Brookings Institution.

Hopkins, Charles Howard. 1940. *The Rise of the Social Gospel in American Protestantism, 1865–1915.* New Haven, Conn.: Yale University Press.

Hoult, Thomas Ford. 1950. "Economic Class Consciousness in American Protestantism." *American Sociological Review* 15 (February): 97–100.

——— 1952. "Economic Class Consciousness in American Protestantism: II." *American Sociological Review* 17 (June): 349–350.

Hudson, Winthrop S. 1953. *The Great Tradition of the American Churches.* New York: Harper Bros.

——— 1955a. "Denominationalism as a Basis for Ecumenicity: A Seventeenth Century Conception." *Church History* 24 (March): 32–50.

——— 1955b. "Are Churches Really Booming?" *The Christian Century* 72 (December 21): 1494–1496.

——— 1961. *American Protestantism.* Chicago: University of Chicago Press.

——— 1965. *Religion in America.* New York: Scribner.

Hull, William. 1889. "A Census Which Ignores Religion and Higher Education." *The Quarterly Review of the Evangelical Lutheran Church* 19 (July): 412–419.

Hutchison, John A. 1941. *We Are Not Divided: A Critical and Historical Study of the Federal Council of the Churches of Christ in America.* New York: Round Table Press.

Hutchison, William R. 1974. "American Religious History: From Diversity to Pluralism." *Journal of Interdisciplinary History* 5 (Autumn): 313–318.

*Information Service.* 1936. "Church Attendance Statistics." Department of Research and Education, Federal Council of the Churches of Christ in America, *Information Service* 15 (December 12): 1–4.

——— 1945. "A 1946 Census of Religious Bodies?" Department of Research and Education, Federal Council of the Churches of Christ in America, *Information Service* 24 (September 8): 4.

——— 1946. "Census of Religious Bodies for 1946." Department of Research and Education, Federal Council of the Churches of Christ in America, *Information Service* 25 (October 5): 4.

——— 1956. "The Rise and Fall of the Census of Religious Bodies." Bureau of Research and Survey, National Council of the Churches of Christ in the United States of America, *Information Service* 35 (June 30): 1–2.

——— 1961. "A Critical Review of Publications on Statistics of Religious Affiliation." Bureau of Research and Survey, National Council of the Churches of Christ in the United States of America, *Information Service* 40 (February 4): 4–8.

——— 1963. "Census of Religious Bodies: Background." Bureau of Research and Survey, National Council of the Churches of Christ in the United States of America, *Information Service* 42 (June 22): 5–6.

Inkeles, Alex, and David H. Smith. 1974. *Becoming Modern: Individual Change in Six Developing Countries.* Cambridge, Mass.: Harvard University Press.

Inverarity, James M. 1976. "Populism and Lynching in Louisiana, 1889–1896: A Test of Erikson's Theory of the Relationship Between Boundary Crises and Repressive Justice." *American Sociological Review* 41 (April): 262–280.

Jacob, Herbert. 1984. *Using Published Data: Errors and Remedies.* Beverly Hills, Calif.: Sage.

Jefferson, Thomas. 1963. "Virginia Statute of Religious Liberty (January 16, 1786)." Pp. 125–126 in *Documents of American History; Volume I: To 1898; Seventh Edition,* edited by Henry Steele Commager. East Norwalk, Conn.: Appleton-Century-Crofts.

——— 1964. *Notes on the State of Virginia.* New York: Harper & Row.

Jensen, Richard. 1971. *The Winning of the Midwest: Social and Political Conflict, 1888–1896.* Chicago: University of Chicago Press.

Johnson, Charles A. 1976. "Political Culture in American States: Elazar's Formulation Examined." *American Journal of Political Science* 20 (August): 491–509.

Johnson, Paul E. 1978. *A Shopkeeper's Millennium: Society and Revivals in Rochester, New York, 1815–1837.* New York: Hill & Wang.

Jones, Charles Edwin. 1974. *Perfectionist Persuasion: The Holiness Movement and American Methodism, 1867–1936.* Metuchen, N.J.: Scarecrow.

Jones, Victor. 1953. "Annexation." Pp. 550–572 in *The Future of Cities and Urban Redevelopment,* edited by Coleman Woodbury. Chicago: University of Chicago Press.

Jordan, Philip D. 1973. "The Evangelical Alliance and American Presbyterians, 1867–1873." *Journal of Presbyterian History* 51 (Fall): 309–326.

    1982. *The Evangelical Alliance for the United States of America, 1847–1900: Ecumenism, Identity, and the Religion of the Republic.* New York: Edwin Mellen Press.

Kaestle, Carl F., and Maris A. Vinovskis. 1980. *Education and Social Change in Nineteenth-Century Massachusetts.* Cambridge University Press.

Karp, David A., Gregory P. Stone, and William C. Yoels. 1977. *Being Urban: A Social Psychological View of City Life.* Lexington, Mass.: Heath.

Kasarda, John D., and Patrick D. Nolan. 1979. "Ratio Measurement and Theoretical Inference in Social Research." *Social Forces* 58 (September): 212–227.

Kennedy, Joseph C. G. 1853. *Report of the Superintendent of the Census for December 1, 1852; To Which Is Appended the Report for December 1, 1851.* Washington, D.C.: Robert Armstrong.

Kennedy, Ruby Jo Reeves. 1944. "Single or Triple Melting-Pot?: Intermarriage Trends in New Haven, 1870–1940." *American Journal of Sociology* 49 (January): 331–339.

    1952. "Single or Triple Melting-Pot?: Intermarriage in New Haven, 1870–1950." *American Journal of Sociology* 58 (July): 56–59.

Kessler, Ronald C. 1977. "The Use of Change Scores as Criteria in Longitudinal Survey Research." *Quality and Quantity* 11 (March): 43–66.

Keyes, Fenton. 1958. "The Correlation of Social Phenomena with Community Size." *Social Forces* 36 (May): 311–315.

Kieffer, George L. 1928. "The Difference Between European and American Methods of Calculating Church Membership." *The Lutheran Church Quarterly* 1 (July): 314–319.

Kincheloe, Samuel C. 1937. *Research Memorandum on Religion in the Depression.* New York: Social Science Research Council.

Kinzer, Donald L. 1964. *An Episode in Anti-Catholicism: The American Protective Association.* Seattle: University of Washington Press.

Klein, Milton M. 1972. "New York in the American Colonies: A New Look." *New York History* 53 (April): 132–156.

1974. *The Politics of Diversity: Essays in the History of Colonial New York.* Port Washington, N.Y.: Kennikat Press.

Kluckhohn, Clyde. 1973. "The Moral Order in the Expanding Society." Pp. 72–83 in *Modernization, Urbanization, and the Urban Crisis,* edited by Gino Germani. Boston: Little, Brown.

Kolb, J. H., and Edmund deS. Brunner. 1935. *A Study of Rural Society: Its Organization and Changes.* Boston: Houghton Mifflin.

Kurland, Philip B. 1962. *Religion and the Law: Of Church and State and the Supreme Court.* Hawthorne, N.Y.: Aldine.

Labovitz, Sanford, and Jack P. Gibbs. 1964. "Urbanization, Technology, and the Division of Labor: Further Evidence." *Pacific Sociological Review* 7 (Spring): 3–9.

Lambert, Richard D. 1960. "Current Trends in Religion – A Summary." *The Annals of the American Academy of Political and Social Science* 332 (November): 146–155.

Land, Kenneth C. 1970. "Mathematical Formalization of Durkheim's Theory of Division of Labor." Pp. 257–282 in *Sociological Methodology, 1970,* edited by Edgar F. Borgatta and George W. Bohrnstedt. San Francisco: Jossey-Bass.

Land, Kenneth C., and Marcus Felson. 1976. "A General Framework for Building Dynamic Macro Social Indicator Models: Including an Analysis of Changes in Crime Rates and Police Expenditures." *American Journal of Sociology* 82 (November): 565–604.

Landis, Benson Y. 1935. "The Church and Religious Activity." *American Journal of Sociology* 40 (May): 780–787.

1940. "A Note on the 1936 Census of Religious Bodies." Department of Research and Education, Federal Council of the Churches of Christ in America, *Information Service* 19 (November 2): 1–2.

1957. "Confessions of a Church Statistician." *National Council Outlook* 7 (February): 3.

1959. "A Guide to the Literature on Statistics of Religious Affiliation with References to Related Social Studies." *Journal of the American Statistical Association* 54 (June): 335–357.

1960. "Trends in Church Membership in the United States." *The Annals of the American Academy of Political and Social Science* 332 (November): 1–8.

Latourette, Kenneth Scott. 1941. *A History of the Expansion of Christian-*

*ity (Volume IV); the Great Century, A.D. 1800–A.D. 1914: Europe and the United States of America.* New York: Harper Bros.

Laurie, Bruce. 1980. *Working People of Philadelphia, 1800–1850.* Philadelphia: Temple University Press.

Laurie, Bruce, Theodore Hershberg, and George Alter. 1975. "Immigrants and Industry: The Philadelphia Experience, 1850–1880." *Journal of Social History* 9 (Winter): 219–248.

Lenski, Gerhard E. 1961. *The Religious Factor: A Sociological Study of Religion's Impact on Politics, Economics, and Family Life.* New York: Doubleday.

Lerner, Daniel. 1957. "Communications Systems and Social Systems: A Statistical Exploration in History and Policy." *Behavioral Science* 2 (October): 266–275.

——— 1958. *The Passing of Traditional Society: Modernizing the Middle East.* New York: Free Press.

——— 1963. "Toward a Communication Theory of Modernization: A Set of Considerations." Pp. 327–350 in *Communications and Political Development,* edited by Lucian W. Pye. Princeton, N.J.: Princeton University Press.

Lichtman, Allan J. 1979. *Prejudice and the Old Politics: The Presidential Election of 1928.* Chapel Hill: University of North Carolina Press.

Lieberson, Stanley. 1964. "An Extension of Greenberg's Linguistic Diversity Measures." *Language* 40 (October-December): 526–531.

——— 1965. "Bilingualism in Montreal: A Demographic Analysis." *American Journal of Sociology* 71 (July): 10–25.

——— 1969. "Measuring Population Diversity." *American Sociological Review* 34 (December): 850–862.

——— 1970. *Language and Ethnic Relations in Canada.* New York: Wiley.

——— 1978. "The Anatomy of Language Diversity: Some Elementary Results." Pp. 32–48 in *Interethnic Communication,* edited by E. Lamar Ross. Athens: University of Georgia Press.

——— 1980. *A Piece of the Pie: Blacks and White Immigrants Since 1880.* Berkeley and Los Angeles: University of California Press.

——— 1981. *Language Diversity and Language Contact: Essays by Stanley Lieberson,* edited by Anwar S. Dil. Stanford, Calif.: Stanford University Press.

Lieberson, Stanley, and Lynn K. Hansen. 1974. "National Development, Mother Tongue Diversity, and the Comparative Study of Nations." *American Sociological Review* 39 (August): 523–541.

Linfield, H. S. 1938. "Statistics of Jews and Jewish Organizations in the United States: An Historical Review of Ten Censuses, 1850–1937." Pp. 61–84 in *The American Jewish Year Book, 5699: September 26,*

*1938 to September 13, 1939; Volume 40,* edited by Harry Schneiderman. Philadelphia: Jewish Publication Society.

Linkh, Richard M. 1975. *American Catholicism and European Immigrants (1900–1924).* Staten Island, N.Y.: Center for Migration Studies.

Lippmann, Walter. 1929. *A Preface to Morals.* New York: Macmillan.

Lipset, Seymour Martin. 1959. "Religion in America: What Religious Revival?" *Columbia University Forum* 2 (Winter): 17–21.

———. 1967. *The First New Nation: The United States in Historical and Comparative Perspective.* New York: Doubleday.

Littell, Franklin Hamlin. 1971. *From State Church to Pluralism: A Protestant Interpretation of Religion in American History.* New York: Macmillan.

Lockridge, Kenneth A. 1974. *Literacy in Colonial New England: An Enquiry into the Social Context of Literacy in the Early Modern West.* New York: Norton.

———. 1981. "Literacy in Early America, 1650–1800." Pp. 183–200 in *Literacy and Social Development in the West: A Reader,* edited by Harvey J. Graff. Cambridge University Press.

Lodge, Martin E. 1971. "The Crisis of the Churches in the Middle Colonies, 1720–1750." *The Pennsylvania Magazine of History and Biography* 95 (April): 195–220.

Loomis, Samuel Lane. 1887. *Modern Cities and Their Religious Problems.* New York: Baker & Taylor.

Lunt, Edward C. 1888–1889. "History of the United States Census." *Publications of the American Statistical Association* 1: 71–93.

Lynd, Robert S., and Helen Merrell Lynd. 1937. *Middletown in Transition: A Study in Cultural Conflicts.* New York: Harcourt, Brace.

Lyon, David. 1981. "Secularization and Sociology: The History of an Idea." *Fides et Historia* 13: 38–52.

———. 1985. "Rethinking Secularization: Retrospect and Prospect." *Review of Religious Research* 26 (March): 228–243.

———. 1987. *The Steeple's Shadow: On the Myths and Realities of Secularization.* Grand Rapids, Mich.: Eerdmans.

McGuire, Meredith B. 1981. *Religion: The Social Context.* Belmont, Calif.: Wadsworth.

MacIntyre, Alasdair. 1967. *Secularization and Moral Change.* New York: Oxford University Press.

McKenzie, R. D. 1933. *The Metropolitan Community.* New York: McGraw-Hill.

McLeish, John. 1969. *Evangelical Religion and Popular Education: A Modern Interpretation.* London: Methuen.

McLoughlin, William G. 1959. *Modern Revivalism: Charles Grandison Finney to Billy Graham.* New York: Ronald Press.

1978. *Revivals, Awakenings, and Reform: An Essay on Religion and Social Change in America, 1607–1977.* Chicago: University of Chicago Press.

MacMillan, Alexander, and Richard L. Daft. 1980. "Relationships Among Ratio Variables with Common Components: Fact or Artifact." *Social Forces* 58 (June): 1109–1128.

Marsden, George M. 1980. *Fundamentalism and American Culture: The Shaping of Twentieth-Century Evangelicalism, 1870–1925.* New York: Oxford University Press.

Marty, Martin E. 1959. *The New Shape of American Religion.* New York: Harper Bros.

1961. "Protestantism Enters Third Phase." *The Christian Century* 78 (January 18): 72–75.

1970. *Righteous Empire: The Protestant Experience in America.* New York: Dial.

1974. "Religious Behavior: Its Social Dimension in American History." *Social Research* 41 (Summer): 241–264.

Marx, Karl. 1963. "On the Jewish Question." Pp. 3–40 in *Karl Marx: Early Writings,* translated and edited by T. B. Bottomore. New York: McGraw-Hill.

Marx, Karl, and Friedrich Engels. 1964. "German Ideology (from Chapter I)." Pp. 73–81 in *Karl Marx and Friedrich Engels: On Religion,* introduction by Reinhold Niebuhr. New York: Schocken.

May, Henry F. 1949. *Protestant Churches and Industrial America.* New York: Harper Bros.

Mays, Benjamin Elijah, and Joseph William Nicholson. 1933. *The Negro's Church.* New York: Institute of Social and Religious Research.

Mead, Sidney E. 1954a. "Thomas Jefferson's 'Fair Experiment' – Religious Freedom." *Religion in Life* 23 (Autumn): 566–579.

1954b. "The American People: Their Space, Time, and Religion." *Journal of Religion* 34 (October): 244–255.

1954c. "Denominationalism: The Shape of Protestantism in America." *Church History* 23 (December): 291–320.

1956. "From Coercion to Persuasion: Another Look at the Rise of Religious Liberty and the Emergence of Denominationalism." *Church History* 25 (December): 317–337.

Merriam, William Rush. 1905. *American Census Taking.* Washington, D.C.: Bureau of the Census.

Meyer, John W., David Tyack, Joane Nagel, and Audri Gordon. 1979. "Public Education as Nation-Building in America: Enrollments and

Bureaucratization in the American States, 1870–1930." *American Journal of Sociology* 85 (November): 591–613.

Miller, Glenn T. 1976. *Religious Liberty in America: History and Prospects.* Philadelphia: Westminster Press.

Miller, Perry G. E. 1935. "The Contribution of the Protestant Churches to Religious Liberty in Colonial America." *Church History* 4 (March): 57–66.

———. 1954. "The Location of American Religious Freedom." Pp. 9–23 in *Religion and Freedom of Thought,* by Perry Miller, Robert L. Calhoun, Nathan M. Pusey, and Reinhold Niebuhr. New York: Doubleday.

Miller, William Lee. 1986. *The First Liberty: Religion and the American Republic.* New York: Knopf.

Moberg, David O. 1962. *The Church as a Social Institution: The Sociology of American Religion.* Englewood Cliffs, N.J.: Prentice-Hall.

Moore, R. Laurence. 1986. *Religious Outsiders and the Making of Americans.* New York: Oxford University Press.

Muller, Dorothea R. 1959. "The Social Philosophy of Josiah Strong: Social Christianity and American Progressivism." *Church History* 28 (June): 183–201.

Murphy, T. F. 1941. *Religious Bodies: 1936; Volume I: Summary and Detailed Tables.* Washington, D.C.: Government Printing Office.

*The Nation.* 1883. "Religious Statistics." *The Nation* 37 (November 29): 443–444.

National Archives. 1950. *Your Government's Records in the National Archives, 1950.* Washington, D.C.: The National Archives.

Nelsen, Hart M., and Hugh P. Whitt. 1972. "Religion and the Migrant in the City: A Test of Holt's Cultural Shock Thesis." *Social Forces* 50 (March): 379–384.

Niebuhr, H. Richard. 1931. "Fundamentalism." Pp. 526–527 in *Encyclopaedia of the Social Sciences: Volume Six, Expatriation-Gosplan,* edited by Edwin R. A. Seligman and Alvin Johnson. New York: Macmillan.

———. 1954. *The Social Sources of Denominationalism.* Hamden, Conn.: Shoe String Press.

———. 1956. *The Kingdom of God in America.* Hamden, Conn.: Shoe String Press.

Noll, Mark A. 1987. "The Eclipse of Old Hostilities *Between* and the Potential for New Strife *Among* Catholics and Protestants Since Vatican II." Pp. 86–109 in *Uncivil Religion: Interreligious Hostility in America,* edited by Robert N. Bellah and Frederick E. Greenspahn. New York: Crossroad.

North, Douglass. 1965. "Industrialization in the United States." Pp. 673–705 in *The Cambridge Economic History of Europe; Volume VI: The Industrial Revolutions and After: Incomes, Population, and Technological Change (II),* edited by H. J. Habakkuk and M. Postan. Cambridge University Press.

Ogburn, William Fielding, and Otis Dudley Duncan. 1964. "City Size as a Sociological Variable." Pp. 129–147 in *Contributions to Urban Sociology,* edited by Ernest W. Burgess and Donald J. Bogue. Chicago: University of Chicago Press.

Ogburn, William F., and Nell Snow Talbot. 1929. "A Measurement of the Factors in the Presidential Election of 1928." *Social Forces* 8 (December): 175–183.

O'Hara, Edwin V. 1922. "Growth of the Church in the United States: 1906–1916." *America* 26 (March 18): 515–516.

Parsons, Talcott. 1960. "Some Comments on the Pattern of Religious Organization in the United States." Pp. 295–321 in *Structure and Process in Modern Societies,* by Talcott Parsons. New York: Free Press.

1963. "Christianity and Modern Industrial Society." Pp. 33–70 in *Sociological Theory, Values, and Sociocultural Change: Essays in Honor of Pitirim A. Sorokin,* edited by Edward A. Tiryakian. New York: Free Press.

Patil, G. P., and C. Taillie. 1982. "Diversity as a Concept and Its Measurement." *Journal of the American Statistical Association* 77 (September): 548–561.

Peach, Ceri. 1980. "Which Triple Melting Pot?: A Re-examination of Ethnic Intermarriage in New Haven, 1900–1950." *Ethnic and Racial Studies* 3 (January): 1–16.

Pearl, Raymond. 1931. "Some Notes on the Census of Religious Bodies, 1926." *Journal of Social Psychology* 2 (November): 417–432.

Pendleton, Brian F., Richard D. Warren, and H. C. Chang. 1979. "Correlated Denominators in Multiple Regression and Change Analyses." *Sociological Methods and Research* 7 (May): 451–474.

Petersen, William. 1962. "Religious Statistics in the United States." *Journal for the Scientific Study of Religion* 1 (April): 165–178.

Pfautz, Harold W. 1956. "Christian Science: A Case Study of the Social Psychological Aspect of Secularization." *Social Forces* 34 (March): 246–251.

1964. "A Case Study of an Urban Religious Movement: Christian Science." Pp. 284–303 in *Contributions to Urban Sociology,* edited by Ernest W. Burgess and Donald J. Bogue. Chicago: University of Chicago Press.

Pointer, Richard Wayne. 1982. Seedbed of American Pluralism: The Impact of Religious Diversity in New York, 1750–1800. Unpublished Ph.D. Dissertation. Department of History, The Johns Hopkins University.

Porterfield, Austin L. 1952. "Suicide and Crime in Folk and in Secular Society." *American Journal of Sociology* 57 ( January): 331–338.

Price, Frank Wilson. 1967. "World Christian Statistics: Some Warnings and Discussion on Their Future Collection." Pp. 48–52 in *World Christian Handbook: 1968,* edited by H. Wakelin Coxill and Kenneth Grubb. London: Lutterworth Press.

Pritchard, Linda K. 1980. Religious Change in a Developing Region: The Social Contexts of Evangelicalism in Western New York and the Upper Ohio Valley During the Mid-Nineteenth Century. Unpublished Ph.D. Dissertation. Department of History, University of Pittsburgh.

———. 1984. "The Burned-Over District Reconsidered: A Portent of Evolving Religious Pluralism in the United States." *Social Science History* 8 (Summer): 243–265.

Rao, Potluri, and Roger LeRoy Miller. 1971. *Applied Econometrics.* Belmont, Calif.: Wadsworth.

Rauschenbusch, Walter. 1897. "The Stake of the Church in the Social Movement." *American Journal of Sociology* 3 ( July): 18–30.

Reimers, David. 1968. "Protestantism's Response to Social Change: 1890–1930." Pp. 364–383 in *The Age of Industrialism in America: Essays in Social Structure and Cultural Values,* edited by Frederic Cople Jaher. New York: Free Press.

Reuss, Carl F. 1943. "An Appraisal of the 1936 Religious Census." *American Sociological Review* 8 ( June): 342–345.

Rigney, Daniel, Richard Machalek, and Jerry D. Goodman. 1978. "Is Secularization a Discontinuous Process?" *Journal for the Scientific Study of Religion* 17 (December): 381–387.

Robertson, Roland. 1971. "Sociologists and Secularization." *Sociology* 5 (September): 297–312.

Robison, Sophia M. 1949. "How Many Jews in America?: Why We Don't Know." *Commentary* 8 (August): 185–192.

Roof, Wade Clark. 1985. "The Study of Social Change in Religion." Pp. 75–89 in *The Sacred in a Secular Age: Toward Revision in the Scientific Study of Religion,* edited by Phillip E. Hammond. Berkeley and Los Angeles: University of California Press.

Ross, Howard N. 1968. "Economic Growth and Change in the United States Under Laissez Faire: 1870–1929." Pp. 6–48 in *The Age of Industrialism in America: Essays in Social Structure and Cultural Values,* edited by Frederic Cople Jaher. New York: Free Press.

Rossiter, W. S. 1919. "The Federal Census." *Publications of the American Statistical Association* 16 (March): 286–292.

Roucek, Joseph S. 1964. "Census Data on Religion in the U.S." *Sociologia Religiosa* 11: 50–60.

Rushing, William A., and Vernon Davies. 1970. "Note on the Mathematical Formalization of a Measure of Division of Labor." *Social Forces* 48 (March): 394–396.

Sanford, Elias B. 1909. *Federal Council of the Churches of Christ in America: Report of the First Meeting of the Federal Council, Philadelphia, 1908.* New York: Revell.

  1916. *Origin and History of the Federal Council of the Churches of Christ in America.* Hartford, Conn.: S. S. Scranton.

Schlesinger, Arthur Meier. 1932. "A Critical Period in American Religion, 1875–1900." *Proceedings of the Massachusetts Historical Society* 64 (June): 523–547.

  1933. *The Rise of the City: 1878–1898.* New York: Macmillan.

Schmeckebier, Laurence F. 1925. *The Statistical Work of the National Government.* Baltimore: Johns Hopkins University Press.

Schnore, Leo F. 1958. "Social Morphology and Human Ecology." *American Journal of Sociology* 63 (May): 620–634.

Schuessler, Karl. 1974. "Analysis of Ratio Variables: Opportunities and Pitfalls." *American Journal of Sociology* 80 (September): 379–396.

Shaughnessy, Gerald. 1925. *Has the Immigrant Kept the Faith?: A Study of Immigration and Catholic Growth in the United States, 1790–1920.* New York: Macmillan.

Shiner, Larry. 1967a. "The Concept of Secularization in Empirical Research." *Journal for the Scientific Study of Religion* 6 (Fall): 207–220.

  1967b. "The Meanings of Secularization." *International Yearbook for the Sociology of Religion* 3: 51–59.

Shortridge, James R. 1976. "Patterns of Religion in the United States." *The Geographical Review* 66 (October): 420–434.

  1977. "A New Regionalization of American Religion." *Journal for the Scientific Study of Religion* 16 (June): 143–153.

Silcox, Claris Edwin, and Galen M. Fisher. 1934. *Catholics, Jews, and Protestants: A Study of Relationships in the United States and Canada.* New York: Harper Bros.

Silva, Ruth C. 1962. *Rum, Religion, and Votes: 1928 Re-examined.* University Park: Pennsylvania State University Press.

Simmel, Georg. 1950. "The Metropolis and Mental Life." Pp. 409–424 in *The Sociology of Georg Simmel,* translated and edited by Kurt H. Wolff. New York: Free Press.

Singleton, Gregory H. 1975. "Fundamentalism and Urbanization: A Quanti-

tative Critique of Impressionistic Interpretations." Pp. 205–227 in *The New Urban History: Quantitative Explorations by American Historians,* edited by Leo F. Schnore. Princeton, N.J.: Princeton University Press.

1979. *Religion in the City of Angels: American Protestant Culture and Urbanization, Los Angeles, 1850–1930.* Ann Arbor, Mich.: UMI Research Press.

1982a. Personal Communication (May 9).

1982b. Personal Communication (August 9).

Smith, David L., and Robert E. Snow. 1976. "The Division of Labor: Conceptual and Methodological Issues." *Social Forces* 55 (December): 520–528.

Smith, George L. 1969. "Guilders and Godliness: The Dutch Colonial Contribution to American Religious Pluralism." *Journal of Presbyterian History* 47 (March): 1–30.

1973. *Religion and Trade in New Netherland: Dutch Origins and American Development.* Ithaca, N.Y.: Cornell University Press.

Smith, T. Lynn. 1947. *The Sociology of Rural Life: Revised Edition.* New York: Harper Bros.

1948. *Population Analysis.* New York: McGraw-Hill.

Smith, Timothy L. 1957. *Revivalism and Social Reform in Mid-Nineteenth-Century America.* New York: Abingdon Press.

1960. "Historic Waves of Religious Interest in America." *The Annals of the American Academy of Political and Social Science* 332 (November): 9–19.

1967. "Protestant Schooling and American Nationality, 1800–1850." *Journal of American History* 53 (March): 679–695.

1968. "Congregation, State, and Denomination: The Forming of the American Religious Structure." *The William and Mary Quarterly* 25 (April): 155–176.

Soltow, Lee, and Edward Stevens. 1977. "Economic Aspects of School Participation in Mid-Nineteenth-Century United States." *Journal of Interdisciplinary History* 8 (Autumn): 221–243.

1981. *The Rise of Literacy and the Common School in the United States: A Socioeconomic Analysis to 1870.* Chicago: University of Chicago Press.

Sorokin, Pitirim A. 1928. "Rural-Urban Differences in Religious Culture, Beliefs, and Behavior." *Publications of the American Sociological Society* 23: 223–238.

Sorokin, Pitirim A., and Carle C. Zimmerman. 1929. *Principles of Rural-Urban Sociology.* New York: Holt.

Sperry, Willard L. 1946. *Religion in America.* Cambridge University Press.

Stange, Douglas C. 1970. "Al Smith and the Republican Party at Prayer: The Lutheran Vote–1928." *Review of Politics* 32 (July): 347–364.

Stark, Rodney, and William Sims Bainbridge. 1979. "Of Churches, Sects, and Cults: Preliminary Concepts for a Theory of Religious Movements." *Journal for the Scientific Study of Religion* 18 (June): 117–131.

1980a. "Towards a Theory of Religion: Religious Commitment." *Journal for the Scientific Study of Religion* 19 (June): 114–128.

1980b. "Secularization, Revival, and Cult Formation." *The Annual Review of the Social Sciences of Religion* 4: 85–119.

1981a. "American-Born Sects: Initial Findings." *Journal for the Scientific Study of Religion* 20 (June): 130–149.

1981b. "Secularization and Cult Formation in the Jazz Age." *Journal for the Scientific Study of Religion* 20 (December): 360–373.

1985. *The Future of Religion: Secularization, Revival, and Cult Formation.* Berkeley and Los Angeles: University of California Press.

1987. *A Theory of Religion.* New York: Peter Lang.

Stark, Rodney, William Sims Bainbridge, Robert D. Crutchfield, Daniel P. Doyle, and Roger Finke. 1983. "Crime and Delinquency in the Roaring Twenties." *Journal of Research in Crime and Delinquency* 20 (January): 4–23.

Stark, Rodney, William Sims Bainbridge, and Lori Kent. 1981. "Cult Membership in the Roaring Twenties: Assessing Local Receptivity." *Sociological Analysis* 42 (Summer): 137–161.

Stead, William Thomas. 1894. *If Christ Came to Chicago!: A Plea for the Union of All Who Love in the Service of All Who Suffer.* Chicago: Laird & Lee.

Stelzle, Charles. 1907. *Christianity's Storm Centre: A Study of the Modern City.* New York: Revell.

1912. *American Social and Religious Conditions.* New York: Revell.

Stinchcombe, Arthur L. 1985. "Macrosociology Is Sociology About Millions of People." *Contemporary Sociology* 14 (September): 572–575.

Stone, Lawrence. 1969. "Literacy and Education in England, 1640–1900." *Past and Present* 42 (February): 69–139.

Strauss, Gerald. 1984. "Lutheranism and Literacy: A Reassessment." Pp. 109–123 in *Religion and Society in Early Modern Europe: 1500–1800,* edited by Kaspar von Greyerz. London: Allen & Unwin.

Strong, Josiah. 1887. "Introduction." Pp. 5–12 in Samuel Lane Loomis, *Modern Cities and Their Religious Problems.* New York: Baker & Taylor.

1891. *Our Country: Its Possible Future and Its Present Crisis; Revised Edition, Based on the Census of 1890.* New York: Baker & Taylor.

1893. *The New Era or the Coming Kingdom.* New York: Baker & Taylor.

1898. *The Twentieth Century City.* New York: Baker & Taylor.

1907. *The Challenge of the City.* New York: Eaton & Mains.

1913. *The Next Great Awakening.* New York: Doubleday, Page.

Stuart, William M. 1898. "Official Statistics." *American Journal of Sociology* 3 (March): 622–630.

Stump, Roger W. 1984. "Regional Divergence in Religious Affiliation in the United States." *Sociological Analysis* 45 (Winter): 283–299.

Sullivan, Teresa A. 1982. "Review Essay: A Supply-Side View of the Melting Pot." *American Journal of Sociology* 88 (November): 590–595.

Swanson, David A. 1973. "A Comment on the Clemente (MFD) and Gibbs-Martin (MID) Measures of the Division of Labor: Their Relation to Amemiya's Index of Economic Differentiation (IED)." *Pacific Sociological Review* 16 (July): 401–405.

Sweet, Douglas H. 1976. "Church Vitality and the American Revolution: Historiographical Consensus and Thoughts Toward a New Perspective." *Church History* 45 (September): 341–357.

Sweet, W. W. 1935. "The American Colonial Environment and Religious Liberty." *Church History* 4 (March): 43–56.

Swift, Arthur L., Jr. 1938. *New Frontiers of Religion: The Church in a Changing Community.* New York: Macmillan.

Teachman, Jay D. 1980. "Analysis of Population Diversity: Measures of Qualitative Variation." *Sociological Methods and Research* 8 (February): 341–362.

Theil, Henri. 1972. *Statistical Decomposition Analysis: With Applications in the Social and Administrative Sciences.* New York: Elsevier North-Holland.

Thernstrom, Stephan. 1968. "Urbanization, Migration, and Social Mobility in Late Nineteenth-Century America." Pp. 158–175 in *Towards a New Past: Dissenting Essays in American History,* edited by Barton J. Bernstein. New York: Pantheon.

Thernstrom, Stephan, and Peter R. Knights. 1970. "Men in Motion: Some Data and Speculations about Urban Population Mobility in Nineteenth-Century America." *Journal of Interdisciplinary History* 1 (Autumn): 7–35.

Thomas, George M. 1978. Institutional Knowledge and Social Movements: Rational Exchange, Revival Religion, and Nation-Building in the U.S., 1870–1896. Unpublished Ph.D. Dissertation. Department of Sociology, Stanford University.

1979. "Rational Exchange and Individualism: Revival Religion in the

U.S., 1870–1890." Pp. 351–372 in *The Religious Dimension: New Directions in Quantitative Research,* edited by Robert Wuthnow. New York: Academic Press.

Thorndike, E. L. 1939. *Your City.* New York: Harcourt, Brace.

Truesdell, Leon E. 1965. *The Development of Punch Card Tabulation in the Bureau of the Census, 1890–1940: With Outlines of Actual Tabulation Programs.* Washington, D.C.: Bureau of the Census.

Turner, Frederick Jackson. 1921. "The Significance of the Frontier in American History." Pp. 1–38 in Frederick Jackson Turner, *The Frontier in American History.* New York: Holt.

Turner, Ralph E. 1940. "The Industrial City: Center of Cultural Change." Pp. 228–242 in *The Cultural Approach to History,* edited by Caroline F. Ware. New York: Columbia University Press.

Tuveson, Ernest Lee. 1968. *Redeemer Nation: The Idea of America's Millennial Role.* Chicago: University of Chicago Press.

Tyack, David. 1966. "The Kingdom of God and the Common School: Protestant Ministers and the Educational Awakening in the West." *Harvard Educational Review* 36 (Fall): 447–469.

——— 1974. *The One Best System: A History of American Urban Education.* Cambridge, Mass.: Harvard University Press.

United States Department of Commerce. 1954. *Appraisal of Census Programs: Report of the Intensive Review Committee to the Secretary of Commerce.* Washington, D.C.: Government Printing Office.

Uslaner, Eric M. 1976. "The Pitfalls of Per Capita." *American Journal of Political Science* 20 (February): 125–133.

VanderMeer, Philip R. 1981. "Religion, Society, and Politics: A Classification of American Religious Groups." *Social Science History* 5 (February): 3–24.

Walker, Francis A. 1872. *A Compendium of the Ninth Census (June 1, 1870), Compiled Pursuant to a Concurrent Resolution of Congress, and Under the Direction of the Secretary of the Interior.* Washington, D.C.: Government Printing Office.

——— 1888. "The Eleventh Census of the United States." *The Quarterly Journal of Economics* 2 (January): 135–161.

Wallis, Roy. 1984. *The Elementary Forms of the New Religious Life.* New York: Routledge & Kegan Paul.

——— 1985. "The Dynamics of Change in the Human Potential Movement." Pp. 129–156 in *Religious Movements: Genesis, Exodus, and Numbers,* edited by Rodney Stark. New York: Paragon House.

Wallis, Roy, and Steve Bruce. 1984. "The Stark-Bainbridge Theory of Religion: A Critical Analysis and Counter Proposals." *Sociological Analysis* 45 (Spring): 11–27.

——— 1986. *Sociological Theory, Religion, and Collective Action.* Belfast,

Northern Ireland: Department of Social Studies, The Queen's University of Belfast.

Ward, David. 1975. "Some Locational Implications of the Ethnic Division of Labor in Mid-Nineteenth-Century American Cities." Pp. 258–270 in *Pattern and Process: Research in Historical Geography,* edited by Ralph E. Ehrenberg. Washington, D.C.: Howard University Press.

Ward, Nathaniel. 1969. *The Simple Cobler of Aggawam in America,* edited by P. M. Zall. Lincoln: University of Nebraska Press.

Waring, George E. 1887. *Report on the Social Statistics of Cities; Part II: The Southern and the Western States.* Washington, D.C.: Government Printing Office.

Warner, Sam Bass, Jr., and Sylvia Fleisch. 1976. "The Past of Today's Present: A Social History of America's Metropolises, 1960–1860." *Journal of Urban History* 3 (November): 3–118.

1977. *Measurements for Social History.* Beverly Hills, Calif.: Sage.

Wasserman, Ira W. 1978. "Religious Affiliations and Homicide: Historical Results from the Rural South." *Journal for the Scientific Study of Religion* 17 (December): 415–418.

Weber, Adna Ferrin. 1967. *The Growth of Cities in the Nineteenth Century: A Study in Statistics.* Ithaca, N.Y.: Cornell University Press.

Weber, Herman C. 1939. "Church-Member Statistics." Department of Research and Education, Federal Council of the Churches of Christ in America, *Information Service* 18 (January 14): 1–6.

Weber, Max. 1946. "The Protestant Sects and the Spirit of Capitalism." Pp. 302–322 in *From Max Weber: Essays in Sociology,* translated and edited by H. H. Gerth and C. Wright Mills. New York: Oxford University Press.

Welch, Kevin William. 1985. Church Membership in American Metropolitan Areas, 1952–1971. Unpublished Ph.D. Dissertation. Department of Sociology, University of Washington.

Welch, Michael R., and John Baltzell. 1984. "Geographic Mobility, Social Integration, and Church Attendance." *Journal for the Scientific Study of Religion* 23 (March): 75–91.

Westhues, Kenneth. 1971a. "An Elaboration and Test of a Secularization Hypothesis in Terms of Open-Systems Theory of Organization." *Social Forces* 49 (March): 460–469.

1971b. "An Alternative Model for Research on Catholic Education." *American Journal of Sociology* 77 (September): 279–292.

1976. "Public vs. Sectarian Legitimation: The Separate Schools of the Catholic Church." *The Canadian Review of Sociology and Anthropology* 13 (May): 137–151.

White, Michael J. 1986. "Segregation and Diversity Measures in Population Distribution." *Population Index* 52 (Summer): 198–221.

White, Ronald C., Jr., and C. Howard Hopkins. 1976. "What Is the Social Gospel?" Pp. xi-xix in *The Social Gospel: Religion and Reform in Changing America,* edited by Ronald C. White, Jr. and C. Howard Hopkins. Philadelphia: Temple University Press.

Whitman, Lauris B., and Glen W. Trimble. 1956. "Series A—Major Faiths by Regions, Divisions, and States: Bulletin Number 1—Introduction," in *Churches and Church Membership in the United States: An Enumeration and Analysis by Counties, States, and Regions.* New York: Bureau of Research and Survey, National Council of the Churches of Christ in the United States of America.

Willis, Cecil L. 1982. "Population Size, Density, Urbanization, and the Division of Labor." *California Sociologist* 5 (Winter): 1–15.

Wilson, Bryan R. 1961. *Sects and Society: A Sociological Study of the Elim Tabernacle, Christian Science, and Christadelphians.* Berkeley and Los Angeles: University of California Press.

1966. *Religion in a Secular Society: A Sociological Comment.* London: C. A. Watts.

1982. *Religion in Sociological Perspective.* New York: Oxford University Press.

Winter, Gibson. 1961. *The Suburban Captivity of the Churches: An Analysis of Protestant Responsibility in the Expanding Metropolis.* New York: Doubleday.

Wirth, Louis. 1938. "Urbanism as a Way of Life." *American Journal of Sociology* 44 (July): 1–24.

Wish, Harvey. 1952. *Society and Thought in Modern America: A Social and Intellectual History of the American People from 1865.* New York: Longmans, Green.

Wolf, Stephanie Grauman. 1976. *Urban Village: Population, Community, and Family Structure in Germantown, Pennsylvania, 1683–1800.* Princeton, N.J.: Princeton University Press.

Wolfe, A. B. 1932. "Population Censuses Before 1790." *Journal of the American Statistical Association* 27 (December): 357–370.

Wonnacott, Ronald J., and Thomas H. Wonnacott. 1970. *Econometrics.* New York: Wiley.

Woodson, Carter G. 1945. *The History of the Negro Church.* Washington, D.C.: Associated Publishers.

Wright, Carroll D., with William C. Hunt. 1900. *The History and Growth of the United States Census: Prepared for the Senate Committee on the Census.* Washington, D.C.: Government Printing Office.

Wuthnow, Robert. 1976. "Recent Patterns of Secularization: A Problem of Generations?" *American Sociological Review* 41 (October): 850–867.

Wuthnow, Robert, and Kevin Christiano. 1979. "The Effects of Residential

Migration on Church Attendance in the United States." Pp. 257–276 in *The Religious Dimension: New Directions in Quantitative Research,* edited by Robert Wuthnow. New York: Academic Press.

Yinger, J. Milton. 1963. *Sociology Looks at Religion.* New York: Macmillan.

Zelinsky, Wilbur. 1961. "An Approach to the Religious Geography of the United States: Patterns of Church Membership in 1952." *Annals of the Association of American Geographers* 51 ( June): 139–193.

Zuckerman, Michael. 1982. "Introduction: Puritans, Cavaliers, and the Motley Middle." Pp. 3–25 in *Friends and Neighbors: Group Life in America's First Plural Society,* edited by Michael Zuckerman. Philadelphia: Temple University Press.

Zunz, Olivier. 1982. *The Changing Face of Inequality: Urbanization, Industrial Development, and Immigrants in Detroit, 1880–1920.* Chicago: University of Chicago Press.

# Index